LAWS AND LEGISLATION

RAPE, TORTURE AND GENOCIDE: SOME THEORETICAL IMPLICATIONS

Laws and Legislation

Additional books in this series can be found on Nova's website under the Series tab.

Additional E-books in this series can be found on Nova's website under the E-books tab.

LAWS AND LEGISLATION

RAPE, TORTURE AND GENOCIDE: SOME THEORETICAL IMPLICATIONS

DANIELA DE VITO

Nova Science Publishers, Inc.
New York

For permission to use material from this book please contact us:
Telephone 631-231-7269; Fax 631-231-8175
Web Site: http://www.novapublishers.com

LIBRARY OF CONGRESS CATALOGING-IN-PUBLICATION DATA
De Vito, Daniela.
Rape, torture and genocide : some theoretical implications daniela de
vito.
p. cm.
Includes index.
ISBN 978-1-61728-501-1 (hardcover)
1. Rape as a weapon of war. 2. Torture. 3. Genocide. I. Title.
K5304.5.D4 2010
345'.02532--dc22
2010025383

Published by Nova Science Publishers, Inc. ✢ New York

ACKNOWLEDGMENTS

I wish to thank Sam Ashenden for her efforts on an earlier manifestation of this book. Her encouragement and gentle 'pushing' to improve, in an analytical sense, were greatly appreciated. I would also like to thank Joni Lovenduski and Alejandro Colás for their help during this stage. Appreciation is extended to Diana Coole, Michael Freeman and Nigel Rodley for their helpful comments.

I am also thankful to Aisha Gill and Damien Short for their support and assessment of the revised work.

I also wish to thank my co-workers at Crucible Centre, Roehampton University for their support during this period.

Thank you to my family and friends – here and abroad – for their support. To my siblings (Lisa, Victor, and Marc), to my Tante Madeleine, and to Richard a special thank you for your support. Thank you to Friederike for the fabulous flat in Highgate! To my brother Marc, who has always believed in reaching for the seemingly impossible – I thank you for this.

Finally, I wish to dedicate the work undertaken for this book to the memory of my parents Alda and Victor. Although they were not part of the journey, their influence was never forgotten.

Hove, East Sussex

CONTENTS

PREFACE

How rape *has been* conceptualized, placed and treated by the various components within international human rights and humanitarian law present both inconsistencies, and in recent times, innovative conclusions. In terms of the former category, inconsistencies, when rape is explicitly mentioned within for instance the context of international humanitarian law it tends to be associated with a woman's honor and not as a crime of violence or it is linked to the protection of women and not with the prohibition of rape. In contrast, the well-established international crime of torture has been conceptualized as a crime of violence and its prohibition is paramount.

Furthermore, beyond being subsumed into an established international crime such as torture, genocide, the grave breaches provisions of the Geneva Conventions (1949), or crimes against humanity, rape currently does not stand on its own as an enumerated international crime. Rape is indeed prohibited under international law, but it has not been conceptualized, placed, and treated as a stand alone international crime.

As such, understanding what *can* occur to rape once it is subsumed into such categories is essential for developing a clearer framework to address this violation. This book will undertake a political analysis approach to what can happen when rape is subsumed into the international crimes of torture and genocide.

When rape is considered a form of torture, it has to not only operate within the realities of international law but, more specifically, within the confines of the current concept of human rights, which emphasizes the importance of the individual. The crime of rape is conceptualized and treated as an act committed against the individual. Torture, as a human rights violation, is also conceptualized and treated as a violation against the individual. When rape is subsumed into the human rights violation of torture it also relates to violations committed against the individual.

In contrast, rape as genocide has to operate within the constraints of genocide with its links to the protection of groups. Since genocide under international law has been conceived, placed and treated as a denial of the right to life of human groups, rape must find its space within this innovative approach.

As such, some of the critical theoretical implications emanating from the consideration of rape as a form of torture and rape as genocide will form the analytical sections of this book.

Chapter 1

OVERALL INTRODUCTION

"...there is no pain that lasts a hundred years,
nor a body that will endure it...
there is no pain greater than the pain of being alive
- a Nicaraguan saying" [1]

OVERVIEW

Within the past few decades, relatively rapid developments have occurred in relation to the promotion, protection, and even at certain levels the enforcement of human rights norms. A plethora of international, regional and national human rights instruments and mechanisms have been established. Despite these critical steps, the human rights discourse, which involves States, international organizations such as the United Nations (UN), non-governmental organizations, the media, individuals, theoretical and legal developments, etc., continues to adapt and to reveal discrepancies between what is required and what in reality occurs.

How rape has been conceptualized, placed, and treated by various institutions and instruments within international human rights and humanitarian law presents both inconsistencies and, in recent times, innovative conclusions. With respect to inconsistency, when rape is mentioned explicitly within, for instance, the context of international humanitarian law, it tends to be associated with a woman's "honor" and not as a crime of violence.[2]

Alternatively, an emphasis is placed on the protection of women and not on the prohibition of rape. As long as there is no single authoritative instrument or provision that exists for defining rape within regional and United Nations (UN) human rights instruments, it will not be possible to point to an overarching definition of rape that can be utilized within the

---

[1] Quote taken from: James Quesada. "Suffering Child: An Embodiment of War and Its Aftermath in Post-Sandinista Nicaragua." P. 51.

[2] Rhonda Copelon has argued that where rape is mentioned in the Geneva Convention (1949) it is conceptualized as an "attack against honour", rather than depicted as a crime of violence. She argues this is problematic, because it marginalizes the seriousness as well as the violent nature, of rape under international humanitarian law. She urges that rape should be viewed as a form of torture, in order to remove the ambiguity that is the legacy of sexism and to place such crimes against women on a par with crimes against men. Rhonda Copelon, 1999: 337.

context of international humanitarian law. However, in 1998, the Trial Chamber for the International Criminal Tribunal for Rwanda (ICTR) included within its Judgement in the case of the Prosecutor v. Jean-Paul Akayesu an attempt to define rape within international law.[3] Highly innovative, this definition has been used as a starting point for subsequent international criminal tribunal reflections on how rape can be . (See also Elements of Crimes, Rome Statute, International Criminal Court, War Crime of Rape and Crime against Humanity of Rape)

In contrast, there is a series of international crimes,[4] such as torture, that have been conceptualized and treated as crimes of violence and as such, their prohibition within international law is considered paramount.[5] Furthermore, beyond rape being subsumed within the categories of such international crimes as torture, genocide, the grave breaches provisions of the Geneva Conventions (1949), or crimes against humanity, rape currently does not stand on its own as an enumerated international crime. Rape is prohibited under international law, but is not specifically designated as an international crime. The result of this process is that rape must be subsumed within an established international crime, such as genocide, crimes against humanity, war crimes, etc. if it is to be prosecuted within an international criminal tribunal or the recently established International Criminal Court.[6] As such, determining and assessing some of the theoretical implications for rape that emerge once it is subsumed into an established international crime will form the crux of this study.

This book determines and assesses some of the theoretical implications for rape that emerge once it is placed within the international crimes of torture and genocide. Specifically, the differences between rape as a form of torture with its emphasis on the individual and rape as genocide, which focuses on violations committed against the group, will form the basis of this theoretical analysis. The question therefore becomes, "does the dynamic of rape alter when it is subsumed within these complex and contrasting international crimes?" Furthermore, it will be argued that any study of group theory, as it relates to rape within the context of international law, must appreciate the relationship between rape as it affects the individual and rape as it affects the group.

In general, rape has been conceptualized as a crime committed against individual victims. In turn, the international crime of torture has been constructed as a human rights violation

---

[3] In its findings, the Trial Chamber defined rape as "a physical invasion of a sexual nature, committed on a person under circumstances which are coercive."

The Chamber also stated rape is a form of aggression and that the central elements of the crime of rape cannot be captured in a mechanical description of objects and body parts. This approach is more useful in international law."

ICTR, Prosecutor v. Jean-Paul Akayesu (Case No. ICTR-96-4-T, 2 September 1998): 598 and 687.

The Akayesu Judgement provided an overarching and potentially progressive definition of rape where none had existed before in instruments of international law. The case also established that rape could be tried as a component of genocide if committed with the intent to destroy a targeted group.

[4] There remains dispute over what is considered an international crime ("crime under international law"?). Overall, an international crime, in relation to State responsibility, may be understood as "…those acts which the 'international community as a whole' considers to be serious breaches of obligations essential for the protection of fundamental interests of that community."

UN Document A/CN.4/453 and Add. 1-3, "Fifth Report on State responsibility by Mr. G. Arangjio-Ruiz, Special Rapporteur," Yearbook of the International Law Commission II (1) (1993): 31.

[5] See Articles 1, 2, 4 and 5 from the United Nations Convention against Torture and other Cruel, Inhuman or Degrading Treatment or Punishment (1984).P.R. Ghandhi, 2000: 109.

[6] For more on this, please refer to the Statutes for the International Criminal Tribunal for Rwanda, the International Criminal Tribunal for the Former Yugoslavia, the Sierra Leone Special Court, and the International Criminal Court.

committed against the individual. The consideration of rape as a form of torture is a recent innovation. At the international level, the first formal association was made by the United Nations (UN) Special Rapporteur in 1986. Rape as torture still emphasizes the individual victim/survivor. In contrast, the critical focus of genocide is the protection of entire human groups. It is the 'right to existence' of human groups and not of individuals, which is the concern. When rape has been considered as genocide [7] which is conceived as a crime, when committed against certain groups its dynamic changes. Rape is no longer just a violation against the individual. Rape becomes part of a notion set up to protect the group. The determination of this book is that there is still a place for the individual victim of genocide or of rape as genocide. However, as with the current concept of human rights, this space is unequal and at times uncomfortable. Crucially, even with innovative jurisprudence there is a need to assess the complex relationship between rape that affects the individual and rape as genocide, which is placed within the group dynamic.

Although the book will touch upon international human rights and humanitarian law, it will not function within a traditional legal framework. Analyzing recent changes achieved within the human rights discourse, in relation to how rape has been conceptualized, placed and treated, will instead be driven by conceptual resources found within the broad discipline of political theory. For instance, when is a human rights violation a public/private matter? Also, when are rights concerns for individuals or for groups?

Underlying the book are two fundamental questions:

1. What are some of the theoretical implications of considering rape as a form of torture when committed within the spheres of international human rights and humanitarian law? and;
2. What are some of the theoretical implications of considering rape as genocide?

Three main areas of discussion, emanating from two real-life international criminal tribunal cases, have been identified to arrive at an understanding of some of the theoretical implications that can affect rape. These two cases, one taken from the International Criminal Tribunal for the Former Yugoslavia (ICTY) and the other from the International Criminal Tribunal for Rwanda (ICTR) offer an opportunity to extract and to assess certain theoretical issues that could affect the understanding of rape. The ICTY case (2001) discusses rape and torture and acknowledges the individual component of rape with references to violations of *sexual autonomy*.[8] In contrast, the ICTR case (Akayesu case, 1998) proposes for the first time that under specific circumstances rape could be genocide thereby constructing rape within the formulation of genocide—a crime against the group (Akayesu case, 1998).

The three main areas of deliberation are: possible tensions within the current concept of human rights between the individual and the group; understanding rape as a violation committed against the individual; and what can happen to rape once it has been subsumed within an established international crime such as torture or genocide. These factors are crucial

[7] See for instance, Prosecutor v. Jean- Paul Akayesu (International Criminal Tribunal for Rwanda (ICTR), Trial Chamber Judgement, 1998). Hereinafter the Akayesu case.

[8] *Prosecutor v. Dragolijub Kunarac, Radomir Kovac and Zoran Vukovic*, ICTY, IT-96-23-T and IT-96-23/1-T, Judgement, 22 February 2001. Hereinafter the Foca Case. Although the Kunarac *et al* cases focuses on Crimes Against Humanity, it has been chosen for analysis due to the discussions of rape and torture and the notion of *sexual autonomy*.

to determining and assessing some of the theoretical implications emerging from recent and innovative international jurisprudence.

1. The Current Concept of Human Rights

As developed from the Enlightenment period with the advent of natural rights and to the post World War II establishment of human rights, certain features of these types of 'rights' continue to affect how these are conceived and to a certain degree implemented. One critical feature in how the current concept of human rights has emerged pertains to an emphasis placed on the rights and the importance of the individual. The current concept of human rights is one that reflects an ongoing and in reality an imperfect relationship – how the State treats individuals within, and at times without, its borders.

One aspect that has influenced this rise in the status of the individual has been the political theory of liberalism. The growing role for the individual and the development of rights attached to the individual, along with an examination of what role the individual should have within the State (or public realm) and even in private matters such as in the family, have been issues taken up by a myriad of thinkers formally or informally associated with liberalism. From Thomas Hobbes' and John Locke's works on certain and limited natural rights for the individual, to the current United Nations (UN), regional, and national human rights instruments, echoes of liberal influences are evident. The UN's Universal Declaration of Human Rights (UDHR, 1948), emphasizes the individual and his/her rights. Articles pertaining to everyone having the right to life, not to be subjected to slavery, to vote, etc. are framed within the needs and the importance of the individual regardless of (in theory of course!) one's standing or role in the State.

However, as with liberal political theory, the current concept of human rights does make limited room for 'the group'. Various international human rights instruments recognize the right of peoples to self-determination. It is not the individuals within a group of 'peoples' that have this right but in fact the peoples as a whole. Although the machinations of this right are still in the process of being worked through under international law and its application has thus far been limited to situations whereby peoples have been living in situations of colonialism, this right does demonstrate some accommodation for the group within the current concept of human rights. Furthermore, Article 16 of the UDHR (1948) relates to the family. Minority rights, as shall be briefly undertaken in Chapter seven of this book, travel the schism between rights of the group as a whole and much more frequently – especially within international human rights law – as the rights of individuals within the group.

This tension, as found within liberalism and within the current concept of human rights, of determining if the emphasis should solely be on the rights of individuals or if the concept of human rights also has room for the group will form the basis for understanding the implications of when rape is considered as torture (a violation against the individual) and when it is considered as genocide (a violation against the group). It is the proposal of this author that accommodation is indeed possible, albeit limited and imperfect, for rape to be considered as both a violation against the individual and as a violation against the group.

2. RAPE

Rape, in general, has been conceptualized as a crime committed against individual victims. Although when brought to trial, be it at the national or international level, it is the Prosecutor who faces the defendant in a rape case it is also the victim's story that is considered. If appropriate, it is the individual victim who testifies before the court. When rape is placed within the realms of international human rights and humanitarian law inconsistencies and problems appear in relation to its conceptualization, placement and treatment. For instance, rape is not explicitly listed in UN human rights treaties. Even in instruments linked to rape this violation is not always mentioned. With reference to international humanitarian law, rape has to be read into several passages and when it is explicitly mentioned it is linked to issues such as a woman's 'honor'.[9] This book proposes that how rape is currently addressed must be acknowledged and analyzed beyond jurisprudence parameters to include theoretical analysis.

3. RAPE AS...

A) Torture

As noted, the international crime of torture has been constructed as a human rights violation committed against an individual. Its considerable status within international human rights and humanitarian law in terms of its perception as a serious human rights violation, of the instruments created, of the implementation regimes, etc., has resulted in the prohibition and the eradication of torture being crucial goals for the international community. Despite reality, the focus and the perception of individual victims of torture have been on those who have been politically active or politically linked (for instance to relatives and friends).[10] The reality is that most victims of torture do not have this connection to the 'political' and in fact, most are common criminals. As the UN Special Rapporteur has commented, one reason for this predominance of cases involving political individuals is that they may have more access to and knowledge of the reporting mechanisms for torture at the national, regional and international levels. (UN doc. A/55/290: 8)

Since the general emphasis has tended to be placed on the political dimensions of the individual victim of torture, it will be critical to work through an understanding of what is meant by the 'political' and what are the effects when this label is attached to these individuals. One option would be to view the political in a more restricted manner whereby the political would mean involvement in a political party, a trade union, etc. It is the opinion

---

[9] For instance, the UN Convention on the Elimination of Discrimination Against Women (CEDAW, 1979) does not specifically mention rape – Article 6.

This formulation can be found within one of the tenets of international humanitarian law, the Geneva Conventions of 1949. For instance, Article 24 from the 1949 Geneva Convention IV Relative to the Protection of Civilian Persons in Time of War states "Women shall be especially protected against any attack on their honour, in particular against rape, enforced prostitution, or any form of indecent assault."

Adam Roberts and Richard Guelff, Documents on the Laws of War, 3rd ed. P. 310.

[10] This 'political' focus and perception of the individual victim of torture is not related to how torture has been defined within international instruments. Rather, the focus can be found in the types of cases that are highlighted by, for instance, NGOs and experts in the field. This issue will be discussed in Chapters 4 and 5 .

of this author that such a restricted perspective of the political is too limited. The risk is that this would exclude a large number of individuals claiming to have been tortured. Rather, I propose an alternative and one that I have developed and named as *a more expansive perspective of the political* that would include issues and activities traditionally placed within the private realm such as *inter alia* familial matters. For instance, throwing a ball to one's dog in a park may not at first glance be considered political. Yet, understanding where the ball used to play fetch was made, by whom, and under what circumstances places this action within the realm of the political. This more expansive notion of the political is not one in which everything is considered to have political undertones or implications, but it does allow for additional activities and associations to be considered when determining if torture has taken place. However, regardless if this more expansive perspective of the political is adopted it is still too restrictive to insist on the placement of a political label onto individual victims of torture.

Rape As Torture

The consideration of rape as a form of torture is a recent innovation. At the international level, the first formal association was made by the UN Special Rapporteur in 1986. Subsequently, more work occurred on this issue and several international and regional cases have confirmed the possibility that if rape occurs in situations where the definition of torture exists then it is possible to subsume rape into the international crime of torture. As with torture, a link will be made in this book between individuals who have suffered rape as a form of torture and the 'political'. Even with a more expansive notion of the political the implications for rape as a form of torture, if the political is emphasized for individual victims, would be too restrictive since this would mask the reality that this crime occurs most often beyond the boundaries of the 'political'.

B) Genocide

The critical focus of genocide, understood as an international crime, is the protection of entire human groups. Often referred to as the most serious of international crimes, genocide is influenced by the 'right to live' of individuals. However, it is the 'right to existence' of human groups and not of individuals, which is the concern. This formulation of genocide seems to contrast with the overall current concept of human rights with its emphasis on the individual. The Convention on the Prevention and Punishment of the Crime of Genocide (1948) lists the following groups that could be targeted for genocide – national, ethnical, racial, or religious.

Despite this built in mechanism for the protection of certain human groups within genocide, an interesting interplay does emerge. That is, genocide is most definitely a violation against the group as a whole. Yet, acts of genocide are in turn committed against individuals within these groups. It is individual members of said groups who are killed, harmed, raped, etc. It is these individual stories, along with what has happened to the group as a whole, that for instance, are told before international criminal tribunals. This interplay, between space for the groups and space for the individual within genocide, is what will be taken from the real life case (Akayesu case, 1998) and assessed.

Rape as Genocide

The ICTR *Akayesu* Judgement (1998) was the first time that an international criminal body has subsumed rape within the international crime of genocide. The Trial Chamber, with reference to the particular circumstances of the case, argued that the women were raped because they were members of the Tutsi ethnic group. As such, some of the rapes related to this case constituted genocide. Individual victims of rape testified within the context of the trial against Jean-Paul Akayesu. It was these individuals who were raped, and they were also members of the Tutsi ethnic group.

The final part of the discussion, outlined above, will examine the *implications for rape* if it is considered as a violation against the individual (as is the case with torture) and if it is subsumed within the group focused crime of genocide. Overall, this book has assessed the role and place of the individual and the group within the current concept of human rights. Although unequal, both aspects do have space within this concept. The individual is still given prime position with his/her rights making up the bulk of human rights instruments and theory. The group element, with some notable exceptions, is most often constructed as rights that individuals as members of particular groups have. When rape is subsumed into an international crime such as genocide, which is conceived as a crime committed against enumerated groups, its dynamic changes. Rape is no longer just a violation against the individual. Rape becomes a part of a notion set up to protect the group. The determination within this book is that there is still a place for the individual victim of genocide or rape as genocide. However, as with the current concept of human rights, this space is unequal and not always comfortable. Crucially, even with innovative jurisprudence such as the ICTR case (Jean-Paul Akayesu, 1998) and literature on this issue, there is a need to assess this complex relationship between rape, which affects the individual, and rape as genocide, which is placed within the group dynamic.

The Approach

This analysis will unfold within an analytical political theory approach that touches upon the current concept of human rights with its focus on the individual. Although the emphasis is on the individual, the concept of human rights also accommodates (albeit in a limited manner) the group. Influenced by liberal political theory, which exists as a separate theoretical entity, the current concept of human rights operates within this potential tension – the rights of individuals as opposed to the 'rights' of groups. This tension may be a by-product of liberalism, of human rights, or perhaps even of political theory in general.

This theoretical overview will involve the examination of human rights violations committed under '*political*' circumstances, such as the torture by means of rape committed by State officials against a political opposition member. Overarching this approach will be an understanding of the distinction between 'public' and 'private' life. The process of bringing rape into the very public human rights violation of torture will be touched upon. As noted, the emphasis of how torture has been addressed within the international law arena has tended to be on victims who are politically active or who have a political association. Throughout more recent and even past periods, the 'political' has most often been associated with the public realm such as the government or the State. Working through what makes up this category of the political is essential for any understanding of rape as a form of torture.

The theoretical analysis will also bring out some of the implications when rape is subsumed within the international crime of genocide, with its emphasis on violations against the group, as opposed to the individual. In other words, the overall process of this book will involve an assessment of possible tensions between the conceptualization of human rights violations committed against the individual and of violations committed against the group. The reason for adopting this two-pronged analytical political theory approach, as will shortly be described, is due to the fact that gaps exist in how rape has been conceptualized and placed within international human rights and humanitarian law. This lack of practical effect in addressing rape within both types of law will be touched upon throughout the book. As mentioned, this book will be limited in its legal scope. International human rights and humanitarian law will be a starting point. On the one hand, international law will assist in understanding how rape has been conceptualized, placed and treated and on the other hand, it will provide a useful foundation for the political theory questions that have emerged from this author's examination of recent developments. Therefore, the issue of rape committed within international human rights and humanitarian law, and the specific consideration of rape as a form of torture and rape as genocide within these two types of law will underscore the book. As such, theoretical implications emerging from recent international cases pertaining to rape, and not the legal consequences, will be prioritized.

In sum, two main theoretical issues have emerged from the discussion thus far. First, there is the possible tension between rape as a human rights violation committed against the individual (in the case of torture) and rape as a violation against the group (in the case of genocide). Second, the manner in which international crime of torture has been addressed tends to focus on victims who have been politically active or who have political affiliations. Understanding what is meant by the 'political' and the implications of this for rape as a form of torture will in turn be addressed. As such, this book will examine rape, torture, genocide, rape as a form of torture and rape as genocide as understood within international human rights and humanitarian law. The implications for rape, within the context of the current concept of human rights with its focus on the individual and on violations committed against the group (genocide), will be analyzed. A similar undertaking will be applied to rape as a form of torture in relation to the 'political' nature of reported victims of torture. Finally, this work will take place within the conceptual resources offered by political theory analysis.

Some critical issues, in terms of rape, will emerge throughout the book. Although relevant to the discussion, these issues must remain within a distinct realm from the specific aims of the book. The reason is to allow for a fuller examination of the main theoretical claims associated with rape as a form of torture and as genocide. For instance, there is a difference between international law as it is set up and the reality of practice. Also, is rape committed within the auspices of international human rights and humanitarian law considered wrong on moral grounds and/or because the perpetrators tend to operate with impunity. Furthermore, there is the misrepresentation that during armed conflicts rape is inevitable.[11]

Finally, there is the important question of why does rape occur. The power that the perpetrator wields over the victim, as opposed to mere sexual motivations that the perpetrator may or may not have, is essential to understanding why rape takes place. This is a complex issue and this author acknowledges its importance.

The book is organized into seven Chapters, including the Overall Introduction.

Chapter 2 discusses a variety of literatures. It begins with a short overview of natural rights and the current concept of human rights. The literature chosen will also articulate

[11] I am grateful to Diana Coole for insisting on these distinctions from the overall themes of the book.

feminist understandings in relation to rape and rape occurring within the context of international and non-international armed conflicts along with relevant gender dimensions. This will be followed by works on the international crime of torture; rape as a form of torture; and genocide. The literature overview is directly linked to the three main areas of discussion identified earlier in this Overall Introduction. [12]

Chapter 3 outlines the essential definitions critical for understanding the theoretical implications emanating from the two international criminal tribunal cases assessed in this book. The definitions chosen relate specifically to the main issues covered: rape, torture, and genocide. In relation to defining rape, this book will specifically assess how definitions of rape have evolved within the context of national and international parameters. The focus will be on consent *versus* coercion definitions of rape, and their influence within international criminal tribunal attempts to define rape. Certain national juridical developments in this area will be utilized while appreciating the particulars of international law and international criminal tribunals. This process will demonstrate some of the influences, for instance feminist perspectives, which have placed the issue of rape more prominently on the international law agenda.

This chapter also assesses how rape has been conceptualized and placed within international human rights and humanitarian law. The book argues that how rape has been conceived and placed within international law is problematic. International human rights treaties, under the UN system, do not explicitly mention rape. Furthermore, even human rights instruments at the UN level that deal with women have not always mentioned the violation of rape. Accepting the possibility of rape as a form of torture is a recent development. Within international humanitarian law, the problems are deeply entrenched. For instance, under the Geneva Conventions of 1949, rape is not explicitly considered a grave breach and so it would have to be subsumed into the crime of torture. In turn, under Convention IV (Article 27) rape has been conceptualized as a crime against one's 'honor' and not as a crime of violence.

This Chapter examines and analyses essential cases pertaining to rape. Due to the scope of this book, only two cases covering the period from 1998-2001 are utilized. Again, the underlying influence of the book is not to present a complete and up-to-date analysis of legal developments in this area. Instead, these cases/decisions will be utilized as a starting point for the political theory inquiry and for the development of the schema noted above. The cases are from the International Criminal Tribunal for Rwanda; and from the International Criminal Tribunal for the Former Yugoslavia. [13]

In addition, this Chapter brings to light *two theoretical implications* identified by this book and emanating from the international criminal tribunal cases assessed. First, rape has to function within the parameters of a violation committed against the individual. This exists with torture, which has generally been understood as a crime against the individual and crucially for this book as a violation that tends to affect individuals who have been politically active. This book argues that a theoretical analysis must occur in relation to how rape can be

---

[12] *These are* the current concept of human rights (the group/individual schism), rape as affecting the individual, and rape within the context of torture or genocide.

[13] *Prosecutor v. Dragolijub Kunarac, Radomir Kovac and Zoran Vukovic*, ICTY, IT-96-23-T and IT-96-23/1-T, Judgement, 22 February 2001. *Prosecutor v. Jean-Paul Akayesu*, ICTR-96-4-T, Judgement, 2 September 1998.

understood as a violation committed against the individual, when it is subsumed within torture, from juridical decisions and judgements. Second, when rape has been linked to a group violation such as genocide this book also insists the theoretical implications of this process must be understood.

Chapter 4 sets out the overall theoretical framework. The general approach used is analytical political theory, alongside international human rights and humanitarian law. This is achieved in two ways. First, I will briefly return to the current concept of human rights. Specifically, this will entail linking liberalism with human rights; discussing the public/private dimensions of human rights; and an overview of the State, the individual and human rights. The purpose is to intertwine some of the key theoretical factors from the current concept of human rights that may affect how rape is understood. Also, discussing the complex relationships that exist between the State, the individual, and human rights will highlight critical factors. Under the international system, States wield an enormous amount of power. Yet, the position of the individual has changed over the centuries. As is argued, the current concept of human rights still places a strong emphasis on the importance of the individual. This chapter will argue that such notions may affect how rape is framed.

Second, the chapter prepares the way to assess the two real life cases taken from the International Criminal Tribunals. The purpose is to place rape firmly within the current concept of human rights, thereby understanding a process whereby rape travels into the respective frameworks presented by the international crimes of torture and genocide.

Furthermore, the nature of harm associated with rape will be outlined while linking this specifically to torture and genocide. The reason is to bring out two important points identified by this book in relation to the complexities surrounding the international crimes of torture and genocide. First, the nature of harm in rape when it is subsumed within torture has to fit within the legal definition, which utilizes the concept of *severe* pain (mental or physical). With genocide, the nature of harm must relate to the group context and that the harm is *serious* (as per the Genocide Convention). Second, the nature of harm in rape has been examined within the realities of armed conflicts (international and non-international) and specifically in connection to rapes that have occurred in public.

Chapters 5 and 6 outline two theoretical concerns emerging from the examination of the cases/decisions under Chapter 3. First, in Chapter 5, the emphasis on 'the political' in relation to individual victims of torture or rape as a form of torture is expanded upon. In turn, a determination unfolds as to whether or not even a broad understanding of 'the political' is adequate when considering rape as a form of torture. Second, in Chapter 6, I return to the notion that the current concept of human rights places an emphasis on the individual and on his/her needs and rights. Also, the autonomy *v.* group dimensions of working through rape, torture, rape as a form of torture and genocide, respectively are considered. These two Chapters seek to not only to highlight the two theoretical implications brought forth by this book, in relation to rape, but also insist on the importance of moving academic discourse beyond judicial assessments, to also include critical theoretical analysis.

The Overall Conclusion represents a synthesis of the discussions and arguments woven into the book. The aim will be to better understand some of the theoretical implications incurred when rape is considered a form of torture and when it is considered as genocide.

Chapter 2

ENGAGEMENT

"Concepts, like individuals, have their histories,
and are just as incapable of withstanding
the ravages of time as are individuals."
Soren Kierkgaard
The Concept of Irony, with Constant Reference to Socrates

OVERVIEW

This Chapter will discuss multiple literatures with the aim of demonstrating their relevance to the book while bringing out its importance and specific contribution. Since the book will be determining and assessing some of the critical theoretical implications that emerge when rape is subsumed within the established international crimes of torture and genocide this review will cover the following three main areas of discussion. [1] First, I discuss key literature relating to the development of the current concept of human rights and with a focus on the rise of the individual, on the influence of liberalism with its approach to the public/private discourse, and on the stresses within the current concept of human rights in relation to the group/individual schism. Second, I discuss feminist contributions to the understanding of rape in order to appreciate recent changes in how rape has been conceptualized, placed and treated within international law. Lastly, I examine literature on the definitions of torture and genocide as background to determine under which circumstances rape can be placed within these respective international crimes.

Literature on the Current Concept of Human Rights

Natural Law and Natural Rights

To fully understand the current concept of human rights outlined in this book, it was necessary to briefly acknowledge the body of literature from and influenced by the

[1] Please note: the topics covered in Chapter Two relate to the three main areas of discussion identified in the Overall Introduction: "...possible tensions within the current concept of human rights between the individual and the group; understanding rape as a violation committed against the individual; and what can occur to rape once it has been subsumed within an established international crime such as torture or genocide."

Enlightenment period. François Furet (cited in Stephen Marks, 1998: 471- 473) has argued that the French Revolution of 1789 is the starting point for human rights. Influences for the advent of human rights may be found in earlier events or writings, but H. Lauterpacht makes a key observation in International Law and Human Rights: "...inalienable rights above positive law of the state, seem to be more recent", that is, not earlier than the Enlightenment period (H. Lauterpacht, 1950: 80). During the Enlightenment, the notion of rights did exist but this was intertwined with natural law and natural rights. Emanating from natural law were natural rights, often viewed as the precursor to human rights. Critically, as Peter Jones in Rights (Jones, 1994: 48) argues, the pivotal role for rights is to determine "...what people are entitled to do and how they are entitled to be treated." Knud Haakonssen (1996: 6) points out rights for the individual did exist during this period (seventeenth and eighteenth centuries) but that these were linked to the fulfillment of duties. That is one had rights to the actions associated with fulfilling one's duties and rights to what others had to do in order to fulfill their respective duties. This can be seen in John Locke's seminal work Two Treatises of Government (edited by Peter Laslett, 1967: 270-271) where he wrote about the natural rights to 'life, liberty and property' and that individuals also had a duty to respect the natural rights of others. [2] In essence, as Richard Tuck (Tuck, 1979: 86) describes, natural rights theories operated beyond the civil laws of societies. The overview of literature pertaining to natural law and natural rights also included working through some of the reasons as to why the idea of natural rights developed. First, there was the challenge to political absolutism and to the divine right of kings to rule (Jeremy Waldron, 1987: 7-11, John Locke, 1967: 202-203). Second, States increasingly began to claim a monopoly over the legitimate use of violence. Third, there was the growth in the notion of the individual as a separate entity from religious and political organs, and later from the State. (John Locke, 1967: 308, Alan Rosenbaum, 1980: 11, Richard Tuck, 1979: 22, Jeremy Waldron: 10) This, in turn, was associated with natural rights such as the liberty of self-preservation and to life, liberty and property. (Darren Obyrne, 2003, Costas Douzinas, 2000) Although Locke does focus on the individual and clearly denotes individual natural rights, the Lockean individual does not live within an atomistic society. Michael Freeman, in Human Rights: An Interdisciplinary Approach, points out this duality within Locke's framework by stating, "There is, therefore, an unresolved tension in Locke's political theory between the natural rights of individuals and the collective good of society." (Freeman, 2002: 21). As later outlined in this book with the overview of rape, torture, and genocide and although not exactly the same as previous manifestations, the tensions between individual rights and the requirements of society still exist.

Finally, as developed over three hundred years, the political ideology of liberalism shall be inserted into the discussion to demonstrate key links with natural rights and eventually with human rights such as ensuring the equal opportunity of individuals to enjoy liberty. (Ball and Dagger, 2006). What follows is not an all-encompassing examination of literature pertaining to liberalism in all its variations. Instead, I merely wish to outline how the individual is perceived within this political ideology. Once again, the current concept of

---

[2] Thomas Hobbes (1588-1679) wrote about the natural right to self-preservation; John Locke (1632-1704) argued for the natural rights to life, liberty and property; and the French Declaration of the Rights of Man and the Citizen (1789) insisted on the rights to liberty, property, security and resistance to oppression. Critiques of natural rights included *inter alia* Jeremy Bentham (1748-1832) who famously referred to these as 'nonsense upon stilts'; Olympe de Gouges (1745-1793) who insisted that women be included in the French Declaration (1789); and Karl Marx (1818-1883) who viewed natural rights as only benefiting the interests of the bourgeois class.

human rights emphasizes the individual. Understanding the development of and changes in the individual's role, in relation to natural rights, and later within the concept of human rights, will be essential to this book. Within the concept of human rights, torture is a human rights violation committed against an individual and rape as a form of torture is committed against the individual. These two violations follow the focus found within the current concept of human rights, that is, an emphasis on the individual and his/her human rights. In contrast, rape as genocide is a violation against a determined group. It is the theoretical implications stemming from these different approaches that will form the analytical portions of the book.

An additional consideration for liberals, although not always so easily demarcated, would be the dichotomy of the private and public spheres. (Sam Ashenden, 2003: 69-72) [3] In other words, where is the individual able to function – within the realities of public life (the state, politics, etc.) or within the realities of private life (the family, the private, the market, etc.)? One concern is determining how deeply government can interfere and if this interference should occur within both spheres. That is, what should be the proper boundaries between the State and the individual? In its earlier manifestations liberalism, along with other Enlightenment thought, was extremely concerned with breaking through the limits found within the authority and tradition that rulers (be it the monarch, State or religion) held over individuals (Anne Philips, 1993: 59-60). A similar, yet more developed, concern will be exposed with the examination of the current concept of human rights. (Joanna Kerr (ed.), 1993)

Another difficulty would be deciding which particular individuals could operate within each sphere. For instance, the precarious position of non-citizens and of women during the Enlightenment period, meant that there was no place (or at best a very limited space) within the perceived more important public sphere for these individuals. [4] The tension, according to Sam Ashenden, was a matter of State authority and its relation to the individual striving for freedom via the channels of autonomy (Ashenden, 2003: 75). However, the realities of how authority manifests itself within the family, as it affects individuals such as women and children, would continue to be problematic during the Enlightenment and even within contemporary debates. For instance, if the accepted head of the family is the father who has authority over his children and over his wife, then how does liberalism maintain the capacity for freedom and autonomy of these individuals. For Barry Hindness, autonomy of the individual, within liberalism, can include inter alia attributes such as 'personal independence, rationality and responsibility' (Barry Hindness, 1993: 65). Hindess also distinguishes between 'natural autonomy', and autonomy that is constructed through interactions within society – autonomy as an 'artifact' (Ibid: 73-74). The issue of autonomy will be addressed in this book in relation to understanding how rape has been conceptualized and treated as a crime against the individual and linking these parameters to the theoretical analysis of rape as a form of torture. Steven Wall navigates similar complex themes in reference to collective rights and

[3] An example of this potential difficulty, regarding human rights, will be discussed in Chapter 5 covering 'What is the Political?'

For an historical overview of why this dichotomy developed within liberalism, please refer to:

Sam Ashenden. Governing Child Sexual Abuse: negotiating the boundaries of public and private, law and science, Routledge, London, 2003: 69-72.

[4] In relation to John Stuart Mill on the public and private spheres "Mill displayed a transitional attitude toward the individual in society, leading eventually to a reconceived individualism. His view reflected the blurred distinctions between the private and public spheres of life, long recognized in liberalism for their uncertain implications on the concept of the individual." Rosenbaum. 1980: 17-18.

adds the notion of 'collective autonomy rights'. He also argues the latter goes beyond traditional notions of the individual right to freedom of association since such rights expand beyond the interests of one individual (Steven Wall, 2007: 236-239). Moreover, recent jurisprudence from the European Court of Human Rights demonstrates the importance of personal autonomy but with an emphasis on upholding one's right to privacy (Jill Marshall, 2008: 345) and on the protection of 'women's sexual autonomy' (Ivan Radacic, 2008: 371-374). Such issues will also be relevant for the discussions on rape understood as a violation against the group and understanding possible tensions between the individual and the group.

A strong association existed between classical liberalism and the distinction of the public and private worlds. Thinkers such as John Locke demarcated attributes such as reason, knowledge and mind as opposed to passion, desire and body. The former set belonged to the public sphere, where the political process occurred, while the latter set was placed within the private sphere. (Hilary Charlesworth, 1992:190-191) For women, especially, attributes found within the private sphere were attached and their place within this sphere was entrenched. (Ibid) It should be noted that thinkers of the time, such as Mary Wollstonecraft and Olympe de Gouges, wrote against the assumption that women only had certain attributes and that their pre-determined roles were found within a small section of the private sphere (namely the family) away from any political or public involvement.

In relation to this book, understanding how the current concept of human rights has been historically influenced by liberalism and subsequently framed (with its emphasis on the individual, with an acknowledgement of the group/community dynamic, and with efforts to determine which human rights could be placed within the public or private spheres), will expand on how rape as a form of torture and rape as genocide should be approached within international human rights and humanitarian law. As will be discussed, influences from liberalism still find resonance within the framework of human rights. For instance, both liberalism and the concept of human rights work within a potential tension between the rights of individuals and the collective good of society. Yet, as Iris Marion Young argues, "The neat distinction between individualism and community thus generates a dialectic in which each is a condition for the other." (Iris Marion Young in Linda J. Nicholson, 1990: 307). Thus, this important point may have an impact on the consideration of rape as a form of torture and as rape as genocide, which are violations against the individual and the group respectively.

Arriving at the Concept of Human Rights

By the late 19th and early 20th centuries, natural rights had lost its form with criticism of their existence and relevance taking hold (Burns H. Weston, 1984: 261). Yet, the idea of rights remained during this period with movements to abolish slavery, support for trade unions and minority issues. It was not until the Second World War and the rise of Nazism that the idea of human rights took hold. This is evident in the UN Charter (1945) and with the UDHR (1948) (Alan Rosenbaum, 1980: 21).

The concept of human rights, from Jack Donnelly's writings, can be understood as "*the rights that one has simply because one is a human being.*" (Jack Donnelly, 2nd Edition, 2003: 10). Alan Gewirth also notes, "human rights are a species of moral rights." For Gewirth something can be considered 'moral' if it can be "based upon or justifiable through a valid moral principle." (Alan Gewirth, 1982: 31). Is the explanation that we have human rights simply because we are human beings a satisfactory one? Michael Freeman points out some inadequacies with this framework in that he asks, *why* exactly one has human rights based on one's status as a human being? For example, and using Article 21 of the UDHR – "...the right to take part in the government of his country..." - he notes out that this right emanates not from our position as human beings. Rather it is due to an individual's standing as an 'adult citizen' and that this tends to exclude children and foreigners. (Michael Freeman, 2002: 60-61). Freeman does pose a critical question in relation to '*why* human beings have these rights'? However, I am not completely convinced that the overall concept of human rights needs to be broken down so thoroughly. As a foreigner studying in the United Kingdom, who cannot participate in national/local government elections as a voter or as a candidate, I do not think this would necessarily create a dilemma within Donnelly's perception of the concept of human rights. Not all the rights listed in the UDHR, and in subsequent human rights instruments, are relevant to me personally. I am not a mother and so Article 25 (2), which addresses motherhood, is not relevant. Additionally, when I return to my country of origin I will be able to participate in my government at several levels. Furthermore, foreigners and children have 'human rights' which may not be relevant to 'adult citizens'. Critically, and this is why the concept of human rights as presented by Donnelly influenced this book, these individuals do not cease to be human beings. It is not, in my opinion, that Donnelly is insisting all human beings are the same and that they all have the same rights. In a similar vein, human rights can be understood and enforced in different ways. This is especially true for the right to a fair trial whose framework can vary according to common law or civil law traditions. Perhaps there is room for the concept of human rights, which at its core is directed to human beings, while understanding a need for flexibility in terms of its wider branches as presented by Freeman. Is it just because we are human that we have human rights? At one level, as argued above, the answer is yes. Yet, going beyond this has also taken place in a theoretical sense. One reason is linked to how human rights can be justified. For Donnelly the term itself points to one way of working through this question: he looks at the source of human rights - one's 'moral nature' – which for him is loosely associated with human nature. Donnelly correctly points out that it is extremely difficult to grasp a clear understanding of human nature. For example, the political ideology of liberalism would view the desire for freedom as being *natural and fulfillable* and that fulfilling this desire would lead to human happiness. (Jack Donnelly, 2nd Edition, 2003: 13-16) Donnelly states that we 'need' human rights "not for life but for a life of dignity." That is, "for a life worthy of a human being, a life that cannot be enjoyed without these rights." (Ibid: 14). For instance, an international human rights instrument - such as the UDHR – notes the "inherent dignity" of the person.[5] The human rights version of dignity would examine the equality and value of each person who has certain inalienable rights. Inalienable rights (certain human rights such as the right not to be subjected to torture are often referred to in this manner) can be understood as rights that cannot be lost if one is to live a life "worthy of a human being" (Ibid: 15-20). However, human dignity is understood/defined in varied ways and, as Donnelly concedes in his book dealing with non-western viewpoints, the aim of human dignity can be achieved in other ways than via human rights. Critically though, Donnelly is adamant that if the human rights version of dignity is changed then the idea of human rights would be challenged (Ibid).

Who has human rights? To put it simply, human rights are for human beings. These are the subjects of human rights. Is it all human beings as a whole or is it individuals that have

[5] UDHR – Preamble: "Whereas recognition of the inherent dignity and of the equal and inalienable rights of all members of the human family is the foundation of freedom, justice and peace in the world, "P.R. Ghandhi: 21.

human rights? Once again, Jack Donnelly has a strong opinion on this. For him "Because only individual persons are human beings…only individuals can have human rights." (Id: 25) In relation to the individual, Donnelly mentions the International Human Rights Covenants where, with one exception - the right of peoples to self-determination, only individual rights are listed. Even this right of 'peoples' is qualified since according to Donnelly groups as a whole do not have rights, only individuals as part of a group have rights. The same argument, for him, is applicable to human rights pertaining to the family (Id: 26-27). Donnelly's viewpoint may not at first reading, leave room for other traditions that focus on the group over the individual. However, as Michael Freeman argues , the concept of human rights

> "…denies neither individual responsibility nor the value of community. It is a concept that affirms human solidarity while respecting individual autonomy." (Michael Freeman, 2002: 75)

A similar approach was outlined with the exploration of early liberalism and natural rights. As the UDHR states in Article 29(1), which includes a blend of the individual, the community and duties, "Everyone has duties to the community in which alone the free and full development of his personality is possible." However, this notion of the community is rare within most documents addressing the current concept of human rights. An important exception is the African Charter on Human and Peoples' Rights (1981) with its multiple references to duties, to the rights of 'peoples', and to the 'collectivity'/ 'community'. (Gene M. Lyons and James Mayall, 2003)[6] For instance, and in reference to this book, this interaction between the individual and the community/group will emerge in the construction of rape and torture as violations committed against the individual and with genocide, which is a violation against the group.

The insights presented above have strongly influenced the broad theoretical underpinnings of this book. Namely, that the current concept of human rights has been developed to protect the individual. At the same moment, it is possible to find traces of a group element within this discourse. By bringing together the individual and group dynamics as understood by the current concept of human rights and placing these within a theoretical analysis of rape as linked to torture and to genocide, this book will add to the existing literature on human rights. In the next section of the literature review, the important contribution of varied feminist theories towards understanding how rape can be conceived and understood will be outlined. This overview will also include recent developments found within international law, including rape that has taken place within the context of international armed conflicts.

---

[6] There is also the Genocide Convention (1948), the Declaration on the Rights of Minorities (1992), and the European Framework Convention for the Protection of National Minorities (1995) and the Convention for Minority Languages ((1992).

Feminist Literature on Rape

Feminist Theories of Rape

Feminist understandings, of rape have evolved from several theoretical perspectives. From liberal feminism, to socialist feminism, and to radical feminism, how rape is perceived and defined include a variety of viewpoints, which have contributed to the overall understanding of why rape occurs and how rape should be defined. Eric Reitan has argued that rape is an essentially contested concept and has written about efforts to attain a balance between developing too broad a definition and the need to expand understandings of rape. (Eric Reitan, 2001: 43-50) These works were important and relevant to the book since a major step within the past few years at the international law level was not only to develop a definition of rape within this context but also included a difficult process which led to an acceptance of the need to effectively prosecute rape that had occurred under circumstances of armed conflict.

In Susan Brownmiller's influential work on rape *Against Our Will: Men, Women and Rape* (1975), she argues that "all rape is an exercise in power" and as such is an act linked to the need to dominate others as opposed to one influenced by sexual desire (Brownmiller, 1975: 256). Critically for the subsequent examination of the two international juridical cases in this book, Brownmiller assesses the history and function of rape under circumstances of armed conflict and links this to the overall subjugation of women (and I would argue girls also) within the parameters of everyday life (Brownmiller, 1975). In addition to Brownmiller, other radical feminists insist that rape is a consequence of patriarchal social, cultural, and political systems that results in men being violent and seeing women as sexual objects (Susan Sorenson and Jacquelyn White, 1992: 1-8). However, an important critique of radical feminism deals with its formulation of rape as an individual to individual act (male to female). As Giles and Hyndman correctly point out, some radical feminist theory has tended to disregard the collective and social parameters of rape – especially within the context of armed conflict (Wenona Giles and Jennifer Hyndman, 2004: 15). Yet, as Brownmiller states:

> "In each historic interlude a mob of men, sometimes an official militia , armed itself with an ideology that offered a moral justification – 'for the public good' – to commit acts of degradation upon women." (Brownmiller, 1975: 124-125)

With reference to this book, the point made by Brownmiller is critical since, and as will be discussed, many of the rapes committed during the armed conflict in the Former Yugoslavia and during the genocide in Rwanda occurred in public situations and with socio-political undertones. For instance, during the conflict in the Former Yugoslavia in the 1990s some of the rapes took place in detention camps whereby some of the women were raped until they became pregnant. The reason was that a belief system existed whereby only the father determined a baby's national heritage and by ensuring pregnancy through rape, the desired nationality was continued and expanded. Despite this critique of radical feminism, it is maintained that such observations linking the issues of power, domination, and sexual violence to rape in general and to rape committed under circumstances of armed conflict offered an important and useful analytical perspective for the book.

In an interesting and relevant assessment of rape, Anne J. Cahill outlines three broad feminist perspectives on rape (Anne J. Cahill, *Rethinking Rape*, 2001). These include the 'second wave of feminism'; the radical feminist approach; and 'feminine agency'. I will now examine these three perspectives, which helped to shape the discussions surrounding how rape has been defined under international law.

First, as mentioned earlier, Cahill focuses on what she terms the 'second wave of feminism', which includes Brownmiller's analysis of rape as political and rape as an expression of power and domination over the victim(s) - women (Cahill, 2001:16-20). In her assessment of Brownmiller, Cahill makes an interesting comment in that although rape takes away the autonomy of a woman in fact "Rapists do not rape individuals, but members of a class." (Cahill, 2001:19) In connection to this book, Brownmiller's assertion that on the one hand rape denies a woman's autonomy while on the other asserting that rape is not individualistic may seem to contradict one of the main tenets of my argument. In this book, I argue that rape is understood as a crime/human rights violation committed against the individual. I further develop that rape attacks the autonomy of a woman as reflected in a recent and important international criminal tribunal judgment. Although Brownmiller's views that rape is committed against and can affect women as a class, I would also insist that the important notion of the individual who has been raped is still relevant. To be precise, this approach will be significant for my examination of what happens to rape, on a theoretical level, when it is subsumed within the group focused international crime of genocide. In other words, will a crime (rape) conceived as something that happens to the individual, lose its way when it is placed within genocide with its emphasis on the group? I do not propose the individual model over the group model but I do argue that tensions exist between the two and these must be addressed and understood in relation to rape.

One important contribution of the second wave of feminist analysis of rape was to insist that rape was not a sexual act but one rooted in the realities of patriarchal political, social, economic and power factors. In other words, rape is violent and not sexual and its objective is to dominate (Cahill, 2001: 20-25). Yet, as Cahill points out, such a clear demarcation between any sexual aspect to rape and its violent nature is not fully reflective of its parameters. As Cahill argues:

> "In other words, the violence and the power present in an act of rape are particularly sexualized; they gain, at least in part and perhaps entirely their meaning from a particular sexual hierarchy. Considering rape free from its sexed and gendered meanings is to miss the mark entirely." (Cahill, 2001: 36)

Rhonda Copelon, in relation to international law, also insists that 'rape is a crime of violence'. (Rhonda Copelon, 1995: 65) Chile Eboe-Osuji expands on this notion by distinguishing between the 'modern view' of rape within certain domestic jurisdictions and the 'traditional enquiry':

> "However, the modern view, increasingly gaining ground in some domestic jurisdictions, is that rape is centrally a crime of violence and domination and not just a crime of sex without consent." (Chile Eboe-Osuji, 2007: 256).

This is an important point, which relates to subsequent sections of the book whereby innovative and at times contradictory definitions of rape have been developed within international criminal tribunals. As will be outlined in Chapter 3, some definitions emphasize the violent aspect of rape while others attempt to work through what constitutes rape within the context of international law.

Second, Cahill pushes this idea of sexuality and rape as separate by outlining the radical feminist approach to rape which has argued that rape is found "...squarely within the confines of so-called normal, but imposed, heterosexuality." (Cahill, 2001: 36) Radical feminist authors such as *inter alia* Catherine Mackinnon and Andrea Dworkin, according to Cahill, correctly connect rape with compulsory heterosexuality. Within this context, heterosexuality is "...defined primarily as a dynamic of masculine domination and female submission." (Ibid: 39) In other words, the violence is not found within the act of rape but within the links to heterosexual sex with its domination of the male over the female (Ibid: 41). In a more recent article, and within the context of commenting on one of the international criminal tribunal cases analyzed in this book (ICTR, Akayesu, 1998), Mackinnon continues with this theme:

> "Illegal rape is commonly defined to revolve around force and unwanted sexual intercourse." (Catherine A. Mackinnon, 2006: 940.)

However, and this refers to the third strand covered in Cahill's overview of rape, Cahill notes that the emphasis of radical feminists such as Mackinnon and Dworkin on the patriarchal formulation of heterosexuality can in turn deny the possibility of, in her words, 'feminine agency'. (Cahill, 2001: 37) Once again the issue of, as I use the term 'sexual autonomy', has influenced the basis for one of the two main theoretical implications identified by this book – namely that rape is constructed as a crime/human rights violation committed against the individual and due to selected international jurisprudence rape must also fit into crimes committed against the group. The violation of personal autonomy, or as Cahill comments 'feminine agency', is an important component of how rape is understood. (Joanne Conaghan, 2005: 156; Rosalind Dixon, 2002: 702) For instance, women in situations of armed conflict are often seen and written about mostly as victims. This can have the effect of precluding the possibility of retaining sexual or political autonomy.

In an insightful critique of the role (both positive and negative) feminists have played in developing recent international jurisprudence on rape (especially within the context of the international armed conflict in the former Yugoslavia), Karen Engle writes about two main feminist debates (or in her words 'camps') which surfaced during the 1990s:

> "Advocates in both camps tended to treat most women as victims of the war. Such treatment had implications for the extent to which women were seen to possess sexual and political agency. Those who focused on rape as genocide were likely to regard all Bosnian Muslim women, raped or not, as victims, and as incapable of fighting in the war, but also of speaking truthfully about whether they had been raped. Those who emphasize that rapes were committed on all sides tended to regard women on all sides as victims of, rather than political or even military participants in, the war." (Karen Engle, 2005: 778).

As Cahill argues:

> "For where previous theories of rape risked defining women solely by their victimization, ignoring women's experiences, or resorting to theoretical dichotomies that no longer hold, contemporary feminist theories of the body resist those problems." (Cahill, 2001: 8)

Reflecting this approach of bringing the discussion beyond victims of rape, in a book entitled "Taking Sexual Autonomy Seriously", Stephen J. Schulhofer insists that law (in this case United States law) needs to protect the autonomy of women who have been raped. This emphasis, as Cahill has promoted in her book, would better reflect the realities of women who have been raped and place less of an emphasis on the victimization of those who are raped. (Stephen J. Schulhofer, 1998: 274-282) An additional component to sexual autonomy, which was mentioned in the previous section on human rights, is the link to liberal theory.

Kirsten Campbell points out:

> "This notion of 'consent' derives from liberal models of contractual sociality, which provide the basis of the modern understanding of the crime of rape as a violation of autonomy, that is, a violation of the right to self-determination." (Kirsten Campbell, 2004: 334)

This issue relates directly to how rape can be defined under international law and especially within situations of armed conflict. An existing association under current international law between 'consent' definitions of rape and autonomy may hinder the possibility of linking 'coercion' definitions of rape with autonomy. As such, which feminist understandings of rape best suit the theoretical analysis within this book? In simple terms, the first and third broad theories of rape reviewed thus far can be found throughout the book. One reason is that within the context of recent international law developments much emphasis has been placed on developing definitions of rape. As I will demonstrate in Chapter 3, some of these definitions are linked to power theories of rape as covered by authors such as Susan Brownmiller. This is evident in definitions of rape that include coercion elements. Other definitions of rape examine consent issues, which it may be argued also involve issues of power. Furthermore, one of the cases assessed in Chapter 5 (ICTY, Kunarac et al, 2001) insists that rape is a violation of sexual autonomy thereby projecting the third understanding of rape outlined. A vast and rich literature exists on feminist understandings of rape.

These cover both theoretical and legal assessments. This book will contribute to the feminist body of literature by engaging in theoretical analysis of recent international cases pertaining to rape. In particular, I will link the tensions present within the current concept of human rights with its focus on the individual and the possibility of the group dynamic existing within this concept. This will unfold within an analysis of hope rape has been conceptualized, placed and treated under international law and its association with the individual along with some of the theoretical implications that can emerge when rape is associated with torture and with genocide. In order to better understand how rape has been conceptualized, placed and treated within recent international law developments, it was necessary to review literature on rape as affected by international law and within the context of armed conflicts. It is to these matters that I now turn.

Rape, International Law and Armed Conflicts

This section includes the examination of key international human rights and humanitarian law instruments alongside relevant feminist authors commenting on how rape has been addressed within international law. Critically, for this examination of rape, it was determined that both types of law are problematic. Human rights treaties at the UN level do not explicitly mention rape. Even human rights instruments that deal with women have not always listed the violation of rape. [7] The UN Declaration on the Elimination of Discrimination against Women (1967) and the Convention on the Elimination of All Forms of Discrimination against Women (CEDAW, 1979) do not even address violence against women, let alone rape specifically. It should be noted that Article 6 of CEDAW does mention the trafficking of women. Despite this, violence against women (and girls) still needs to be 'read into' the Convention. [8] As Felice D. Gaer points out:

> "Although violence against women is not specifically discussed in the text of CEDAW, the CEDAW committee members had discussed the problem in a brief general recommendation in the 1980s." (Felice D. Gaer, 1998: 23)

In 1993, the UN General Assembly adopted the Declaration on the Elimination of Violence Against Women. Article 2 (a) outlines "sexual and psychological violence"; the "sexual abuse of female children in the home"; and "marital rape". Whereas Article 2 (b) states "...including rape, sexual abuse..." (Ian Brownlie and Guy S. Goodwin-Gill (eds), 2002: 64) [9] Notwithstanding its lack of status as legally binding, the Declaration (1993) was the first time that violence against women, and rape in particular, had been placed within a UN human rights instrument. In turn, the Vienna Declaration of the World Conference on Human Rights also mentions rape (UN Doc. A/CONF.157/DC/1/Add. 1, 1993).

The Rome Statute, establishing the International Criminal Court (ICC, 1998), incorporates rape and other forms of sexual violence within established international crimes. However, this treaty only entered into force as of 1 July 2002 and the ICC is underway at the time of writing.[10] At the regional level, the Inter-American Convention on the Protection, Punishment and Eradication of Violence Against Women (1994) explicitly addresses rape. The treaty entered into force on 5 March 1995. Article 2 (b) outlines acts of violence against women including *inter alia* rape. (P. R. Ghandhi, 2001: 323)

To conclude this section on international human rights law and rape, the net effect of this absent or even late establishment of said instruments has been a fragmented reality in terms of reporting, understanding, and working towards the eradication of rape under the auspices of human rights law. For example, it was not until 1985 at the UN Conference for Women held in Nairobi, that violence against women was substantially placed within the human rights discourse. However, some positive changes did occur which emerged during the 1980s, whereby the issue of violence against women was slowly interwoven into the broader human

---

[7] There is a difference between 'instruments' and 'treaties and mechanisms'. Overall, and in a general sense, the former are "...international law documents, whether legally binding or not." Camille Giffard, 2000: iv.

[8] The Beijing Declaration and the Platform for Action (1995), resulting from a UN Conference held in 1995, defined violence against women and girls such as 'sexual or physical harm'. For more on this document and the follow-up conference held in New York during 2000, please refer to Daniela De Vito, 2001 : Section III (p. 3).

[9] The 1974 UN Declaration on Women and Children in Emergency and Armed Conflict does not mention rape. UN doc. G.A. Res. 3318 (XXIX) of 14 December 1974.

[10] The ICC also covers situations of armed conflict and individual criminal responsibility.
The ICC trial of ICC-01/04-01/07: The Prosecutor v. Germain Katanga and Mathieu Ngudjolo Chui began on November 2009. The accused have been indicted on charges of rape under article 8(2)(b)(xxii) of the Statute - War crimes and rape under article 7(1)(g) of the Statute - Crimes against humanity.

rights context. [11] (Felice D. Gaer, 1998: 16-19) This last point is critical in terms of how rape has been perceived and understood, even at the international law level. Lisa Sharlach, writing as recently as 2000, notes:

> "First, only within the last decade have many begun to treat rape as a human rights violation, and courts have the power to help shape public opinion on this matter."(Lisa Sharlach, 2000: 90)

The process by which rape enters the human rights discourse is relevant since it demonstrates the difficulty that rape has faced for recognition within international law. As Catherine A. Mackinnon assesses:

> "What is done to women is either too specific to women to be seen as human or too generic to human beings to be seen as specific to women. Atrocities committed against women are either too human to fit the notion of female or too female to fit the notion of human." (Catherine A. Mackinnon, 1994: 6)

One such tension is the process by which rape is subsumed within torture – an established human rights violation and one that has tended to be *perceived* as a violation against men who are politically active.

Regarding *international humanitarian law*, or the law of armed conflict, the prohibition against rape has existed for over one hundred years. (Ruth Jacobson et al, 2000; BRIDGE, 2003; International Expert Meeting, 2007) Furthermore, and as noted in *States of Conflict*, the gendered aspects of armed conflict, power and the State are intertwined. (Ruth Jacobson et al, 2000) In 1847 under Order No. 20, which was a supplement to the United States (US) Rules and Articles of War, rape was prohibited. [12] (Kelly Dawn Askin, 1997: 33-34) An important and influential step in the eventual international codification of the rules of warfare was the Lieber Code (1863). Although formulated in relation to US Army regulations, the Code nonetheless formed the basis of future international efforts to formalize the conduct of war. Article 44 states "all rape…(is) prohibited under the penalty of death." (Askin, 1997: 35-36) According to Askin the prohibition of rape in the Lieber Code, which was based on *customary international law*, not only meant the criminalization of rape but also that its prohibition became part of 'customary humanitarian law'. (Ibid: 36) In 1864, the initial Geneva Convention appeared. Like the earlier Lieber Code, it influenced the development of international humanitarian law.

The Geneva Convention was innovative since it "…aimed at regularizing in a permanent manner, a situation which until then had only been haphazard." (Ibid: 37-38) In an interesting analysis of international humanitarian law, Doris E. Buss insists that this type of law "…in effect, regulates, rather than prohibits, wartime rape." (Doris E. Buss, 1998: 179) One reason for this assessment, according to Askin, could be linked to what is actually emphasized within international humanitarian law – namely the needs of the military rather than protecting

[11] For an overall view of why the rights of women have not always been placed on the human rights agenda (within international organizations, within non-governmental organizations, etc.) please refer to Felice D. Gaer, 1998: 20-22.

[12] The laws of war existed during the eighteenth and nineteenth centuries, yet these were 'uncodified' and varied from nation to nation. As such, the laws of war in existence were within customary law. Treaties pertaining to war were eventually developed during this period.

civilians. (Askin, 1997) However, feminist writers have correctly insisted that how rape (committed under circumstances of armed conflict) is conceptualized has affected its lack of effective prosecution in international law. In 1949, the Four Geneva Conventions were established. Again, the prohibition against rape is included but it is formulated as an attack on a woman's 'honor' and not as a crime of violence. The result of this is an understanding of rape, in situations of armed conflict that does not reflect the realities of those who suffer this crime.

For Doris E. Buss this formulation within the Geneva Conventions is of serious concern since:

> "The characterization of rape as an attack on a woman's honor, and the positioning of the prohibition against rape in the context of 'family rights', 'religious convictions' and 'customs' is problematic." (Doris E. Buss, 1998: 181)

For instance, it could be asserted that only women considered to be honorable are raped. (Ibid) Rhonda Copelon goes on to add that rape has been approached with the labels of not only 'honor' but also of 'dignity' rather than emphasizing its violent nature. (Rhonda Copelon, 1995: 65) As Kelly Askin tellingly points out "Then, as now, rape was considered an effective weapon of war, a 'spoil' of war, and an inevitable consequence of war." Furthermore, "(the) laws of war are only as strong as those who insist that they be observed." (Kelly Dawn Askin, 1997: 33-36) In addition, the connection to 'family rights' distances the individual and emphasizes the group which in turn may impact the violation of rape.

In 2000, Resolution 1325 was adopted by the UN Security Council. The resolution focuses on civilians, especially women and children, affected by armed conflict. Point 10 refers to protecting women and girls "...from gender-based violence, particularly rape and other forms of sexual abuse." (UN Doc. S/RES/1325, 2000). This was the first UN Security Council resolution which considered in detail the impact of armed conflict on women. (www.peacewomen.org/un/sc/1325.html Accessed January 2010)

The final point covered in this section is that of *armed conflict*. It is only within the past fifteen years that more of an emphasis has been placed on the examination of rape within the context of international and non-international armed conflicts. (In relation to the 'gender dynamics of armed conflict' – (BRIDGE, 2003: 11-12; International Expert Meeting, 2007; 3; Golie G. Jansen, 2006). This new work emerged in the early 1990s after the international armed conflict in the Former Yugoslavia. The genocide in Rwanda in 1994, whereby mass and public rapes occurred, also initiated such literature. Terms such as 'ethnic cleansing', 'sexual violence as a weapon of war' (Marleen Bosmans, 2007: 1-3) and attempts to understand the impact of multiple and public rapes along with forced impregnation resulted in significant and at times groundbreaking literature. (Catherine A. Mackinnon, 1994: 6-11; Rhonda Copelan, 1995: 64-65) For instance, assessing how rape can be used as a strategic weapon of war used to carry out ethnic cleansing – as witnessed in the Former Yugoslavia - expanded the knowledge base of rape in times of armed conflict. (Jennifer Green, 2004: 97-116)

In addition, the international community had to change its perceptions of rape occurring in situations of armed conflict. It was not until the 1990s that the issue of rape committed within armed conflict was addressed in a broader and more effective manner. One hurdle to overcome was the perception, such as covered in Susan Brownmiller's work, that rape was a by-product of war. One perspective was that 'soldiers will be soldiers' while another recognized that at times wartime rape could be organized and ordered regardless of its prohibition under international humanitarian law. (Brownmiller, 1975: 31; Simon Chesterman, 1997: 324-330)

As the UN Special Rapporteur Linda Chavez has concluded:

> "(Rape) is an unfortunate and widespread phenomenon which has particularly devastating consequences on the enjoyment of the basic right to dignity and security of person of women, who comprise the greatest number of victims of rape…Rape committed by soldiers has been prohibited by law for centuries. None the less, in many situations, soldiers have been given license to rape as an instrument of policy." (Ms. Linda Chavez, U.N. Doc. E/CN.4/Sub.2/1996/26, 16 July 1996: paragraph 5)

Why has this marginalization of rape during armed conflicts occurred? One reason is linked to a process by which rape cannot solely be understood within the parameters of violence. For example, after the Second World War and as M. Cherif Bassiouni points out, sexual violence was returned to the private sphere whereby the topic of rape, which involved shame and humiliation, could not be discussed in public especially not at an international trial. (M. Cherif Bassiouni, 1999) As such, rape occurring during armed conflicts should remain a private matter. (Judith G. Gardam and Michelle J. Jarvis, 2001; Kelly Dawn Askin, 1997; Hannah Pearce, 2002; Katharine Fortin, 2008) Once again, the tensions formulated by not allowing rape and discussions about rape to operate within the public realm have hindered its effective prohibition and enforcement. Another reason why rape has been marginalized under international law relates to its perception as a gender specific crime committed by men. In an interesting warning, Simon Chesterman argues if only certain rapes are placed within the public realm then in his words "By defining certain rapes as public acts, this act of inclusion implicitly operates to exclude other rapes (those not referable to state policy)." (Simon Chesterman, 1997: 336) Although an interesting observation and one that can be placed within the discussions of this book pertaining to which acts can amount to torture or to genocide, I must emphasize that not all acts can be considered as human rights violations. Or, in this case as rapes that do not have a state policy connection but which are nonetheless acts that are significant and must be addressed but under other jurisdictions than international law or international criminal tribunals. With this background of ignoring wartime rape or of addressing the issue in limited circumstances, and with attitudes perceiving rape during armed conflict as inevitable or as something that should not be discussed or addressed publicly, the international community during the 1990s had to overcome significant barriers. This shift, beginning with the rapes during the armed conflict in the Former Yugoslavia, took place due to a variety of influences and initiatives. The increase in media reports worldwide (UN Final Report of the Commission of Experts, 1992), and the influence of non-governmental organizations such as Amnesty International and Human Rights Watch helped to transform international law and to influence the burgeoning international criminal tribunals for both the Former Yugoslavia and Rwanda (Afra Afsharipour, 1999: 129-172; Helen Durham, 1999: 819-843). Finally, the testimony of individual victims heard by the media, non-governmental organizations and eventually by the international criminal tribunals reflected an important and significant step in international law whereby wartime rape gained a firmer footing than what was possible pre and post World War II. Rape during armed conflict has the effect of being extremely destructive and harmful. One reason is that rape has the capacity to demoralize a so-called conquered group. Rape or even the threat of rape, during armed conflict can result in populations being displaced due to people having to flee internally or beyond international borders. Rape also produces shame and trauma which can hinder marriages, incur divorce, divide families, or compel women to abandon or even terminate children born/conceived as a result of rape, sexual diseases, etc. (Christine Chinkin, 1994: 3-5)

In addition, as Doris Buss has noted, in some cultures the idea of 'woman' is directly linked to the notion of the community. If a woman is raped then it means that the nation/culture has also been raped. (Doris E. Buss, 1998: 195-197) Rape in times of armed conflict can also be used to control a civilian population. Rapes committed against targeted populations, such as Muslims in the Former Yugoslavia or the Tutsi in Rwanda, in public or in front of relatives, occur to intimidate and to ensure compliance with military demands or aims. As Claudia Card poignantly writes, such rapes in armed conflicts are comparable to a form of terrorism, in terms of the varied victims, which are targeted and used to intimidate and ensure compliance from others. (Claudia Card, 2002: 181.) Women are targeted in armed conflicts because of their gender and membership in a particular racial/ethnic group or political affiliation. Rape under these circumstances can act as a conduit for racism, for class reasons and xenophobia against the enemy group and via the abuse of women. As Grayzel correctly points out, the female body becomes the symbolic place where cultural and geopolitical differences are played out, and where new forms of hatred are created for revenge in the future. (Susan Grayzel, 1999: 245.) Within the realities of the genocide in Rwanda (1994), Llezlie L. Green has written about propaganda targeted against Tutsi women prior to the genocide commencing:

> "…'We want to see how sweet Tutsi women are. You Tutsi women think that you are too good for us. We want to see if a Tutsi woman is like a Hutu woman…' These statements reveal that propagandists' efforts successfully demonized Tutsi women, thus increasing their vulnerability to sexual violence throughout the genocide." (Llezlie L. Green, 2002: 18)

Critically, in the words of Christine Chinkin, "Public rape terrorizes and traumatizes the civilian population. There is also only just beginning to be some understanding of the psychological damage caused by the trauma of violent sexual abuse." (Chinkin, 1994: 5) This is linked to the harm or trauma that can result in rapes which have occurred within international or non-international armed conflicts. (Charli Carpenter, 2000; Patricia A. Weitsman 2008) Lastly, Mukamana and Collins develop an important argument in that Western understandings and approaches to addressing rape do not always fit into wartime realities and/or in other areas of the world. Beyond the individual having to be accommodated within the group and commenting on the rapes that took place in Rwanda during 1994 they state:

> "These dominant understandings of sexual violence (Western) begin to weaken when dealing with wartime, where communities rather than individuals are attacked and the social fabric is directly threatened…Further differences may exist in cultural specifics such as meanings of sexual violence, modes of experiencing and articulating traumatic crises, and conventional healing practices." (Donatilla Mukamana and Anthony Collins, 2006: 142)

Literature on Torture and Genocide [13]

There is much literature covering definitions of and the philosophical and social foundations of both the prohibition against torture and of genocide. As such, this book will fill a significant gap that has emerged from the literature review. This contribution relates to what can occur on a *theoretical basis* when rape is subsumed within torture or genocide. As noted, the book considers, among other issues, how rape can be understood within the framework of torture, which is constructed as a human rights violation committed against the individual, and how/if rape can function when it is associated with the international crime of genocide, which has been defined and presented as a violation against a group. In doing so, the book will contribute to a greater understanding of some of the theoretical implications that can emerge from international jurisprudence cases and judgements. It is this author's argument that merely assessing juridical decisions within legal parameters does not offer a complete picture of the implications involved. That is, by adding theoretical analysis to legal assessment a broader understanding of how rape can be conceived, placed, and treated within international human rights and humanitarian law will be possible.

Literature on Torture

Writings on the well-established international crime of torture are detailed and tend to focus on the international legal prohibition of this crime. There is also a vein of literature that relates to philosophical discussions, for instance, examining whether or not torture can be justified. In the aftermath of the 9/11 (New York), 7/7 (London) and subsequent terrorist attacks, the 'ticking time bomb' scenario with links to the philosophical standpoints of utilitarianism, and its counterpoint of consequentialism, is one such approach which has gained prominence. (Sanford Levinson (ed.), 2004; Michael Ignatieff, 2005; Bob Brecher, 2007; Thomas C. Hilde, 2007; Yuval Ginbar, 2008) For this approach, however, the literature reviewed and used focused on how torture has been defined under international law, the importance of the prohibition against torture, and recent efforts to link rape as a possible form of torture under specific conditions.

As noted, literature on the *definition(s) of torture* is quite extensive. Some of the focus is on how torture is defined under international or regional human rights regimes while other discussions stay within the parameters of international humanitarian law. (See in general Nigel Rodley, 1999; Antonio Cassesse, 1996; Duncan Forest, 1996: 1-20; Bertil Duner 1998: 3-62; Michael Peel (ed.) 2005: 7-19) In an extensive overview of the historical background of how the prohibition against torture has been developed under international law and its definitions, Nigel Rodley's book *The Treatment of Prisoners Under International Law* is an excellent starting point for understanding this complex process. In an important passage, Rodley notes the critical distinction between torture and other inhuman treatment since not all acts amount to torture. This distinction was an important aspect as to how the United Nations Convention Against Torture and other Cruel, Inhuman or Degrading Treatment or Punishment (1984) was formulated. As Rodley writes:

---

[13] As noted in the Overall Introduction, the definitions of torture and genocide will be detailed in Chapter 3.

> "The separation of the terms of the formula was therefore much reinforced by the creation of a distinction of obligations or consequences incurred by the two branches." (Nigel Rodley, 1999: 76-77)

The 'two branches' cited refer specifically to Torture as opposed to Other Cruel, Inhuman or Degrading Treatment or Punishment from the UN Declaration against torture (1975) and subsequently from the UN Convention (1984). In other words, torture in terms of both scope and consequences is at the high end of the scale, while the remaining notions such as inhuman treatment fall below torture. More than one definition of torture exists. It was therefore necessary to review instruments at both the international and regional levels in order to understand which definition could be used throughout the book. (This will be worked through in greater detail in Chapter 3). In addition, recent developments from the international criminal tribunals for Rwanda and the former Yugoslavia meant reviewing several cases and Judgements relating to how torture is defined when committed during international and non-international armed conflicts. (ICTY, Celibici case, 1998; ICTY, Foca case, 2001; Women's Caucus (ICC), "Grave Breaches: The Torture Cluster, 1999)

As such, the understanding of torture varies. For example, the UN Convention (1984, Article 1) mentions that torture involves the infliction of 'severe' pain or suffering while the Inter-American Convention (1985, Article 2) leaves out the element of severity. In contrast, the European Convention (1987) does not include a definition of torture (OSCE, 1999). The Medical Foundation for the care of victims of torture, in a report entitled Rape as a Method of Torture has offered the following understanding of torture which will be utilized at this stage in the book:

> "Torture is the deliberate infliction of physical or psychological pain. In the context of human rights law...to be tortured, the infliction of pain must be in the custody of, or under the control of, a state agent, or by a non-state agent acting in an organized group...Most human rights instruments have required there to be a purpose for an act to be categorized as torture, such as gaining a confession (whether true or false), punishing, or intimidating..." (Michael Peel (ed.), 2005: 11)

This literature and the juridical cases reviewed proved invaluable for determining a definition of torture that could be used in this book within the context of international human rights law and humanitarian law and as linked to the specific issue of rape as a method of torture.

With reference to the importance of the *prohibition against torture* (UN Doc, CAT General Comment No. 2, CAT/C/GC/2, 2008), its use over the centuries, and continued use in approximately seventy countries, along with its devastating physical and psychological effects, have contributed to the establishment of several international and regional mechanisms, human rights, and medical entities working towards its abolition. (Nigel Rodley, 1999; Antonio Cassesse, 1996; Ducan Forest, 1996; Bertil Dunér (ed.), 1998; Camille Giffard, 2000; Michael Peel (ed.) 2005)

Beyond this established understanding of the importance of ensuring the full abolition of torture worldwide, I have encountered an underlying yet not well-established notion within the literature. As Deborah Blatt boldly argues, torture is different from other human rights violations:

> "Since torture triggers broader protective and compensatory obligations under the Convention (1984), identification of a particular offence as torture, as opposed to inhuman treatment, has enormous significance for the victim." (Deborah Blatt, 1994: 829)

As I will outline subsequently, the human rights violation of torture in contrast to the human rights violation of rape is well established and addressed within current human rights instruments and mechanisms. Despite significant recent changes at the international law level, the same is not true for rape. (Evelyn Mary Aswad, 1996; Katherine Lusby, 1995; E. Baines, 2003: 488) In fact, as noted earlier, it was not until the 1990s that rape during situations of armed conflict was given a more prominent and effective standing under international law. Asserting that torture rates higher than other human rights violations is an extremely loaded and complex issue. As such, this book will only refer to this observation in connection to innovations associated with the consideration of rape as a form of torture under circumstances that fit within the definition of torture.

This idea that torture can be placed on the higher end of the human rights violations scale due to not only its status under international law but also due to the nature of the violation in terms of effect and trauma was evident with a European case dating from the 1970s. Such a link and in relation to rape considered to be inhuman treatment, as opposed to the more serious violation of torture, can be found in the European Commission of Human Rights Opinion pertaining to *Cyprus v. Turkey* (1976). The European Commission concluded, through evidence submitted, that during the invasion of Cyprus by Turkish armed forces in 1974 there were "...strong indications of rapes (of Cypriot women and girls) committed on a large scale" by said forces. (European Human Rights Reports (EHRR). Volume 4. 1982: 537 - 373 and 374). [14] For the European Commission these rapes were viewed as constituting 'inhuman treatment' and not torture. In another section of the *Cyprus v. Turkey* Opinion, rape as inhuman treatment is placed at the same level as a lack of sufficient food or water. As the European Commission notes, "The withholding from prisoners of an adequate supply of food and drinking water and of adequate medical treatment constituted 'inhuman treatment' in the sense of Article 3." (EHRR: 483 (7. (a) and (c)). Bringing out this point has not been done to make light of such treatment. Nevertheless, the European Commission in its Opinion did not analyze how the acts and effects associated with rape differ from the acts and effects of being deprived of adequate levels of food and drinking water. In correctly commenting on this approach Deborah Blatt (1994: 884) adds that the Commission did not even consider why the rapes did not amount to torture.

The European Commission, which voted by 12 against 1, in reaching this decision, referred to Article 3 (Prohibition of torture) of the European Convention for the Protection of Human Rights and Fundamental Freedoms (1950). This article states, "No one shall be subjected to torture or to inhuman or degrading treatment or punishment." (P.R. Ghandi, 2000: 193) Torture is not defined in this article. Technically, this meant that the European Commission had no working definition of torture at its disposal that would have allowed it to distinguish this crime from other acts and to understand whether rape could be considered as a form of torture. Additionally, the UN Convention (1984) and the European Convention for the Prevention of Torture and Inhuman or Degrading Treatment or Punishment (1987), with only the former including a definition of torture, were not in force or in existence when the

[14] The brackets have been inserted by this author.

Commission's Opinion was produced. However, as Blatt (1994: 821) argues, a definition of torture did exist at the time albeit in the form of the UN Declaration (1975). [15] Moreover, in an earlier case (*The Greek Case* of 1969), the European Commission of Human Rights mapped out a definition of torture that the European Commission could have referenced in relation to the events in Cyprus. Blatt, 1994: 821). In its Report, the European Commission of Human Rights referred to an example of torture as "*falanga* (the beating of the feet), or severe beatings", and that such treatment was committed with a 'purpose', such as, extracting confessions. (Yearbook of the European Convention on Human Rights. Vol. 12. 1969. *The Greek Case*: 504) However, the Commission also noted that other forms of torture existed such as 'mock executions', etc. (Ibid: 500). This has led Deborah Blatt to assert that due to the particulars of these rapes, and the criteria which existed at the time for determining what constitutes torture, these factors should have enabled the Commission to state that the rapes had indeed amounted to a form of torture. (Blatt, 1994: 844-846) [16]

One final observation must be noted from the literature review of torture which relates to earlier sections on feminist literature and gender dimensions, and which will have an impact on the theoretical examinations within this book. There is the tension between how international law and various bodies such as the UN have approached the formulation of a torture definition and how these entities have focused on certain aspects which are detrimental to women who have been victims of torture. For instance, in relation to how the definition of torture, as developed in the UN Convention (1984), and how it has been perceived, the World Organization Against Torture (OMCT) has written:

"The definition of torture has been interpreted narrowly and, consequently, has led to a gender-biased image of the torture victim as a male prisoner of conscience: it is the male who pervades the political/public sphere, thus it is the male who is likely to be targeted by state violence and repression. Such an image, however, neglects women's experiences as victims and survivors of torture." (OMCT, 1999: 41) Also (Lois M. Kois, 1998: 88)

Rape as Torture

From the literature reviewed, there is a concern that if rape cannot be placed within the category of torture and its broader protective and compensatory elements then it may be viewed as less serious. As the Women's Caucus, assessing the Elements of Crimes that were developed for the International Criminal Court, insisted

> "...it is also essential to have an explicit direction to integrate crimes of sexual and gender violence in the prosecution of the grave breaches ... in order to avoid their marginalization. Otherwise, sexual violence might not be included ..." when torture is

[15] Article 1 of the Declaration on the Protection of All Persons from Being Subjected to Torture and Other Cruel, Inhuman or Degrading Treatment or Punishment (1975)

[16] An example of how the particulars of the rapes could begin to fit into the definition of torture, as outlined in the UN Declaration (1975), is referenced within the allegations (made by the Applicant Government – Cyprus). This is evident whereby the perpetrators (the Turkish army) is not disputed, and where the purpose(s) linked to the acts are hinted at in the following excerpt "In certain cases 'members of the same family were repeatedly raped, some of them in front of their own children. In other cases women were brutally raped in public." The European Commission concluded that Turkish forces committed rapes 'on a large scale'. The allegations could have been investigated to determine why some of the rapes occurred in public or in front of family members. This process may (emphasis added) have resulted in a different conclusion being reached by the European Commission, including rape as a form of torture. EHRR 1982, Vol. 4: 536 (Paragraph 358).

charged. (Women's Caucus (ICC), "Grave Breaches: The Torture Cluster". 12-26 February 1999: 2)

In addition, Katherine Fortin writes:

> "Torture is a peremptory norm of international law from which no derogation is permitted. As such, when rape is seen as torture, it is treated under one of the strongest protections that international law can offer." (Katherine Fortin, 2008: 145; Hannah Pearce with reference to 'elevating' the status of rape by associating it with torture – Hannah Pearce, 2002: 534)

Rape as a form of torture is not a distinct crime under international law. Rape is prohibited, torture is a separate international crime, and rape must be subsumed into torture for the act of 'rape as a form of torture' to be recognized. One of the earliest references to rape as a form of torture at the UN level was in a report by the former UN Special Rapporteur on Torture P. Kooijmans. [17] In a 1986 report, Mr. Kooijmans offered a non-exhaustive list of methods that could constitute 'physical torture'. In this list, the Special Rapporteur outlined a section on 'Sexual aggression', which included rape. At this stage, rape was described as the "insertion of objects into the orifices of the body." (UN doc. E/CN.4/1986/15. Report of the Special Rapporteur on Torture: 29)

In 1992, the Special Rapporteur on Torture noted in an oral introduction to his annual report:

> "Since it was clear that rape or other forms of sexual assault against women held in detention were a particularly ignominious violation of the inherent dignity and right to physical integrity of the human being, they accordingly constituted an act of torture." (UN doc. E/CN.4/1992/SR.21. Report of the Special Rapporteur on Torture: 8)

During this period, other voices also began to note that under certain circumstances rape could be a form of torture. In 1991, the human rights organization Amnesty International (AI) produced a report which argued that rape "whether the women are in actual or effective custody (could be) torture." (Amnesty International Document (1991). 'Rape and Sexual Abuse: Torture and the Ill-Treatment of Women in Detention: 5)

Commenting on the case listed in 1995 of Dianna Ortiz, a nun who was raped by government officials in Guatemala, Evelyn Mary Aswad insists that rape under certain circumstances should be considered as torture since "...the separation of rape from torture perpetuates myths about rape and denies women an equal right to dignity, as protected by international human rights law." (Evelyn Mary Aswad, 1996: 1913) A concern, as it relates to this particular case, is how the violations were listed in the legal brief. This is evident in Sister Ortiz's 'Declaration' (Xuncax v. Gramajo, Nos. CIV. A. 91-11564-DPW, CIV.A. 91-11612-DPW, 1995 WL254818 (D. Mass., Apr. 12, 1995), 886 F. Supp. 162) directed against Hector Alejandro Gramajo who was the Guatemalan defense minister during the period in question. Sister Ortiz was kidnapped and repeatedly raped by several individuals. She also received

[17] UN Special Rapporteurs are created and appointed by the UN Human Rights Council (Prior to 2006 it was the UN Commission on Human Rights). The first Special Rapporteur on Torture, Peter Kooijmans was appointed in 1985.

cigarette burns during her interrogation, which were charged as torture. Again, this separation of torture and rape in Sister Ortiz's complaint does not allow for the possibility that rape could be considered a form of torture since the crimes of rape and torture (the cigarette burns) were listed separately. (Evelyn Mary Aswad, 1996: 1914 at note 7 and 1919 at note 34)

Critically, as Deborah Blatt adds:

> "The semantic separation of the terms 'rape' and 'torture' has arguably led to substantive distinctions between the two terms and the perception that they should be read as definite and different…Rape becomes the one physical act a torturer may employ which is not identified as torture." (Blatt, 1994: 849)

As will be outlined in later Chapters, more cases and references to rape as a form of torture emerged in subsequent years at the UN and regional human rights levels. (For an overview of UN CAT jurisprudence please see Katherine Fortin, 2008: 147-149)

The literature review of rape as a form of torture brings out three issues. First, it outlines an evolutionary process as with the European Commission of Human Rights Opinion on the rapes in Cyprus *v.* Turkey (1976) whereby rape was understood as 'inhuman treatment', and later as with the UN Special Rapporteur on Torture and other commentators rape was considered a form of torture. Second, the overall focus when rape has been considered as a form of torture seems to avoid the language of 'honor' and 'protection' generally associated with rape under international humanitarian law. As such, this approach is able to bring out more effectively the violent nature of rape in general and of rape as a form of torture specifically. Third, the focus of this process has been to subsume rape into the crime of torture.

As Simon Chesterman critically points out with reference to the International Criminal Tribunal for the former Yugoslavia (ICTY)

> "…the status of rape as a crime independent of other violations remains unclear. The idea that rape is essentially a 'private' act – only constituting a 'valid' international crime when linked to another more 'serious' offense or when explicitly tied to 'public' policy – has been imported into the jurisprudence of the Tribunal." (Simon Chesterman, 1997: 334)

As mentioned in the Overall Introduction, underlying this book is the fundamental question of "What are the theoretical implications of considering rape as a form of torture when committed within the spheres of international human rights and humanitarian law?". In other words, what are the theoretical implications of considering rape as a method of torture? Several of the literature linking rape as a form of torture (and even on the general topic of torture) insisted on a political association or link to the victims of rape as torture. (Catherine A. Mackinnon, 1993: 25-27; Mary Aswad, 1996: 1930; Deborah Anker, 1995: 784; Deborah Blatt, 1994: 846; Duncan Forest (ed.), 1996: 189; Human Rights Watch, 1999; Hannah Pearce, 2002: 537 and 557; Michael Peel (ed.), 2005: 22; Ruxandra Cesereanu, 2006: 120; Clare McGlynn, 2008: 73-75) Unlike the established literature reviewed, this work will challenge the notion of associating a political element or connection with individual victims of rape as torture. The work will also significantly contribute to existing literature via theoretical analysis, which develops an understanding of the political in order to determine if a broader or narrower perspective of the political can accommodate rape when it is considered as a form of torture.

Literature on Genocide

There is much literature on the histories of genocide and on the development of a definition within international law. Recently, there are enquiries into the relevance of the term and concept itself. (See for instance Luke Glanville, 2009: 467-469) Since the definition of genocide is relevant to the theoretical analysis undertaken in Chapter 6, it was useful to examine some of the existing work assessing the process of formulating the notion of genocide, the definition found within the Genocide Convention (1948), and current concerns with the elements of genocide. As Martin Shaw notes, this assessment involves *inter alia* legal, sociological and political disciplines (Martin Shaw, 2007: 8). Although the innovation and importance of the UN Convention on the Prevention and Punishment of Genocide (1948) cannot be underestimated, it is also evident from the scholarship that concerns exist in relation to its *definition* and to how the international community has, or has not, dealt with circumstances after World War II. With reference to the genocide definition [18], areas of concern include which groups should or should not be protected, which actions constitute genocide, the ambiguities of understanding what is meant by 'intent to destroy' or 'in whole or in part'. (Damien Short, forthcoming publication; Shaw, 2007: 28 and 33) For instance, in an early definition of genocide 'political groups' and 'other groups' were included thereby broadening who could become a victim of genocide (UN General Assembly Resolution, 91-1, 11 December 1946) Much debate ensued at the UN and the final version of the Genocide Convention (1948) omitted political groups and the phrase 'any other group'. (Damien Short; William A. Schabas, 2001) An additional debate within genocide studies relates to the need for or the dangers of expanding the list of groups protected within the Genocide Convention. Martin Shaw (2007) and Adam Jones (2006) refer to the "many 'cides…' of genocide. These include politicide, urbicide, culturalcide and gendercide. The restrictions of the Genocide Convention (1948) in this respect has the effect of excluding many groups which may or may not be permanent or entail specific attributes. These limits were, for instance envisioned by Raphael Lemkin the architect of the term Genocide and the individual who pushed for the Convention. As a result, several authors have argued for either a more flexible approach to accepting which groups should be considered victims of genocide, or have offered different definitions of genocide, that go beyond the Convention. (1948) – (Jones, 2006: 14 and 22; Leo Kuper, 1981; Helen Fein, 1993; Shaw, 2007; Damien Short, forthcoming publication) Which groups should be included? Political groups are often the first to be targeted by States.

---

[18] As the Genocide Convention (1948) outlines:

"Article II

In the present Convention, genocide means any of the following acts committed with intent to destroy, in whole or in part, a national, ethnical, racial or religious groups, as such:

(a) killing members of the group;
(b) causing serious bodily or mental harm to members of the group;
(c) deliberately inflicting on the group conditions of life calculated to bring about its physical destruction in whole or in part,
(d) imposing measures intended to prevent births within the group;
(e) forcibly transferring children of the group to another group."

Although the permanence of these groups could be questioned, the omission from the Genocide Convention (1948) has been strongly contested. (Damien Short)

What about women and the possibility of 'gendercide'? Gender could be considered a specific attribute and barring medical intervention a permanent one. Some are actively using the term 'gendercide' and monitoring events that fall within the category. (Gendercide Watch at wwww.gendercide.org) In more recent times and as witnessed by the genocides of Rwanda and in the former Yugoslavia and as discussed within this book, women were targeted in the lead up to and during the genocides not only because of their membership in a particular ethnic or religious group but more specifically since they were women and because their victimization contributed to the overall intent and policies of the respective regimes.

What is the solution? Through the literature reviewed, it is obvious that changing the Genocide Convention (1948) would be extremely difficult if not impossible. Also, layers of additional groups or of expanded contexts may result in diluting the international crime of genocide. (Luke Glanville, 2009: 467) A parallel can be seen with torture in that acts that do not amount to torture are incorporated into the language. Some are innovative such as with domestic violence while others such as mere personal reflections – "The exam was *torture*!" – take away from the gravity and impact of torture. This author has not developed another definition of genocide. However, perhaps the path undertaken by the trial Chamber of the International Criminal Tribunal for Rwanda in its 1998 Akayesu Judgement offers a concrete and more flexible approach in that both the individual and the group are addressed:

"…the Chamber is satisfied that the acts of rape and sexual violence described above were committed solely against Tutsi women…and specifically contributing to their destruction and to the destruction of the Tutsi group as a whole." Jean-Paul Akayesu v. Prosecutor. International Criminal Tribunal for Rwanda (ICTR). Case No. ICTR-96-4-T. Judgement. 1998: 165-166).

Moving beyond the issue of groups, Martin Shaw makes an interesting point with his discussions of how the term 'ethnic cleansing', used for instance during the armed conflict in the former Yugoslavia during the 1990s, can be substituted for genocide.

For Shaw the term:

> "…'Ethnic cleansing' was a *perpetrators'* term, embedding rather than criticizing their particular meaning of 'cleanliness' or 'purification', while failing to indicate the destructive character of the removal of groups from territories where they lived." (Shaw, 2007:52)

However, as Shaw notes, the term has been adopted within the media and by other entities to denote a negative or destructive policy. (Shaw, 2007: 49) Why then would it matter if one term is used over another? One concern relates to if indeed the two terms are different. Shaw points out the 'exterminatory concept of genocide' versus simply removing a people from an area without 'intentionally killing off'. (Shaw, 2007: 51-52).

Shaw goes on to argue that developing and more importantly accepting the new terminology of 'ethnic cleansing' was not an appropriate step:

> "Looking closely at the language brings into focus the crassness of the proposed analytical distinction. The words were all synonyms for the 'destruction' of a group, understood as the essence of genocide." (Shaw, 2007: 52)

Furthermore, As Catherine Mackinnon wrote in 1994 in relation to the conflict in the former Yugoslavia:

> " 'Ethnic cleansing' is a euphemism for genocide." (Catherine A. MacKinnon, 1994: 8)

An interesting overview connecting the role of the media and how the term 'ethnic cleansing' was problematic in relation to the conflict in Bosnia can be found in Gregory Kent's book *Framing War and Genocide* (2006: 276-295).

One important concern in pushing for and adopting a term such as 'ethnic cleansing' is *if* it is used by the international community (especially by States) to defer responsibilities outlined under the Genocide Convention (1948) such as prevention and prosecution. That is, if a situation is deemed to be 'ethnic cleansing' and not genocide then important and yet complex aspects to the Genocide Convention (1948) are not applicable. (Gregory Kent, 2009: 295; Luke Granville, 2009: 446-449) A related tension can be seen with the recent conflict (since around 2003) in the Darfur region of Sudan whereby certain ethnic groups have been killed, raped or displaced by the Sudanese government or the militia known as the 'Janjaweed'. (Martin Shaw, 2007: 162-171) The crisis has been called a humanitarian issue or a serious human rights concern, involves violations of international humanitarian law and even as 'ethnic cleansing' by the UN and other organizations and governments. (Shaw, 2007: 162-164). To date, only the United States (US Senate Foreign Relations Committee, 9 September 2004, Colin Powell) has referred to the overall situation as genocide (Ibid: 166-167) The politics and national interests of member States of the UN is one reason why genocide has not been linked to the Darfur crisis. A similar reality occurred during the time leading up to the genocide in Rwanda (1994) and the delay of weeks by the UN Security Council to use the word genocide once the killings, rapes and other acts had unfolded. Lastly, an interesting link to the torture sections of this book unfolded within this portion of the literature review. That is, similar tensions and limitations surrounding an association between 'ethnic cleansing' and genocide can be replicated and are addressed in the portions of the book examining the connection between torture and the political (Chapter 5).

Rape as Genocide

One of the first pieces of academic literature reviewed that made the link between rape and genocide under particular circumstances was Catherine Mackinnon's 1994 article entitled "Rape, Genocide, and Women's Human Rights." (See also: Christine Chinkin, 1994: 6) In this piece, Mackinnon writes about the conflict in the former Yugoslavia and how the international community had up to that point misunderstood what was happening in relation to the type of conflict – beyond civil war or ethnic conflict – and the background to the rapes occurring during the armed conflict. As Mackinnon argued:

> "One result of this approach is that the rapes in this war are not grasped as either a strategy in genocide or a practice of misogyny, far less both at once. They are not understood

as continuous both with this particular ethnic war of aggression and with the gendered war of aggression of everyday life." (Catherine MacKinnon, 1994: 8)

She goes on to describe that the situation in the former Yugoslavia at the time was genocide and that rape was "...a tool, a tactic, a policy, a plan, a strategy, as well as a practice." (Ibid: 9) Mackinnon also uses the terms 'rape as genocide' and 'genocidal rape'. (Ibid: 9 and 11)

As with writers such as Deborah Blatt, who have criticized the separation of the terms rape and torture, the use by the international community of either genocide or rape during this period was challenged by MacKinnon. (Ibid) Although an important piece of literature which has influenced this book, it should be noted that placing rape within an international crime such as torture or genocide in turn requires a more in depth analysis of the respective conventions where definitions can be found. (In relation to forced impregnation and the Genocide Convention (1948) - Christine Chinkin, 1994: 8) This was the approach taken by the International Criminal Tribunal for the former Yugoslavia four years later in its Prosecuter v. Jean-Paul Akayesu judgement (1998).

From the Akayesu Judgement, whereby due to the specifics of the case the rapes were considered genocide, several interesting and relevant articles have appeared. Some relate to the juridical implications of the Judgement in terms of subsuming rape into genocide, international law, and how rape has been addressed. (Kelly Dawn Askin, 2005; Christine Stumpen-Darrie, 2006; Catherine A. MacKinnon, 2006; Chile Eboe-Osuji, 2007) Although the Akayesu Judgement (1998) has been viewed as a positive and significant step for rape within international law, there are still concerns. Catherine MacKinnon focuses on the definitions of rape developed (either consent or coercion focused) and this issue will be discussed subsequently in the book. (Mackinnon, 2006: 941; Eboe-Osuji: 252-254).

Another issue relates to the debate about the "intent to destroy a 'substantial' part of a group". In her article "Rape as genocide: some questions arising", Chile Eboe-Osuji analyses rape as genocide in conjunction with what is the minimum number of group members protected by the Genocide Convention (1948) "...intended for destruction." The debate highlighted refers to the phrasing of 'in whole or in part' from the Genocide Convention (1948). (Chile Eboe-Osui, 2007: 260- 265) Eboe-Osui notes that an emphasis on the 'substantial' requirement to numbers has influenced the jurisprudence of the international criminal tribunals. There is also a warning of the "...hazardous effect..." that this emphasis will have on the preventative aspects of genocide and the need to reject the understanding that 'in part' actually means 'substantial part'. (Ibid: 261) A similar concern was raised when the exact numbers of rapes during the conflict in the former Yugoslavia were debated. The point was that unless a substantial number of rapes could be reported and verified, then the impact of the situation would not be considered as serious and the international community would not react effectively. [19] Kelly Dawn Askin's concerns relates to how, in her view, the international community has failed to seize upon the innovations of the Akayesu judgement (1998). That is, many of the subsequent indictments from the ICTR have not included rape charges.

[19] The influence for this section comes from earlier readings of Catherine MacKinnon and personal reflection from this author's informal conversations with individuals helping victims of rape during the conflict in the former Yugoslavia.

The reason, in her words:

> "...primarily because there has been very little genuine and rigorous investigation of the crime by the Prosecutor's Office." (Kelly Dawn Askin, 2005: 1007-1008)

Another area of the post-Akayesu Judgement literature had a strong influence on this book. This body of work explores the more theoretical aspects of the 1998 understanding of rape as genocide. Important themes such as the trauma and social stigma of rape and of rape within the context of genocide (Erin K. Baines, 2003: 488); the shame (Llezlie L. Green, 2002); the effect on communities (Lisa Scharlach, 2000: 91); and especially the voices of those who have been raped within circumstances of genocide and of rapes that have taken place in public (Donatilla Mukamana and Anthony Collins, 2006) have been interwoven within various sections of this book. To conclude, the international crimes of torture and of genocide are well established within international human rights and humanitarian law. In turn, torture is most definitely presented as a crime of violence within international human rights and humanitarian law. In contrast, rape seems to gain status when associated with torture. This may also be the case when rape is subsumed within genocide due to its place within international law. In addition, under international human rights law rape is at times absent or it has been mentioned only recently within human rights documents, resulting in a fragmented reality. International humanitarian law emphasizes the honor of a woman and their protection from rape and not the violent aspect of rape or its prohibition. While these writings on rape as torture and rape as genocide are insightful, extremely useful and at times innovative, they do not address theoretical implications for rape once it is subsumed within international crimes such as torture and genocide. Although theoretical approaches do exist, such as *inter alia* understanding the social and cultural back drop to rape in general and to rape during armed conflicts, the literature reviewed does not use as a starting point theoretical implications emanating from juridical decisions pertaining to the conceptualization of rape as torture and rape as genocide. This significant gap in the literature is what this book endeavors to fill and contribute to the existing body of work.

Chapter 3

ESSENTIAL DEFINITIONS AND INTERNATIONAL CASES PERTAINING TO RAPE

OVERVIEW

In this Chapter, essential definitions for the book will be outlined. These include definitions of rape, torture, and genocide as human rights violations. This is in contrast to 'crimes' that would be dealt with under the domestic judicial systems of respective States. Such a distinction can be understood with the notions of torture as a crime v. torture as a human rights violation as outlined in regional and international human rights instruments. The current concept of human rights does not include all acts. For instance, domestic violence may be a crime under domestic legislation but it is not considered to fall within the remit of human rights. However, if a particular State in its acts or omissions does not take steps to prosecute individuals accused of committing domestic violence then a human rights violation has occurred in direct reference to the State in question.

With specific reference to defining rape, this Chapter will assess how definitions of rape have evolved within certain national jurisdictions and within international parameters. The focus will be on distinguishing between consent and coercion definitions of rape. This will demonstrate some of the key influences which have enabled the issue of rape to gain a firmer footing at the international law level. Finally, each definition will be accompanied by a brief overview of the significant sources and instruments associated with these concepts. The focus, due to the cases/decisions chosen, will be international instruments as opposed to regional instruments. Regional instruments emanate from the Inter-American, African and European human rights regimes, while international ones come from the United Nations. This approach, however, does not dismiss the relevance and influence of national or other regional provisions for human rights violations. Working definitions of key terms are necessary, although the essential contestability and contextuality of such terms must also be kept in mind. [1] Additionally, it is not productive to be limited when operating within a constraining definition. As Nigel Rodley, in reference to precisely formulating a legal definition of torture, insists:

---

[1] I am grateful to Costas Douzinas, who during a conversation suggested this approach in relation to definitions.

> "It is obvious, however, that a juridical definition (of torture) cannot depend upon a catalogue of horrific practices; for to do so would simply provide a challenge to the ingenuity of the torturers, not a viable legal prohibition." (Rodley, 1999: 77) [2]

Yet, as will be outlined during the examination of rape within the context of international humanitarian law, a lack of a definition or vague language has contributed to misunderstandings and to misinterpretations harmful for those who have suffered this crime. As Stanley Cohen mentions:

> "There must be sharable definitions of minimum prison standards, a fair trial, torture or rape. The definition will have some ambiguities, but should be able to exclude official interpretations that are evasions made in bad faith." (Stanley Cohen, 2002: 106)

Therefore, the process of defining essential terms and concepts is included in this section. However, this procedure also involves a flexible approach and a certain level of openness within the formulations that will add to the issues in hand. The chapter will also give a brief overview of the cases covered and extract the relevant theoretical implications. Specifically, I shall discuss how rape has been conceptualized and placed within two cases taken from the International Criminal Tribunals for the former Yugoslavia and Rwanda. The aim is to bring forward critical conceptual concerns with how international law addresses rape.

Rape

As assessed in Chapter Two (Rape, international law and armed conflicts), international human rights law at the regional and United Nations levels and international humanitarian law have created a fragmented reality whereby rape on its own is at times absent from documents, or it is associated with a woman's honor as opposed to an act of violence, or it has only been discussed in a meaningful way very recently. A significant by-product of this process is that no single authoritative law or provision exists for defining rape within regional and UN human rights mechanisms. It is more a matter of accepting that a variety of shifting and not always consistent understandings function within numerous sections of UN and regional human rights levels. One cannot point to a single overarching definition of rape that can be utilized within this context. As such, it was necessary to identify important conceptual differences between rape committed within the context of criminal and national legislative parameters and rape that takes place under the auspices of international law. For instance, understanding that rape committed by a soldier in uniform and during an armed conflict as opposed to the same soldier committing rape out of uniform and outside a nightclub may require different definitions of rape, was essential for this section of the book. 3

The United Nations Special Rapporteur on violence against women, its causes and consequences, has used the term violence against women to include:

---

[2] Parenthesis inserted by this author.

[3] I am grateful to Andrea Loux Jarman for making this important distinction.

> "...any act of gender-based violence that results in, or is likely to result in physical, sexual or psychological harm or suffering to women, including threats of such acts, coercion or arbitrary deprivation of liberty, whether occurring in public or in private life." (UN document E/CN.4/1999/68/Add. 4: 3) [4]

Documents emanating from the Fourth World Conference on Women (Beijing, China 1995) and the five year follow-up Conference (Beijing Plus Five) elaborate on the concept of violence against women (and girls).

The *Platform for Action* (Beijing) follows this definition and

> "...a non-exhaustive list of acts follows which are placed within the following categories: acts occurring in the family or in the community, committed or condoned by the State, and that take place during armed conflict." (Daniela De Vito, 2001: 3)

In the follow-up document to the *Platform for Action*, the Beijing Plus Five *Final Outcome Document* insisted that violence against women and girls "Is a human rights issue and under certain circumstances a human rights violation" and that it is "...linked to the enjoyment of their human rights and fundamental freedoms." Domestic violence would be an impairment to the enjoyment of human rights and freedoms but not a human rights violation *per se*. Sexual violence, including rape, can be understood as "...any violence, physical or psychological, carried out through sexual means or by targeting sexuality." Some examples of this type of violence, which can be inflicted on both men and women, include "...forcing a person to strip naked in public, mutilating a person's genitals or slicing off a woman's breast, etc." (UN document E/CN.4/Sub.2/1998/13: 6) [5]

Within the framework of international law, until 1998, there was no accepted definition of rape. This is not to say that no definitions were ever offered, but it was true that no "...commonly accepted definition of this term" existed before 1998. (ICTR. *The Prosecutor v. Jean-Paul Akayesu*. Case No. ICTR-96-4-T. 1998: 596) In a landmark decision the ICTR Trial Chamber, in *The Prosecutor v. Jean-Paul Akayesu* (hereinafter referred to as the 'Akayesu case') offered a definition of rape. The Trial Chamber defined rape as "...a physical invasion of a sexual nature, committed on a person under circumstances which are coercive." (Ibid: 598) The Chamber also insisted that:

> "...rape is a form of aggression and that the central elements of the crime of rape cannot be captured in a mechanical description of objects and body parts. This approach is more useful in international law." (Ibid: 597)

In the Judgement, the Trial Chamber also makes a comparison between rape and torture. That is, the UN Convention (1984) does not list specific acts that amount to torture. In other words, the Convention "...is focusing rather on the conceptual framework of State sanctioned

---

[4] The quote used by the UN Special Rapporteur on violence against women is taken from Article 1 of the Declaration on the Elimination of Violence against Women (1993).

[5] Human Rights Watch has also added to the process of defining sexual violence.

"Acts such as rape, sexual assault, sexual slavery, forced prostitution, forced sterilization, forced abortion, and forced pregnancy may all qualify as crimes under national and international laws."

Human Rights Watch. "Kosovo Backgrounder: Sexual Violence as an International Crime." May. 1999. Paragraph 1.

violence." (Ibid) This means that the UN Convention (1984) does not represent a framework for outlining the exact and varied methods of torture developed and used throughout the world. Instead, the Convention (1984) sets limits and degrees in relation to how the State uses violence. The Akayesu case also compared this methodology to the crime of rape.

The Akayesu case and its definition of rape was an important development for international law especially since subsequent cases have referred to and have added to its formulation. It will be the starting point, used throughout the book, of how rape is currently being defined under international law. [6] However, tensions in relation to how terminology is defined do exist. For instance, in the above-noted definition of sexual violence the UN Special Rapporteur on Systematic rape, sexual slavery and slavery-like practices during armed conflict, also used the phrase "...any violence physical or psychological." In contrast, the Trial Chamber in the Akayesu case does not incorporate a psychological component in its understanding of sexual violence. An example of this could be a threat to commit rape. The Akayesu Judgement was innovative by offering for the first time a definition of rape within the parameters of international law. However, two key issues have been linked to this and subsequent definitions of rape: 'what are some of the influences that have affected such definitions of rape?' and within this overview 'what are some of the tensions that may result in developing definitions of rape within the confines of international law?' It is to these questions that I now turn.

National and International Influences on Definitions of Rape

International definitions of rape have focused on coercion or consent approaches. Within feminist analysis, the former approach emphasizes power, domination, and violence while the latter focuses on the victim proving non-consent and on the mental state of the perpetrator. (Catherine A. Mackinnon, 2006: 940) According to Catherine A. Mackinnon:

> "Coercion definitions by distinction turn on proof of physical acts, surrounding contexts, or exploration of relative position: who did what to whom and sometimes why. This crime basically takes place on the material plane. Accordingly, while consent definitions tend to frame the same events as individuals engaged in atomistic one-at-a-time interactions, coercion definitions are the more expressly social, contextual, and collective in the sense of being group-based." (Ibid: 940-941)

Mackinnon distinguishes between consent and coercion definitions of rape as understood within national and international law systems. For Mackinnon, coercion definitions of rape are expressed socially, contextually and collectively. Consent definitions of rape emphasize whether or not the victim has consented to the sexual act or acts. In addition, the victim should have the capacity to exercise this consent freely. In contrast, coercion definitions of rape – especially within the context of international law and with reference to situations of genocide, armed conflict, crimes against humanity and mass rapes - focus on the fact that coercive realities are placed upon victims. In other words, within the framework of genocide (or other mass violations of human rights) which are coercive in nature the need for a court or tribunal to determine whether or not a victim has freely consented to a sexual act(s) should

[6] Several definitions of rape exist under national laws of respective States. For an overview of legislation pertaining to rape and the issue of 'force or threat of force' from several civil and common law States please refer to the Foca Case.Foca Case, 2001.

not be relevant. In turn, Mackinnon argues that coercion definitions of rape are more reflective of international law since most international crimes – due to their nature – are coercive and should not require the discussion of consent. (Id; ICC Elements of Crimes: Article 7 (1)(g)-1 Crime against humanity of rape: 2)

Before examining recent international definitions of rape, it is necessary to understand influences from national jurisdictions that have affected such developments. Feminist influences during the 1970s and 1980s brought to public attention the harm (physical and psychological) of domestic violence, rape, marital rape, and sexual assault. As Vera Mackie notes, these efforts and results provided a "conceptual vocabulary" whereby women could express their experiences of victimization. (Vera Mackie, 2000: 37-59) In particular, feminist efforts focused on ensuring that criminal justice systems offered respect and dignity to women who had been raped or abused. Many efforts in terms of law reform and the recognition of harm within criminal trials occurred. Yet despite reforms and changes in attitudes, as Stephen J. Schulhofer argues and within the context of the United States:

> "After decades of intense scrutiny and repeated attempts at ambitious reform, our laws against rape and sexual harassment still fail to protect women from sexual overreaching and abuse."(Stephen J. Schulhofer, 1998: ix)

Schulhofer goes on to add that some of the roots of this failure to effectively reform rape laws can be located in what he describes as "...the intensely personal – and intensely controversial – character of sexual behavior." (Ibid: 17) Questions surrounding sexual behavior and different approaches between men and women to sex along with moral values and social perceptions have affected how the law and courts have addressed rape over the centuries. For example, the 'marital exemption' set in the seventeenth century meant that husbands could impose sex on his wife even if he used physical force. It was not considered rape. During the eighteenth century, rape was defined in England as "carnal knowledge of a woman forcibly and against her will." (Id: 18) Moving away from the idea that a woman could only be raped if there was force involved was a difficult process and one that continued well into the twentieth century. (Id: 19)

Although by the 1970s rape law in the United States and other countries had been examined and reformed to varying degrees, crucial difficulties still existed. These included the perception of how women should behave – for instance, what she was wearing, had she been drinking, was she 'asking for it'. In addition, the courts did not always allow for different understandings of force such as women who are in dependent relationships with men. Finally, there were other hurdles such as police attitudes when interviewing victims of rape. (Id: 25) In turn, even if a case went to court, the victim was challenged, not believed or subjected to public scrutiny leading to more humiliation and loss of dignity. (Catherine A. Mackinnon: 1989: 171-183)

Despite changes to rape laws during the 1980s and 1990s in the United States, such as moving away from notions of force and behavior, Schulhofer observes from certain court cases:

> "Disappointing results such as these have convinced large numbers of anti-rape activists of the need for new and far more ambitious reforms." (Stephen Schulhofer, 1998: 46)

The evolution of changes demonstrates an ongoing and at times fragmented approach to initiate and to achieve legal and attitudinal advancements for rape laws, how rape is addressed within societies, and how victims are treated. (Ivana Radacic, 2008: 368 at notes 52 and 373) Critically is the need to understand what national jurisdictions have included in their respective definitions of rape in terms of coercion or consent. This is important since definitions under international law have had to choose between these understandings and subsequently place them within the complex context of human rights violations such as genocide, torture or systematic rape and within the realities of armed conflicts. As such, and using recent international criminal tribunal Judgements, I shall briefly overview which definitions selected national legal jurisdictions have placed on their statute books and then return to the tensions of deciding with approach (consent or coercion) best fits the circumstances addressed by international law.

Although the Akayesu Judgement (ICTR, 1998) offered a definition of rape, subsequent international criminal tribunal judgements have offered their own versions while reflecting on the Akayesu version. As the Trial Chamber in the Celebici case observed there:

> "...is no convention or other international instrument containing a definition of the term itself...no commonly accepted definition of the term in international law." As such, the Trial Chamber "draws guidance from the discussion in the recent judgement of...Akayesu." (ICTY. *Prosecutor v. Zejnil Delali and Hazim Deli.* ICTY, IT-96-21-T, Judgement, 16 November 1998. (Celebici Case): 478).

It is for these reasons that international criminal tribunals have developed definitions of rape and why the tribunals have examined national jurisdictions. In December of 1998, the Trial Chamber of the ICTY in the Prosecutor v. Anto Furundzia extensively outlined a variety of national statutes that have defined rape. In its overview, the Trial Chamber acknowledged that if international criminal rules did not offer a definition of a concept then utilizing national legislation is permitted. [7] However, the Trial Chamber also insisted on two critical conditions. First, unless an international rule exists then reliance on only one legal system should not be made. That is both civil-law and common-law legal systems should be used. (Ibid: 178) Second, international trials operate differently from national criminal proceedings. Recognizing this would avoid, in the words of the Tribunal, "...a mechanical importation or transposition from national law into international criminal proceedings." (Id)

As such, the Trial Chamber was attempting to find 'common denominators' within the national legislation examined and it concluded:

> "...that a trend can be discerned in the national legislation of a number of States of broadening the definition of rape so that it now embraces acts that were previously classified as comparatively less serious offences, that is sexual or indecent assault." (Id: 179)

The Trial Chamber in the Furundzija case also asserted that most legislation reviewed [8]

---

[7] The Trial Chamber found that the elements of the crime of rape could not be found in 'international treaty or customary law', in 'general principles of international criminal law, nor in 'general principles of international law.'ICTY. Prosecutor v. Anton Furundzija, ICTY IT-95-17/1-T10, Judgement, 10 December 1998, at 177.

[8] For the list of national legislation (both common and civil law) reviewed by the Trial Chamber, please refer to Paragraph 180 and Endnotes 207-214.

varied but these understood rape to involve "...the forcible sexual penetration of the human body by the penis or the forcible insertion of any other object into either the vagina or the anus." [9] This conclusion by the Trial Chamber from its review of national legislation brings out an important potential tension in arriving at any definition of rape, namely that rape must be understood as something that is forced. For instance, and although the Trial Chamber acknowledged different degrees of force including incapacitating the victim, this notion may prove to be problematic. (Id: 180) There are circumstances, some of which have been covered by international criminal tribunals, whereby force does not enter into the realities of rape. For example, a woman in a refugee camp may have to 'agree' to sexual intercourse in order to receive food aid for her family. In turn, a woman during situations of armed conflict may be placed in a house to service soldiers – in some instances these women could go out of the house to get provisions.

In a further case, Foca case (2001), the conclusion offered by the Furundzija Case Trial Chamber that rape in national jurisdictions involves force was challenged by the Trial Chamber in its Judgement. Specifically, the Foca Case Trial Chamber asserted that although the definition of rape offered by the Furundzija Judgement was relevant to that case, it was also too narrow for international law. (ICTY, Prosecutor v. Dragolijub Kunarac, Radomir Kovac and Zoran Vukovic, ICTY, IT-96-23-T and IT-96-23/1-T, Judgement, 22 February 2001. (Foca Case): 438) Specifically, the Foca Judgement focused on the 'force, threat of force or coercion' elements from the Furundzija definition of rape. (Ibid: 440) Once again, the Foca Trial Chamber reviewed several national jurisdictions 10 to determine some common features and concluded that these could be divided into three broad categories: 1) 'Force or threat of force'; 2) 'Specific circumstances which go to the vulnerability or deception of the victim'; and 3) 'Absence of consent or voluntary participation'. (Ibid: 443-460) In the first category, some national jurisdictions such as Korea, China, Norway, Austria, Spain and Brazil required 'violence, force, or a threat of force'. (Id: 444) The second category relates to criminal codes that include not only violence or force or threat of force, but also circumstances whereby the victim is rendered incapacitated in their definitions of rape. For instance, the victim was surprised or not mentally or physical capable to resist. (Id: 446) For the third category, the Trial Chamber notes that most common law systems (and some civil law traditions such as Belgium) reflect "...the absence of the victim's free and genuine consent to sexual penetration which is the defining characteristic of rape."(Id: 453) From its examination, the Trial Chamber decided to focus on the 'consent' aspect within its definition of rape. (Id: 456-459) Reflecting on the Furundzija Case definition of rape:

> "Given that it is evident from the Furundzija case that the terms coercion, force, or threat of force were not to be interpreted narrowly and that coercion in particular would encompass *most* conduct which negates consent, this understanding of the international law on the subject does not differ substantially from the Furunzija definition." (Id: 459)

Although national jurisdictions that have defined rape are extremely useful to the journey undertaken by international law in its nearly ten year attempts to define rape it must be noted

---

[9] The Trial Chamber also recognized the difficulties with accepting oral sex as a possible for of rape since some States view this act as sexual assault while others understand it as rape.
Id at 181 and 182.

there are constraints for international law. As Kirsten Campbell in her assessment of the Foca Case Judgement (2001) notes:

> "For this reason, the Tribunal held that 'rape as a crime against humanity or a violation of the laws or customs of war requires proof of elements that are not included in national penal codes, such as attack upon any civilian population…or the existence of an armed conflict." (Kirsten Campbell, 2004: 335)

Definitions of Rape Developed Under International Law

To date, there is still no definitive definition of rape within international law. Rather international criminal tribunal cases from the Akayesu Judgement (1998) have crossed between 'consent' (non-consent) or coercion' definitions of rape or have meshed the two approaches. Returning to Catherine A. Mackinnon, the Akayesu Judgement (1998) definition of rape – "a physical invasion of a sexual nature, committed under circumstances which are coercive." (Akayesu case: 478-479) - was critical since:

> "Crucially, 'coercive circumstances need not be evidenced by a show of physical force' but 'may be inherent in certain circumstances', such as armed conflict or the military presence of threatening forces on an ethnic basis." (Catherine A. Mackinnon, 2006: 941)

Commenting on the Akayesu Case (1998) definition of rape which focused on coercion, Mackinnon forcefully argues for this approach under international law and states:

> "And, arguably for the first time, rape was defined in law as what it is in life." (Ibid)

Since Akayesu (1998) several international Judgements have developed or utilized existing definitions of rape from previous international cases. As Mackinnon notes, the ICTY and ICTR in post-Akayesu definitions have tilted towards non-consent definitions of rape. (Id: 941-942)

In 2003, the ICTR Trial Chamber in the case of Semanza offered a definition that stated the:

> "…mental element for rape as a crime against humanity is the intention to affect the prohibited sexual penetration with the knowledge that it occurs without the consent of the victim." (ICTR. *Prosecutor v. Laurent Semenza*, ICTR-97-20-T, Judgement, 2003: 346) However, as Mackinnon acknowledges, the Trial Chamber understood that consent should be "…assed within the context of the surrounding circumstances." (Catherine Mackinnon, 2006: 943)

Why is this tension, between non-consent and coercive approaches to defining rape under international law, so problematic? As Mackinnon so eloquently argues in her overview of ICTY and ICTR definitions of rape and in relation to crimes against humanity:

---

[10] For the list of national legislation reviewed by the Foca Trial Chamber, please refer to Paragraphs 443-460.

> "No other crime against humanity has ever, once the other standards are met, been required to be proven non-consensual. With sex, it seems, women can consent to what would otherwise be a crime against their humanity, making it not one." (Ibid: 944-945)

As such, which definition of rape will be utilized. As a start, I agree that the Akayesu case 'coercive' definition of rape is extremely important. It does not offer an all-encompassing solution, but as with definitions of torture, this flexibility is better suited for international law. However, completely removing the issue of 'non-consent' may not be so beneficial. It is perhaps for this reason that the recently established International Criminal Court in its elements of rape, as Mackinnon argues, "straddles the definitional divide rather than resolves it."(Id: 945) This tension cannot be resolved here. However, I will understand the definition of rape under international law to be influenced by the Akayesu Judgement (1998) while allowing for other variations of this more flexible approach to infiltrate.

Lastly, is rape an international crime? Since international crimes only emanate from three sources of international law (conventions, customs – State practice, and general principles – recognized by civilized nations), there are constraints when determining if rape qualifies. Rape is indeed prohibited under international humanitarian law. Furthermore, rape could be an international crime if committed within the framework of other crimes such as war crimes, torture, genocide, or as crimes against humanity. (Human Rights Watch, 1999: 1-2) Rape, if incorporated into the grave breaches provisions (I.e. torture) of the Geneva Conventions (1949) and of Additional Protocol I (1977), and if considered as genocide or as crimes against humanity could incur universal jurisdiction. (Ibid: 2-3) Yet, beyond being subsumed into one of these established categories of international crimes, rape currently does not stand on its own as an enumerated international crime. The impact of this reality on rape within international human rights and humanitarian law will be examined during the theoretical portions of this book.

Torture and Genocide Briefly Defined

Torture

The right not to be subjected to torture is listed in several international and regional human rights instruments. [11] The non-derogable nature of this right, meaning that even under declared states of emergency it can never be suspended, is well founded within several regional and international human rights instruments and within international humanitarian law. Its position within what is referred to as 'general international law' is commonly accepted. Briefly on this subject, through various international, regional, and even domestic developments achieved since the establishment of the UN, the prohibition of torture fits into

---

[11] For example, this right is explicitly noted in the Universal Declaration of Human Rights (1948), Declaration on the Protection of All Persons from Being Subjected to Torture and Other Cruel, Inhuman or Degrading Treatment or Punishment (1975), Convention against Torture and Other Cruel, Inhuman or Degrading Treatment or Punishment (1984), Inter-American Convention to Prevent and Punish Torture (1985), European Convention for the Prevention of Torture and Inhuman or Degrading Treatment or Punishment (1987), Body of Principles for the Protection of All Persons under any Form of Detention or Imprisonment (1988), Code of Conduct for Law Enforcement Officials (1979), etc.

the category of general international law which emanates from certain established sources of international law such as treaties or custom. (Nigel Rodley, 1999)

What constitutes torture? More than one definition of torture exists, such as those outlined under the UN and the Inter-American human rights regimes. The understanding of torture varies. For example, the UN Convention (1984) mentions that torture involves the infliction of 'severe' pain or suffering while the Inter-American Convention (1985) leaves out this element of severity. [12] In contrast, the European Convention (1987) does not include a definition of torture. Torture, as outlined in the *Greek Case* [13], can be understood from the perspective of a 'sliding scale' with a series of phases surpassed in order to arrive at this international crime:

> "So, for torture to occur, a scale of criteria has to be climbed. First, the behavior must be degrading treatment: second, it must be inhuman treatment; and third, it must be an aggravated form of inhuman treatment, inflicted for certain purposes." (Nigel Rodley, 1999: 77-78. See also: OSCE, 1999: 37; Duncan Forrest, 1991: 1-20; Bertil Duner, 1998: 3-62; and Michael Peel, 2005: 7-19)

According to the European Commission of Human Rights, in its report on the Greek case (1969), degrading treatment can mean "humiliation or action against will or conscience". Inhuman treatment must include "(a) mental or physical suffering; (b) the suffering must be severe; (c) it must be deliberately inflicted; and (d) it has (seemingly) to be unjustifiable in the particular situation." [14]

For the Commission, then, torture would be inhuman treatment that also had a 'purpose' such as obtaining information or gaining a confession, or to punish an individual. In addition, torture can be viewed as "...an aggravated form of inhuman treatment." (Nigel Rodley, 1999: 77) An act amounting to 'cruel, inhuman or degrading treatment or punishment' is often referred to as 'ill-treatment.' (OSCE, 1999: 37 Duncan Forrest, 1991: 1-20 Bertil Duner, 1998: 3-62 and Michael Peel, 2005: 7-19)

---

[12] Article 1 of the UN Declaration (1975) reads, "...torture means any act by which severe pain or suffering, whether physical or mental, is intentionally inflicted..."

Article 1 of the UN Convention (1984) reads "1. For the purposes of this Convention, the term 'torture' means any act by which severe pain or suffering, whether physical or mental, is intentionally inflicted on a person..."

Article 2 of the Inter-American Convention (1985) reads "...torture shall be understood to be any act intentionally performed whereby physical or mental pain or suffering is inflicted..."

P.R. Ghandhi. Pp. 109 and 315.

N. Rodley. P.389.

[13] The Greek Case was, in 1967, brought before the European Commission of Human Rights by four member States alleging violations committed by the Greek Government of human rights violations – including torture- under the European Convention for the Protection of Human Rights and Fundamental Freedoms (1950).

In the words of the Commission:

"...for all torture must be inhuman and degrading treatment, and inhuman treatment also degrading. The notion of inhuman treatment covers at least such treatment as deliberately causes severe suffering mental or physical, which, in the particular situation, is unjustifiable. The word torture is often used to describe inhuman treatment, which has a purpose, such as the obtaining of information or confessions, or the infliction of punishment, and it is generally an aggravated form of inhuman treatment."

Yearbook of the European Convention on Human Rights (The Greek Case). V. 12. 1969: Introduction and 186.

[14] Yearbook of the European Convention on Human Rights (The Greek Case). V. 12. 1969: Introduction and 186

The inclusion, by the Commission, of an element of justifiability has been criticized since it could be construed that in particular circumstances such acts could be acceptable. Nigel Rodley, 1999: 78-84.

A more contemporary examination of these degrees of acts can be found in the International Criminal Tribunal for the Former Yugoslavia (ICTY) Trial Chambers decision in the 'Celebici' case. Due to how the charges of rape were formulated, namely under the heading of 'Torture and Cruel Treatment', the Trial Chamber had to work through not only what constituted torture and cruel treatment, but also into which category rape should be placed in this particular case. In a detailed analysis the Trial Chamber, albeit within the context of an international armed conflict, examined the various components of torture; willfully causing great suffering or serious injury to body or health; inhuman treatment; and cruel treatment. It is important to outline that in the Celibici case the ICTY Trial Chamber was attempting to categorize torture and other ill-treatment within the specifics of 'grave breaches' and of Common article 3 of the Geneva Conventions (1949). In turn, although the Trial Chamber has asserted the existence of an "inter-relationship of the mistreatment offences" it has also outlined important distinctions between the offences within the context of international humanitarian law – namely within 'grave breaches' or under the auspices of Common article 3. One such distinction, used by the Trial Chamber, can be found in the use of the word 'severe' or 'serious' when describing the level of suffering incurred. [15]

It is beyond the scope of this study to analyze in a detailed manner whether the Celibici case or the Greek case examinations of torture and other ill-treatment can be replicated under all circumstances. The key is that while torture is at the top end of the scale, both torture and other offences, also constitute inhuman or cruel treatment, depending on the particular situation.

Which definition of torture, then, will be most useful for this book? The two cases mentioned emanate from the UN human rights system and address situations of international or non-international armed conflicts. It is not set in stone that the UN Convention (1984) and its definition of torture must be followed for situations of armed conflict. Yet, in an interesting assessment, the ICTY Trial Chamber has argued:

> "It may therefore be said that the definition of torture contained in the Torture Convention (1984) includes the definitions contained in both the Declaration Against Torture and the Inter-American Convention and thus reflects a consensus which the Trial Chamber considers to be representative of customary international law." (Celebici case, 1998: 459)

In contrast, however, the ICTY Trial Chamber in another decision concludes:

> "...that the definition of torture under international humanitarian law does not comprise the same elements as the definition of torture generally applied under human rights law. In particular, the Trial Chamber is of the view that the presence of a state official or of any other authority-wielding person in the torture process is not necessary for the offence to be regarded as torture under international humanitarian law." [16]

As such, the Foca case Trial Chamber used customary international law to define torture within the confines of international humanitarian law as involving

[15] *Prosecutor v. Zejnil Delali et al.* ICTY, IT-96-21-T, Judgement, 16 November 1998. Hereinafter the *Celibici case*) 440-445 and 452-474.

[16] *Prosecutor v. D. Kunarac (et al).* IT-96-23-T and IT-96-23/1-T (hereinafter the 'Foca case'). Judgement. 22 February 2001.

I. The infliction, by act or omission of severe pain or suffering, whether physical or mental.
II. The act or omission must be intentional.
III. The act or omission must aim at obtaining information or a confession, or at punishing, intimidating or coercing the victim or a third person, or at discriminating, on any ground, against the victim or a third person." (Foca case, 2001: 497)

Furthermore, in the Rome Statute for the recently established International Criminal Court there has been a shift away from the requirement of an 'official link' in the commission of torture and under certain circumstances (Crimes against humanity) a specific 'purpose' is not required. [17] Regardless, the definition of torture as found under the UN Convention (1984) will be used for relevant cases. In other circumstances, the appropriate instrument or interpretation will be referenced on a case-by-case scenario.

The strict definition of torture, under the UN Convention (1984), can be broken down into three main components:

1) The act must cause "severe pain or suffering, whether physical or mental..."
2) Torture is committed under the auspices of a prohibited purpose. For instance the Torture Convention (1984) under Article 1 elaborates:

> "...for such purposes as obtaining from him or a third person information or a confession, punishing him for an act he or a third person has committed or is suspected of having committed, or intimidating or coercing him or a third person, or for any reason based on discrimination of any kind."

Critically, as the Medical Foundation for the care of victims of torture insists:

> "The only requirement is that the violence should not be completely purposeless." (Michael Peel, 2004: 11) There must also be an official link in that the pain or suffering "...is inflicted by or at the instigation of or with the consent or acquiescence of a public official or other person acting in an official capacity." (P.R. Ghandhi, 2000: 109)

In addition to these three elements, the act(s) in question must be inflicted with intention. [18]

To conclude this section, for an act to qualify as torture under this interpretation it must include each of these three elements and it must have been intentionally carried out. [19]

---

[17] The UN Human Rights Committee, in reference to Article 7 of the ICCPR has also argued this point in 1992. "It is the duty of the State party to afford everyone protection...against acts prohibited by article 7, whether inflicted by people acting in their official capacity, outside their official capacity or in a private capacity Foca Case: 481.See also the Rome Statute for the International Criminal Court (ICC) – Elements of Crimes – in relation to the issue of an 'official capacity' and 'purpose'. Articles 7 and 8.

[18] The OMCT has broken down the definition of torture into five main components. The additional element includes "exclusion of torture related to pain arising from lawful sanctions". OMCT. *Violence Against Women: A Report*. 1999. P. 40.

[19] For a more detailed assessment of particular acts that various regional and international human rights mechanisms have stated amount to torture, please refer to Nigel Rodley's book. One example reads, "In the view of the Human Rights Committee, he 'was subjected to severe...psychological torture, including the threat that...(his) hands would be cut off by an electric saw, in an effort to force him to admit subversive activities." Nigel Rodley. Pp. 85-101.

Then, there is the issue of 'broader protective and compensatory obligations' associated with the prohibition against torture within the UN Convention (1984). The UN Convention (1984) offers to those who have suffered torture, protection and compensation.

For instance:

- States must, in their domestic law, ensure that torture is a crime;
- States have an obligation to punish or extradite those involved in torture;
- States cannot return or send (*refouler*) an individual to a State where he/she is in danger of being subjected to torture; and
- States must provide for redress and 'fair and adequate compensation' to those subjected to torture. [20]

Under Article 14, a victim of torture should have effective access not only to redress but also he/she has 'an enforceable right to fair and adequate compensation'. States that are party to the Convention have an obligation to ensure these measures are put into place. [21] Furthermore, and in relation to 'other ill-treatment', States that are party to the UN Convention (1984) are only obligated to prevent such treatment; educate against its commission; and ensure that an effective investigation takes place. (Evelyn Mary Aswad, 1996: 1917)[22] At the UN level, only the International Covenant on Civil and Political Rights (1966) (ICCPR) includes articles ensuring an explicit right to compensation for victims of 'unlawful arrest or detention' and for individuals whose criminal convictions have been 'reversed' or 'pardoned' due to a miscarriage of justice. [23] Article 2 of the ICCPR outlines the right for victims of a violation of the rights and freedoms listed within this treaty, the opportunity to seek an 'effective remedy' within their respective States. [24] In addition, the (First) Optional Protocol to this treaty provides an avenue for individuals (from States Parties to this Protocol) to approach the UN's Human Rights Committee with complaints of human rights violations if, inter alia, all domestic remedies have been exhausted. The Human Rights Committee can only forward its 'views' to the State Party in question and to the individual

[20] Torture Convention (1984) – Articles 2 to 8 and Article 14.
P.R. Ghandhi.Pp. 110-112.

[21] Article 14 – "1. Each State Party shall ensure in its legal system that the victim of an act of torture obtains redress and has an enforceable right to fair and adequate compensation…"
If death takes places due to an act(s) of torture, then the victim's 'dependants' can receive the compensation. This obligation is applicable to an act(s) of torture and not to 'other cruel, inhuman or degrading treatment or punishment'. P.R. Ghandhi. P. 112.

[22] See also Article 16 and Articles 10-13 of the UN Convention (1984).
P.R. Ghandhi. Pp. 111-112.

[23] ICCPR, Article 9(5) and Article 14(6).

[24] Briefly, a remedy (redress, relief) refers to "Any of the methods available at law for the enforcement, protection, or recovery of rights or for obtaining redress for their infringement." In turn, compensation can be understood as "Monetary payment to compensate for loss or damage."
Under international law, reparations are "Compensation for injuries or international torts (breaches of international obligations). Whenever possible, international courts or arbitration tribunals will rule that reparations be made by means of restitution in kind; if this is not possible, compensation is by payment of a sum equivalent to the value of the restitution in kind. The aim of the reparations is to eradicate the consequences of the illegal act."
Critically, and for this examination of torture, the definition of reparations given goes on to add, "It is not clear, however, whether there is an obligation to make reparations for all breaches of international law." Elizabeth A. Martin (ed.). *Oxford Dictionary of Law*. Pp. 90, 395, and 398.

who formulated the complaint. There is no explicit right to compensation. In addition, the UN Special Rapporteur can investigate cases without the need to exhaust domestic remedies.

Regional mechanisms, as found in the European and Inter-American human rights systems, also include provisions for victims of human rights violations to seek an effective remedy and in some cases proceed further than the UN human rights system – excluding the UN Convention (1984). [25] Under the Inter-American system, its Court of Human Rights can order compensation for victims who have suffered violations of the many rights and freedoms enumerated in the American Convention on Human Rights (1969). [26] The European Court of Human Rights, in a case involving rape as a form of torture (Aydin Judgement of 25 September 1997), awarded the applicant the amount of £25,000. This was for compensation in regards to Turkey's violation of Article 3 (Torture) of the European Convention for the Protection of Human Rights and Fundamental Freedoms (1950). [27] In addition, the influence of the UN Convention (1984) on the international law of armed conflict is still critical. As will be outlined in subsequent Chapters the higher status afforded to the international crime of torture, as witnessed by its stronger protection and compensatory obligations at the UN level, may affect how rape is understood. This does not, however, diminish any developments formulated at the regional level that expand State obligations in relation to a broader set of human rights and freedoms. [28]

Beyond the strong protective and compensatory elements found within the prohibition of torture, this international crime is understood to be part of general international law. The

sources of international law, as outlined under Article 38(1) of Statute of the International Court of Justice (ICJ) [29], include the following:

> "an international conventions, whether general or particular, establishing rules expressly recognized by the contesting states; **b.** international custom, as evidence of a general practice accepted as law; **c.** the general principles of law recognized by civilized nations; and **d.** judicial decisions and teachings of the most highly qualified publicists…" [30]

---

[25] Article 13 (Right to an effective remedy) of the European Convention for the Protection of Human Rights and Fundamental Freedoms (1950).

The African Charter on Human and People's Rights (1981) only includes a prohibition against torture in Article 5. However, the Protocol on the Establishment of an African Court on Human and Peoples' Rights has just entered into force during 2003. Under Article 27 (Findings) the court will be able to remedy a violation of the Charter (1981) "…including the payment of fair compensation or reparation."

P.R. Ghandhi. P. 196 and P. 328 and P. 341.

[26] Article 63 (1) of the American Convention on Human Rights (1969) in part reads "If the Court finds that there has been a violation of a right or freedom protected by this Convention…It shall also rule, if appropriate…that fair compensation be paid to the injured party.

Article 41 (Just satisfaction) of the Convention for the Protection of Human Rights and Fundamental Freedoms (1950) states "…if the internal law of the High Contracting Party concerned allows only partial reparation to be made, the Court shall, if necessary, afford just satisfaction to the injured party." P.R. Ghandhi. Pp. 200 and 304.

[27] European Court of Human Rights. Reports of Judgements and Decisions. Case of Aydin v. Turkey. Judgement of 25 September 1997. No 50. Pp. 1902-1903 (Para. 126-131).

[28] See, for example, the UN Convention Article 1(2) on this topic. P.R. Ghandhi. P. 109.

[29] The ICJ is, as denoted in the UN Charter, the 'principal judicial organ of the United Nations'. UN Charter. Article 92.

[30] W. Van Der Wolf and J. Oppenheim (eds.). International Courts and Tribunals: Selected Documents and Materials. . P. 159.

Peter Malanczuck. Akehurts's Modern Introduction to International Law. P. 3, Pp. 35-62, and Pp. 91-108.

Treaties and custom are considered principal sources of international law, while general principles of law, judicial decisions, and the opinions of publicists are subsidiary sources.

General International law then "…refers to that law that may be derived from any one or combination of these sources." [31] Torture, it has been argued, falls within this principle.

This means that States not party to any international or regional conventions addressing torture are nonetheless obligated to uphold its prohibition. As Nigel Rodley writes, in relation to the prohibition of torture, "…the prohibition is one of general international law, regardless of whether a particular state is party to a treaty expressly containing the prohibition." [32]

In sum, the international crime of torture has evolved around several definitions developed within regional and UN instruments and from cases with reference to what constitutes an act of torture. For the purpose of this book, the UN Convention (1984) and its three-part understanding of torture will be the starting point. When necessary references will be made to developments, such as those outlined in cases from the International Criminal Tribunals, for additional elements to the crime of torture. Any consideration of torture must also understand its broad protective and compensatory attributes along with its substantial standing within general international law.

Genocide

Considering rape as genocide may have an impact on the prohibition of rape and on rape as a form of torture. As such, the international crime of genocide needs to be defined along with a brief examination of current international criminal tribunals that have brought forward such cases. The ongoing International Criminal Tribunal for the Former Yugoslavia (ICTY) was originally established via a UN Security Council Resolution in the aftermath of the armed conflict in the former Yugoslavia during the 1990s, which resulted in its dissolution. On 22 February 1993, the Security Council passed Resolution 808, which outlined the idea of establishing an international criminal tribunal to prosecute individuals "responsible for serious violations of (international) humanitarian law committed in the territory of the former Yugoslavia since 1991." (Virginia Morris and Michael P. Scharf , 1995: 31) The ICTY 'Statute', which covers the crimes to be addressed and the rules by which the tribunal should function, was also passed by the Security Council a few weeks later. (Id: 184) A similar tribunal and Statute were established by the Security Council in the aftermath of the 1994 Genocide in Rwanda - the International Criminal Tribunal for Rwanda (ICTR). [33] Since two cases from these international criminal tribunals will be utilized, four points should be noted. First, these are *ad hoc* tribunals created under Book VI of the UN Charter (international peace and security). Second, each tribunal operates within specific limits in terms of 'temporal and territorial jurisdiction'. (Gabriel Kirk McDonald *in* Sienho Yee and Wang Tieya (eds.). The

[31] There is also debate as to whether or not UN General Assembly resolutions can be understood as a source of international law. Nigel Rodley. P. 62.

[32] Rodley also uses the phrase the prohibition of 'torture and other ill-treatment' as being part of general international law. Id. P. 74 and p. 75. Additionally, and due to the non-derogability standing of torture (and other ill-treatment), Rodley adds this may "…permit acceptance of the view that the prohibition is itself a norm of jus cogens or 'a peremptory norm of general international law' which is 'a norm accepted and recognized by the international community of states as a whole as a norm from which no derogation is permitted and which can be modified only by a subsequent norm of general international law having the same character.' "Nigel Rodley. P. 74.

[33] UN Security Council Resolution 995 of 8 November 1994.

ICTY can only deal with violations that took place in the territory of the former Yugoslavia since 1 January 1991 and the ICTR covers violations in Rwanda (and relevant external territories) from 1 January 1994 to 31 December 1994. Third, the armed conflict in the former Yugoslavia was international in nature while the conflict in Rwanda was considered non-international in scope despite crossing its borders. For example, some international crimes were committed in refugee camps in neighboring States. These tribunals are also temporary entities. Fourth, both Statutes have their roots in international criminal law – focusing on individual criminal responsibility. Under the ICTY Statute, the wording of Articles 4(2) and (3) - Genocide is taken *verbatim* from the Convention on the Prevention and Punishment of the Crime of Genocide (1948) – hereinafter the Genocide Convention (1948). In particular, these sections refer to Articles II and III of that Convention. The ICTR Statute, in its Article 2 – Genocide, also reflects the Genocide Convention. The Genocide Convention (1948) has been listed by the Secretary General of the UN as one aspect of conventional international humanitarian law that has developed into international customary law. [34] A few key points need to be made about the crime of genocide in general and about Article 4 of the ICTY Statute more particularly. Unfortunately, humanity has a long history of witnessing genocide - it is not a modern phenomenon. Yet, it was not until the end of World War II (WWII) and in the aftermath of the Holocaust that genocide was systematically examined and the term coined. (Chalk and Jonassohn, 1990:8)

Why is it necessary to formulate a definition of genocide? Such definition making is critical for any attempt to understand what has taken place in a particular situation. Without a definition, it is not possible to determine if genocide was/is present. However, Helen Fein is correct in asserting that at times the term genocide is overly used, thereby watering down its meaning. (Helen Fein, 1993:4) A definition is also necessary for prevention in the face of "… a potential or developing crisis…" (George J. Andreopoulos (ed.), 1994: 4) Despite the need to define genocide, its formulation is fraught with difficulties. That is, "There is no single correct definition of genocide waiting to be discovered." (Michael Freeman, 1991: 186) This is not to say that the more definitions of genocide exist, the better. Rather, as witnessed by the Genocide Convention (1948), gaps can exist or clarifications need to be made in terms of what constitutes genocide. One key difference from earlier episodes of genocide is that the twentieth century versions had increasingly involved genocide committed by the State against its own citizens under situations outside inter-State wars. In other words, conditions not necessarily involving conflict between States. (Chalk and Jonassohn, 1990: 9) Therefore, genocide has taken place, more and more, within the parameters of intra-State - within the State - realities. [35] The push to place the prevention and punishment of genocide within the paradigm of post W.W.II international legal norms originated with Raphael Lemkin. Specifically, he wanted the newly formed United Nations (UN) - 1945 - to tackle the subject. However, the roots of trying to deal with some of the issues involved in 'genocide' can be traced centuries earlier to even the 17th Century. The religious wars and "inhumane

---

[34] UN Doc. S/25704. Report of the Secretary General Pursuant to Paragraph 2 of Security Council Resolution 808 (1993). Article 1 (A)(33-35) – hereinafter referred to as the Secretary General Report. Specifically, this viewpoint emanates from the International Court of Justice's Advisory Opinion on Reservations to the Convention on the Prevention and Punishment of the Crime of Genocide, 1951.Bassiouni, M. Cherif and Manicas, Peter. *The Law of the International Criminal Tribunal for the Former Yugoslavia*. (1996) P. 522.

[35] This fact could have important implications, for example, in relation to the tensions between State sovereignty and the issue of humanitarian intervention under international law.

international conditions" in Europe during the 1600s prompted the legal theorist Hugo Grotius (1583-1645) to push for reforms. He urged the powers at the time to resolve conflicts via legal structures rather than wars. He believed that this method would promote, "...co-operation, peace and more humane treatment of people."(Kegly and Wittkopf, 2003: 481) In his examination of genocide, Raphael Lemkin determined that it was the "...denial of the right of entire groups to exist (and that) the punishment of the crime of genocide is a matter of international concern." Raphael Lemkin, 1948) In December 1948, the UN's General Assembly unanimously adopted the Genocide Convention (1948). [36] It entered into force in January 1951. Precisely defining what constitutes genocide was not only difficult in 1948, but is still contentious today. (Damien Short, forthcoming; Adam Jones, 2006; Martin Shaw, 2006 and Martin Shaw, 2007) One of the most serious problems is deciding what constitutes a victim group of genocide. (Alexander Laban Hinton, 2004) [37] For example, the Genocide Convention (1948), under article II, attempts to define potential victim groups. It sees that genocide is the crime of "...acts committed with the intent to destroy, in whole or in part, a national, ethnic, racial or religious group." One ongoing concern is that this definition does not provide protection to those who do not technically fall into these categories, such as members of 'political' groups. In turn, Kelly Dawn Askin proposes that 'gender'- in particular "women as a gender" - be added as one of the groups outlined in the Genocide Convention. [38] She notes that gender, as it is understood, would not go beyond the intentions of those who framed the Genocide Convention since they wanted "…to extend protection to stable groups only – groups having an enduring identity". (Kelly Dawn Askin, 1997: 342) In the Akayesu case (ICTR), rape constituted genocide since it was a method used against Tutsi women. The aim was to 'destroy in whole or in part' the ethnic group of Tutsis via rape. The effects of being raped, of witnessing relatives being raped, and of unwanted pregnancies contributed to this 'destruction'. According to the ICTR Trial Chamber, the women were targeted due to their membership in the Tutsi group. However, and with the understanding that the Genocide Convention (1948) is the basis for any examination of genocide, only focusing on the fact that these women were Tutsi and putting aside the idea that they were raped because they were women or individuals may present an incomplete overview of the crimes that occurred in Rwanda. Even with a working definition of genocide, the Genocide Convention does not include all potential acts. The issue of 'cultural genocide' as an 'enumerated act' under the Genocide Convention (1948), such as "prohibiting the use of a language and destroying or preventing the use of libraries", was discussed at the General Assembly and at the UN's Economic and Social Council (ECOSOC). This section was not included in the final draft of the Genocide Convention passed in 1948. [39] In addition, the

[36] GA Res. 260A(III), UN Doc. A/760.
Ratner and Abrams, 2001: 27-28 and n. 11.

[37] Other concerns stem from the precise meaning of "in whole or in part" and how to determine "intent".
For more on these issues, please see below and also refer to George J. Andreopoulos.

[38] The connection is between sex crimes and genocide: "The sex crimes against women occur specifically because of their gender."
Kelly Dawn Askin, 1997: 342 and n. 1072.

[39] One concern was that a definition of 'cultural genocide' would be difficult to develop and therefore could be open to "…abusive and illegitimate claims of genocide". Cultural genocide had been included in two earlier drafts of the Genocide Convention.
Ratner and Abrams, 2001: 31.

tension created by defining 'who' is a potential victim and what genocide could reflect, highlights the need to move beyond an understanding of the subject that is solely framed by the horrible events of the Holocaust. (Alan J. Rosenbaum, 2001: 22) In other words, genocide can involve several types of groups and methods/realities beyond only "...the complete biological destruction..." of a group. (Ratner and Abrams, 2001: 22) Away from a working definition of genocide, what are some of the other issues that the Genocide Convention (1948) outlines? Under article III, the 1948 Convention provides for the punishment of genocide. [40] It also provides for the prevention of this crime. Under article VIII, any "Contracting party" may ask the UN to take "...action under the UN Charter (1945) for the prevention and suppression of acts of genocide or any of the acts in article III." (P.R. Ghandi, 2000: 20) Once again, Article 4 of the ICTY Statute borrows language from the relevant sections of the Genocide Convention (1948). Furthermore, genocide is considered an international crime whether it occurs during war or during peacetime. [41] Although this provision of the Genocide Convention (1948) is not explicitly found in Article 4 of the ICTY Statute, the 'Final Report of the Commission of Experts' for the Former Yugoslavia highlights both when genocide can take place and that it is an international crime. [42] Article II of the Genocide Convention (1948) – which is repeated in the ICTY Statute – mentions the important component of 'intent'. [43] That is, for genocide to be proven it must be demonstrated that the perpetrator(s) had the intent to destroy in whole or in part a group(s). [44] The individual on its own is not the focus. Rather, several individuals as members of a national, ethnical, racial or religious group "as such" are the concern. [45] The 'Final Report of the Commission of Experts' describes intent overall as "…the subjective or mental constituent element of a crime". [46] In relation to genocide, the Commission focused on whether there was enough evidence to show reasonably that the perpetrator would have been

[40] In relation to genocide and permissive universal jurisdiction.

[41] Article I of the Genocide Convention reads "…genocide whether committed in time of peace or in time of war, is a crime under international law." P.R. Ghandhi, 2001: 19.

[42] In particular, the Commission noted "Thus, irrespective of the context in which it occurs (for example, peace time, internal strife, international armed conflict or whatever the general overall situation) genocide is a punishable international crime." Bassiouni and Manikas. Quoting from the 'Final Report of the Commission of Experts pursuant to Security Council Resolution 780 (1992), UN SCOR (Security Council Official Record), Annex, UN Doc. S/1994/674 (27 May 1994): 523.

[43] The ICTY Statute reads "Genocide means any of the following acts committed with intent to destroy, in whole or in part, a national, ethnical, racial or religious group, as such:"

Ibid: 521.

Social and political groups are also excluded from protection under Art 4 of the ICTY Statute.

Id. 526.

[44] Article 4 (2) of the ICTY Statute includes a list of act(s) - actus reus (guilty act) - which inter alia are killing (a), causing serious bodily or mental harm (b), the forcible transfer of children (e), etc. Id. 521-522.

[45] According to the 'Final Report of the Commission of Experts' the wording of "as such" allows for an understanding of genocide to include "…the crimes against a number of individuals must be directed at them in their collectivity or at them in their collective character or capacity." Id. 524.The categories of 'national', 'ethnic' and 'racial' be understood as follows: "…the term 'national group' as a set of individuals whose identity as such is distinctive in terms of nationality or national origins…The difference between the terms 'ethnic' and 'racial' is perhaps harder to grasp. It seems that the ethnic bond is more cultural…The racial element, on the other hand, refers more typically to common physical traits." Morris and Scharf, 1998: 173 at n. 698-700.It should be noted that membership in a particular group may also involve a subjective element. This means that a person may consider himself or herself as being part of a group even if technically they do not fit all the parameters.

ICTR, Prosecutor v. Alfred Musema, ICTR-96-13-A, 27 January 2000, Judgement, 161.

[46] UN Final Report, 1992: 521-526

"...aware of the consequences" that his or her actions would have inflicted onto the target group(s). [47] For the Commission this would reveal intent but not necessarily the motive behind the acts or omissions. [48] Despite this attempt to work through what constitutes intent, it nonetheless remains unsettled. (Ratner and Abrams, 2001: 36) One area of debate relates to the issue of evidence, since often it may be circumstantial or indirect. [49]

Using the Genocide Convention (1948) as a starting point, what does genocide consist of? Steven Ratner and Jason Abrams outline "three main elements".

They are as follows:

- "the commission of at least one of the acts enumerated in Article II(a) through (e);
- the direction of that act at one of the enumerated types of groups; and
- the intent to destroy the group in whole or in part." [50]

Thus, the process of defining genocide continues today. The very real tensions created by this debate must be addressed. If not, and unless workable definitions exist in international law and in relevant academic disciplines, acting on the prevention and punishment of this crime will continue to be bogged down by situations such as States incorrectly claiming that genocide is not "technically" taking place as defined by the Genocide Convention (1948). The measures undertaken during 2004 at the UN and within the broader international community, regarding whether or not the human rights violations that occurred place in the Darfur region of Sudan constitute genocide is one example of this difficulty. The purpose of illustrating these shifting debates is not intended as a precursor to solving the tensions involved.[51] Rather, it is meant to elucidate the point that definitions of genocide do not offer a complete picture of what genocide can constitute. The same can be true for any definition of rape, torture, and rape as a form of torture. [52]

Three types of international law can have an impact on the issue of rape, rape as a form of torture and rape as genocide. These include international human rights law, international humanitarian law and in some cases international criminal law with its connections to

---

[47] Ibid.Intent, in relation to genocide, is described as "...the criminal *mens rea*".Kelly Dawn Askin, 1997: 338.*Mens rea* (guilty mind) involves "The state of mind that the prosecution must prove a defendant to have had at the time of committing a crime in order to secure a conviction." Elizabeth A. Martin (ed.). *Oxford Dictionary of Law*. P. 290.

[48] UN Final Report, 1992. To elaborate, "...most commentators agree that so long as the requisite intent is established, underlying motives are irrelevant." Ratner and Abrams, 2001: 38.

[49] Ibid and *Supra* n. 47 in relation to the lack of a 'plan' *per se*.

[50] Ibid: 27. In terms of 'who' can commit genocide – that is, does it have to be the 'State' or can other actors through their acts also commit genocide? - during the deliberations to formulate the Genocide Convention it was decided by the *Ad Hoc Committee* "...not to insert in definition any words to the effect that genocide must be committed, encouraged or tolerated by heads of state or by those who lawfully or factually exercise governmental authority." Bassiouni and Manikas, 1999: 527 and n. 100.

[51] For example, the 1985 Whitaker Report of the UN "...called for decisive amendment of the Convention to include all political mass murders. "George J. Andreopoulos, 1994: 75.Whitaker Report: "*Revised and updated report on the question of the prevention and punishment of the crime of genocide prepared by Mr. B. Whitaker, Review of Further Developments in Fields with which the Sub-Commission Has Been Concerned*". UN Doc. E/CN.4/Sub.2/1985/6 (2 July 1985).Also, the International Criminal Tribunal for Rwanda (ICTR) Trial Chamber in the *Akayesu Judgement* (at para. 516) "...stated that the list of four groups in the Convention (Genocide) is not exclusive insofar as the Convention's drafters sought to protect 'any stable and permanent group'. "Ratner and Abrams, 2001: 42.

[52] I am grateful to Nigel Rodley for insisting on this point.

individual criminal responsibility. Although these types of law do overlap in certain and in constrained ways, a separate identity for each remains and will affect how rape is conceptualized, placed and treated within the respective categories. The further notion of international crimes, and specifically those considered to have jus cogens status, also impact on the study in hand. The importance placed on these crimes, including torture and genocide, and the fact that rape on its own is not considered an international crime means that it must be subsumed into inter alia torture or genocide to gain this special status within international law. The theoretical implications of the process whereby rape is subsumed into rape and genocide will form the analytical portions of this book.

International Cases Pertaining to Rape

The final section of this Chapter outlines, the issue of rape within the context of international humanitarian law, and where necessary, relevant portions of international human rights law. To reiterate, International human rights treaties under the United Nations (UN) system do not explicitly mention rape. Furthermore, even human rights instruments at the UN level that deal

with women have not always included the violation of rape. [53] In 1993, and for the first time in a UN human rights instrument, the Declaration on the Elimination of Violence against Women explicitly mentions rape. Within international humanitarian law, the problems for rape are deeply entrenched. For example, under the Geneva Conventions of 1949 rape is not explicitly considered a grave breach. Rape, for example, would have to be subsumed into the crime of torture to qualify for this serious violation of humanitarian law. Furthermore, under Article 27 of the Fourth Geneva Convention rape has been conceptualized as a violation against one's 'honor' and not as a crime of violence. When rape has been explicitly mentioned or implicitly inferred in international humanitarian law, its conceptualization can be problematic.

The overarching issue stems from associating rape with the 'honor' and the 'protection' of women. Under Geneva Convention IV (Article 27) the wording used includes "Women shall be especially protected against any attack on their honor, in particular against rape..." (Roberts and Guelph, 2000: 311) Furthermore, Additional Protocol 1 (Article 76(1) states "Women shall be the object of special respect and shall be protected in particular against rape..." (Ibid: 466)

Two concerns are present in this formulation. First, although the prohibition against rape and other types of sexual assault exists under international humanitarian law, the language used in the Geneva Conventions prioritizes protection rather than the prohibition of these acts. (Judith Gardham, 1997: 57) In contrast, the UN Convention Against Torture (1984) places great emphasis on the prohibition of this crime. There is a sense, from the use of language in these documents, that rape occurs as an inevitable by-product during armed conflicts and there is no focus to ensure that it does not take place. In contrast, this is the case with the formulation surrounding torture conventions. Second, the issue of honor is problematic. On the one hand, this means that rape is associated with the morality of the victim. On the other,

[53] For instance, the UN Declaration on the Elimination of Discrimination against Women (1967) and the Convention on the Elimination of All Forms of Discrimination against Women (CEDAW, 1979).

this masks the violent nature of rape. When rape is understood as a crime against an individual's honor or morality, it is often assumed that shame results for the victim and even that the community views the victim as 'dirty' or 'spoiled'. (UN document E/CN.4/1998/54: 5) Given the relationship between conceptions of 'honor' and the community, and as will be explored later in the Chapter, at times links to matters of religion and ethnic identities, this process seems to place rape as violence against the community rather than as an attack against the individual victim. The discussion at the international level of violence against women and its understanding as a human rights violation is a recent, ongoing and slow development. In sum, this section has briefly outlined how rape has been conceived and placed within various aspects of international human rights law. Key concerns were highlighted such as the need to sometimes read rape into existing human rights instruments; the focus within international humanitarian law on a woman's honor and protecting women; and the lack of emphasis on the violent nature and the prohibition of rape.

The final section of the Chapter focuses on two cases from the ICTY and ICTR that have addressed rape and torture or as a form of genocide. The cases, in chronological order, are:

1. Jean-Paul Akayesu v. Prosecutor. International Criminal Tribunal for Rwanda (ICTR). Case No. ICTR-96-4-T. Judgement. 1998.
2. Prosecutor v. Dragoljub Kunarac, Radomir Kovac and Zoran Vukovic, ICTY, IT-96-23-T and IT-96-23/1-T, Judgement, 22 February 2001.[54]

This will also introduce some of the theoretical implications identified by this book and emanating from these two cases that will be analyzed in Chapters five and six.

1) Prosecutor V. Jean-Paul Akayesu, ICTR-96-4-T, Judgement, 2 September 1998

Prior to the genocide that occurred in Rwanda during 1994, the accused Jean-Paul Akayesu was a 'bourgemestre' , which is an appointed administrator whose duties included responsibility for the police/gendarmes in the commune. [55] As such, Akayesu was found to have had both *de facto* and *de jure* authority for the police/gendarmes in the Taba commune. The former type of authority was considered to exist in a greater amount than the latter by the Trial Chamber of the ICTR. (Ibid) During the period in question, 1 January 1994 to 31 December 1994, a state of internal armed conflict existed in Rwanda. (Id) In the Indictment, Akayesu was charged with a variety of offences under the ICTR Statute pertaining to several events in Taba. The charges included *inter alia* sexual violence committed toward and the killings and beatings of Tutsis who had requested refuge at the 'bureau communal'. As the Indictment reads, "At least 2,000 Tutsis were killed in Taba between April 7 and the end of June 1994, while he (Akayesu) was still in power." (Id: 12) Several instances of sexual violence that had taken place in the Taba commune were described in the Judgement. The Trial Chamber remarked that with few exceptions, most of the rapes and other acts of sexual

[54] Once again, the Kunarac *et al* case has been chosen since it critically links rape as a violation of *sexual autonomy* that has influenced the explorations of the individual and of rape as torture covered in Chapter 5. In addition, this author acknowledges the existence of further and more recent juridical judgements affecting the issues in hand. However, the Akayesu and Celebici cases have been chosen as a starting point for the theoretical underpinnings of this book.

[55] At the time, each bourgemestre was appointed by the President of the Republic upon the recommendation of the Minister of the Interior. *Prosecutor v. Jean-Paul Akayesu* (hereinafter, the Akayesu Case). Judgement. 1-12.

violence had been committed by the 'Interahamwe'.[56] The Chamber found there was sufficient evidence that during 1994, Tutsi women and girls were victims of sexual violence, beatings, or killings in and near the Taba bureau communal. The Judgement describes the rapes and other acts of sexual violence. In terms of the latter, these acts included "...the forced undressing and public humiliation of girls and women." (Id: 449) With reference to the accused, Jean-Paul Akayesu, the Chamber found that he had "...ordered, instigated and otherwise aided and abetted sexual violence." He had however, not actually carried out any of the acts of rape or sexual violence. (Id: 452) Regarding rape, the Chamber offered an understanding of what it can entail since no agreed upon definition was available under international law (humanitarian or human rights). While working through a formulation of a definition, the Chamber made certain links between rape and torture. In particular it stated "...rape in fact constitutes torture when inflicted by or at the instigation of or with the consent or acquiescence of a public official or other person acting in an official capacity." (Id: 687) This follows the definition of torture as found in the UN Convention (1984). The Chamber then defined rape as "...a physical invasion of a sexual nature, committed on a person under circumstances which are coercive." (Id: 688) It also insisted that "...rape is a form of aggression and that the central elements of the crime of rape cannot be captured in a mechanical description of objects and body parts. This approach is more useful in international law." (Id: 597) Again, a link was made to the UN Convention (1984) whereby the definition of torture does not include a list of acts and methods. As the Chamber argued, the UN Convention (1984) is "...focusing rather on the framework of State-sanctioned violence." That is, the process is not centered on creating a limited list of acts or methods of torture. (Id: 687)

The Akayesu case was an important and innovative development for rape on several levels. The Trial Chamber, recognizing that no accepted definition of rape existed under international law, worked through the formulation of a definition. Despite the wording used, the Chamber noted that rape may also include acts "...which involve the insertion of objects and/or the use of bodily orifices not considered to be intrinsically sexual." For instance, one of the witnesses described the Interahamwe as 'thrusting' a piece of wood into the sexual organs of a woman as she was dying. For the Chamber, this act also constituted rape. (Id: 686)

The Akayesu case and its definition of rape, was an important development for international law. In the Chamber's description of rape, it was understood as a 'form of aggression'. This description correctly shifts the conceptualization of rape away from issues of 'honor' and more towards reflecting its reality as a violent act. This case was also significant since for the first time under international law, rape was considered as a component of genocide. In addition, rape was seen as causing both physical and psychological harm. Critically, an association was made between acts of rape committed against individual women and the fact that these women were also part of the Tutsi ethnic group. Individuals were raped. Yet, according to the Trial Chamber, the crime of genocide occurred because these individuals were part of a group – the Tutsi. This overlap, between the individual and the group, is the first of two theoretical issues to be noted from the assessment

[56] The Interahamwe: "The MRND militia (Mouvement révolutionnaire national pour le développement), known as the Interahamwe...They were later join by the militia of other parties or wings of Hutu extremist parties." Ibid: 99.

of these cases. As such, the question to be addressed in Chapter 6 of this book will be whether the *current concept of human rights*, with its emphasis on the individual, creates a tension when placed within *the international crime of genocide*. Finally, a word about rape as a form of torture. Rape was not charged as a form of torture in this case. This is not to say that the Trial Chamber was not aware of the possibility to make this connection. For example, and as mentioned earlier, the Chamber did recognize that under certain circumstances rape could be a form of torture. However, in its findings the Chamber did not state that the rapes at Taba commune amounted to a form of torture. It could be argued that the description of 'thrusting' a piece of wood into a woman's sexual organs could constitute torture if the remaining criteria of this crime had also been met.

The Chamber was aware of possible omissions and remarked in its Findings:

> "The Tribunal also notes that on the basis of acts described in paragraphs 12(A) and 12(B), the Accused is charged only pursuant to Article 3(g) (rape) and 3(i) (other inhumane acts) of its Statute, but not Article 3(a) (murder) or Article 3(f) (torture). Similarly, on the basis of acts described in paragraphs 12(A) and 12(B), the Accused is charged only pursuant to Article 4(e) (outrages upon personal dignity) of its Statute, and not Article 4(a) (violence to life, health and physical or mental well-being of persons, in particular murder as well as cruel treatment such as torture, mutilation or any form of corporal punishment). The Tribunal notes, however, that paragraphs 12(A) and 12(B) are referenced in Counts 1-3, Genocide and it considers the beatings and killings, as well as sexual violence, in connection with those counts." (Id: 689-690) [57]

In conclusion, two comments must be made about the Chamber's Findings. First, the Chamber outlined *how* the sexual violence including rape was formulized within the Indictment. As such, it could only consider these acts within a prescribed set of concepts. Second, and linked to the first comment, how the ICTR Statute has placed rape – since 'other sexual violence' is not explicitly mentioned in the Statute – constrains how rape can be addressed. That is, when rape is explicitly mentioned in the ICTR Statute it is placed outside most of the traditional terminology associated with torture. As the Statute is currently written, the crimes of torture and rape are considered separately and there is no clear indication that they could overlap. [58] The net effect of this conceptualization and placement of rape within the Statute, along with how the Indictment in the Akayesu case was presented, has been to restrict the consideration of rape as a form of torture. For instance, the Chamber when discussing the particulars of crimes against humanity in this case stated "The Tribunal finds that rape and other inhuman acts which took place on or near the bureau communal premises of Taba were committed as part of this attack." (Id: 695) With specific reference to the Akayesu case, it could be argued that many of the rapes should have also been charged as a form of torture. The question thus becomes, which will be left open for the moment, does this lack of flexibility in potentially presenting rape as a form of torture while solely placing it within the crime of genocide take away from the individual victim?

---

[57] Akayesu was found guilty on several charges including rape as genocide and was sentenced to a single life sentence on 2 October 1998. This sentence was upheld on appeal by the ICTR Appeals Chamber Judgement of 15 June 2001.

[58] I have used the phrase 'most of the traditional terminology associated with torture' since the Chamber maintained, "Like torture, rape is a violation of personal dignity." Id: 597.

2. *Prosecutor V. Dragoljub Kunarac, Radomir Kovac and Zoran Vukovic, ICTY, IT-96-23-T And IT-96-23/1-T, Judgement, 22 February 2001* [59]

This case deals with three individuals who are Serbs and who were soldiers during the international armed conflict in the former Yugoslavia in the early part of the 1990s. They were convicted of several charges in relation to the rapes of Muslim women in the city and municipality of 'Foca'. In early April of 1992, fighting broke out in this region between the Serbs and Muslims. By mid-April the Serbs had taken control, and in the words of the Trial Chamber, "Muslim inhabitants were systematically subjected to the pattern of abuses…" [60] For instance, Muslim inhabitants were systematically expelled, brought together and sent to collection points from where they were taken to buildings or schools to be detained. In these conditions, Muslims were beaten and sometimes killed. Others were killed in the villages. (Ibid: 25-28) Women and girls were placed in houses, apartments, gymnasiums or school and were often raped by Serb soldiers and others. Two of these places of detention were the Foca High School and the Partizan Sports Hall. According to witnesses, the conditions in the latter place were worse. There was less food, no hygiene facilities and rapes were more frequent. [61] Before the conflict began, Foca municipality had a population of 40, 513 inhabitants of whom 52% were Muslim. By the end of the conflict, only ten Muslims remained in the area. (Id: 47) The accused in this case were Serb soldiers. Dragoljub Kunarac was the leader of a 'permanent reconnaissance group', which was part of the Foca brigade. (Id: 49) The other two accused, Rodomir Kova and Zoran Vukovi were part of military units during the conflict. Witnesses in the case gave testimony that they had been raped by one or several of the accused and by others. Witness FWS-87 stated that she, and three other women, were taken to a house in Foca by Kunarac. At this house there were several other soldiers waiting. [62] On that particular night, FWS-87 testified that she was raped by Kunarac and by two other soldiers. (Id) Under the Indictment, rape has been charged as a violation of the laws or customs of war under Article 3 of the ICTY Statute and as a crime against humanity under Article 5 of the Statute. It is interesting to note that rape, as a violation of the laws or customs of war, was placed 'in part' within Common Article 3 of the Geneva Conventions. [63] To elaborate, there is Article 3 1(c) of the Geneva Conventions 'outrages upon personal dignity, in particular humiliating and degrading treatment.' In contrast there is Article 3 1(a) of the Geneva Conventions that covers 'violence to life and person, in particular murder of all kinds, mutilation, cruel treatment and torture'. (Id) Regardless that rape may at times be considered a violent act or as an outrage upon personal dignity, the Trial Chamber confirmed that rape, torture and outrages upon personal dignity involve criminal responsibility under customary

---

[59] Hereinafter referred to as Foca case.

[60] Foca case: 21.It should be noted that Muslim forces also committed violations against Serb villages and villagers in the area.

[61] Witness FWS-51 stated that they only received a 'jar of soup and slices of bread'. Id: 30 at note 91.

[62] Id: 53-75. At the Kalinonovik school, where women were held, one of the guards told witness FWS-191 that he could not help her since Kunarac was in 'overall control'. Id: 255.

[63] Article 3, common to all the Geneva Conventions (1949), includes certain minimum standards such as the prohibition against torture and the passing of sentences without proper judgements by a recognized court that each Party to an international conflict should adhere. Roberts and Guelff. Geneva Conventions (1949) I-IV.

international law. [64] Rape in the Indictments, was charged in part, under the auspices of common Article 3 to the 1949 Geneva Conventions. The Trial Chamber found that common Article 3 was applicable under customary international, and especially within the parameters of this case, it does not need to be linked to treaty law. Following this logic the Chamber noted that rapes placed under common Article 3 do not need to be based within treaty law. [65] As such, some of the rapes charged under Article 3 of the ICTY Statute could be understood within the requirements of common Article 3 to the 1949 Geneva Conventions. (Id: 400-419) For the Chamber rape, torture, and outrages upon personal dignity constituted serious violations of common Article 3. Such violations brought out criminal responsibility under customary international law. (Id) Rape was charged as a violation of the laws or customs of war under Article 3 of the ICTY Statute and as a crime against humanity under Article 5 of the Statute – rape is explicitly mentioned in Article 5(g). As with many cases dealing with rape and presented to the international criminal tribunals, the fact that the exact elements of rape (definition of) are not set out in their respective Statutes, or international humanitarian law, or in international human rights law, means developing or extracting from existing international cases that have attempted to define this crime. (Id: 437) Citing previous cases, namely the *Furundzija* and the *Akayesu* Judgements, the Trial Chamber examined various definitions of rape. In the latter case, the Trial Chamber also reviewed the national legislation pertaining to rape of several states. (Id) With its examination of the *Furndzija* case rape definition, the Foca case Trial Chamber argued that rape should not be so narrowly formulated. In particular, the former Chamber presented that rape could only take place if it is '...accompanied by coercion or force or threat of force against the victim or a third person.' The concern is that the *Furundzija* definition does not leave room for other reasons that would make '...an act of sexual penetration *non-consensual or non-voluntary* for the victim.' (Id: 438) From the *Furundzija* overview, in search of 'common denominators' found in national legislation, the Chamber in the Foca case emphasized that the underlying principle was the aim to penalize 'violations of sexual autonomy'. Issues such as force, the threat of force, coercion and a lack of the ability to give consent or to participate on a voluntary basis all contribute to this violation of sexual autonomy, as suggested within the *Furundzija* findings:

---

[64] Id: 400-409.Jean-Paul Akayesu (Akayesu case) was, under Count 15, also charged with rape as an outrage upon personal dignity (under Article4(e) of the ICTR Statute and based on violations of Article 3 common to the 1949 Geneva Conventions). He was found not guilty of this count.

[65] Id: 405-406.Common Article 3 reads: "In the case of armed conflict not of an international character occurring in the territory of one of the High Contracting Parties, each Party to the conflict shall be bound to apply, as a minimum, the following provisions: (1) Persons taking no active part in the hostilities, including members of armed forces who have laid down their arms and those placed *hors de combat* by sickness, wounds, detention, or any other cause, shall in all circumstances be treated humanely, without any adverse distinction founded on race, colour, religion or faith, sex, birth or wealth, or any other similar criteria. To this end, the following acts are and shall remain prohibited at any time and in any place whatsoever with respect to the above-mentioned persons: (a) Violence to life and person, in particular murder of all kinds, mutilation, cruel treatment and torture; (b) Taking of hostages; (c) Outrages upon personal dignity, in particular humiliating and degrading treatment; (d) The passing of sentences and the carrying out of executions without previous judgement pronounced by a regularly constituted court, affording all the judicial guarantees which are recognised as indispensable by civilised peoples. (2) The wounded and the sick shall be collected and cared for. [...]"

"…all jurisdictions surveyed by the Trial Chamber require an element of force, coercion, threat, or acting without the consent of the victim: force is given a broad interpretation and includes rendering the victim helpless." [66]

The Foca case Chamber goes on to note that this interpretation is correct and that it focuses on 'serious violations of sexual autonomy'. Although the Trial Chamber chose to highlight the 'serious violations of sexual autonomy' nature of rape, it goes on to add that the repeated rape of four girls kept in Radomir Kovac's apartment was '…perpetuating the attack upon the Muslim civilian population.' (Foca Case: 587) Furthermore, the Chamber commented on the three accused and stated "…all their criminal actions were clearly part of and had the effect of perpetuating the attack against the Muslim civilian population." (Ibid: 592) In addition it was observed, in domestic law, for acts to become the crime of rape three components are involved:

1) " the sexual activity is accompanied by force or threat of force to the victim or a third party;
2) the sexual activity is accompanied by force or a variety of other specified circumstances which make the victim particularly vulnerable or negated her ability to make an informed refusal; or
3) the sexual activity occurs without the consent of the victim. (Id: 442)

As the Trial Chamber found, several national jurisdictions – such as Switzerland, France, Portugal, etc. - allow for factors beyond 'force' or 'threat of force' to encompass rape. These situations include '…that the victim was put in a state of being unable to resist, was particular vulnerable or incapable of resisting because of physical or mental incapacity, or was induced into the act by surprise or misrepresentation.' (Id: 446-447)

Thus, the Trial Chamber presented a two-part definition of rape. First, the *actus reus* of rape in international law involves: 'the sexual penetration, however slight: (a) of the vagina or anus of the victim by the penis of the perpetrator or any other object used by the perpetrator; or (b) of the mouth of the victim by the penis of the perpetrator; where such sexual penetration occurs without the consent of the victim. Consent for this purpose must be given voluntarily, as a result of the victim's free will, assessed in the context of the surrounding circumstances.' Second, the *mens rea* of rape '…is the intention to effect this sexual penetration, and the knowledge that it occurs without the consent of the victim.' (Id: 460) Beyond this definition of rape, the Trial Chamber commented on rape and on torture. The Chamber discussed several definitions of torture within international human rights law and cases from the International Criminal Tribunals. Unlike the definition used earlier in this book, the Trial Chamber argued that the UN Torture Convention (1984) and its particular definition should only be used as an 'interpretational aid'. (Id: 482) The Chamber *inter alia* was concerned with the criterion, within the UN Torture Convention (1984) definition, that a perpetrator of torture must be an official or someone acting in an official capacity. Namely, due to the nature of this case, there needs to be a distinction between the responsibility of States and their agents on the one hand and the responsibility of individuals, who can incur 'individual criminal responsibility' on the other. International human rights norms tend to fall

[66] Quoting *Prosecutor v Furundzija*, Case IT-95-17/1-T, Judgement, 10 Dec 1998, par 178. Id: 440 .

within the former category (State and their agents responsibility), while international humanitarian principles fall within the former (State and their agents responsibility) and within the latter (individual/criminal responsibility) or at times even a blend of the two legal norms. (Id: 489) The Chamber also stated that torture found within conventions only address torture, while under the ICTY Statute torture is represented as a war crime, a crime against humanity, or as a grave breach. (Id: 496) It also noted that under international humanitarian law the definition of torture does not include the same elements as the definition of torture under human rights law. Specifically, under international humanitarian law it is not necessary for the perpetrator of torture to be a state official or someone acting in an official capacity. This assessment is based on customary international law. (Id: 497) Lastly, in an interesting paragraph, the Trial Chamber compared rape and torture. It observed that a distinct element of rape, under Article 3 or Article 5 of the Statute, is the 'sexual penetration element'. In contrast, a distinct element of torture is the 'severe infliction of pain or suffering aimed at obtaining information or a confession, punishing, intimidating, coercing or discriminating against the victim or a third person'. (Id: 557) Recalling the Akayesu Judgement whereby the Trial Chamber acknowledged that a form of rape (such as the thrusting of a piece of wood into a woman's sexual organs) does not have to be 'intrinsically sexual' in nature, reveals that the Foca Judgement has not considered this important point. With reference to rape, the three accused were found guilty of under several charges including 'torture and rape' and enslavement (Id: 544-822).

With reference to sentencing, Dragoljub Kunarac received 28 (twenty-eight) years, Radomir Kova received 20 (twenty) years, and Zoran Vukovic 12 (twelve) years. The convictions and sentencing were upheld by the Appeals Chamber on 12 June 2002. [67]

The Foca case focused on a situation during the conflict in the former Yugoslavia, whereby the rape of women occurred on a large scale and was organized. The accused soldiers were found guilty of several rapes and other violations of the ICTY Statute. The Trial Chamber, in its exploration of defining the elements of rape, demonstrated a flexible and innovative approach that resulted in an expanded definition of rape within international law. Specifically, in its Judgement the Chamber understood that factors beyond force or threat of force could result in a victim of rape not being able to give consent to a sexual act. This aspect of the nature of rape, brought out by the Chamber, has added to existing definitions of rape recently developed under international law. This evolution is evident with the initial attempt as outlined in the ICTR case (*Akayesu*) and with subsequent international criminal tribunal cases such as *Furundzija* and others. This demonstrates that finding the elements of a crime must involve a flexible process and that it is ongoing. Another example of this approach is how the Trial Chamber in the Foca case argued that the well-established international crime of torture does not under specific circumstances such as situations of armed conflict need to be committed by a state official or by someone acting in an official capacity.

A further important innovation in the Foca case Judgement is the Trial Chamber's insistence that rape is a 'serious violation of sexual autonomy'. This process understood that rape, like torture, should be conceptualized as a crime committed against the individual. With this understanding, rape is an act perpetuated against the individual and it specifically violates

[67] Appeals Chamber Judgement in the Kunarac, Kovac and Vukovic (Foca) case. The Hague, 12 June 2002, CVO/P.I.S./679-E.

the sexual component of this individual. The individual is not free to give consent. The circumstances surrounding the inability of an individual to give consent may vary, and according to the Foca case Judgement do not need to involve force or a threat of force. It could be argued that most if not all violations of human rights and a large number of violations of the laws or customs of war challenge one's autonomy. For instance, Nigel Rodley has presented that for torture to gain a foothold the perpetrator must "...deny the humanity of his (*sic*) victim." [68] This process, in turn, involves stripping away the 'inherent dignity' of the individual. (Ibid: 15) The individual, in the eyes of the torturer, etc., becomes solely an enemy or worse an object such as when the Tutsis prior and during the genocide in Rwanda were described as 'cockroaches'. What makes up an individual, such as traits, tastes, aspirations, experiences, family links, qualifications, pursuits, etc. is erased in the mind of those who carry out such violations. With rape the added dimension of sexual autonomy, the ability to decide when and under what circumstances one wishes to participate in a sexual act, is removed from the individual. As such, rape is a violation of sexual autonomy.

Despite the positive achievements within the Foca case and Judgement there are some concerns. First, when the Trial Chamber compared rape and torture it observed that the critical difference between the two, is the 'sexual penetration element' of rape and the 'severe infliction of pain' carried out for a specified purpose. In this assessment, there is no acknowledgement that a critical element of rape can involve severe pain or suffering - physical or psychological. As such, the emphasis is on the sexual nature of rape and it leaves out the potentially violent aspects of this crime. Second, and this concern is linked to the first, the Trial Chamber in its decision on the charges for the three accused consistently separated rape and torture. That is, under certain circumstances, rape was linked to torture only due to the circumstances surrounding some of the rapes. However, rape was never presented as a form of torture. Similar to the Akayesu case, rape and torture were represented separately within the Indictment and within the ICTY Statute. Separating the two crimes, or not allowing for the possibility that rape could be used as a form of torture has the effect of distancing rape from torture. There was an acknowledgement that torture did at times take place while rape was committed. However, as noted in the Akayesu Judgment, the Trial Chamber in that case made an important link between rape and genocide, and it acknowledged that it was restricted by how rape was prescribed within the Indictment in terms of presenting rape as torture. Yet, this clear distinction between rape and torture within the Foca Judgement *may* make it more difficult to perceive rape as a form of torture in future cases.

Third, the Trial Chamber associated some of the rapes to the idea of 'degrading' the victim. In one instance, the Chamber stated that since Dragoljub Kunarac 'took away' the virginity of one of the witnesses the rape resulted in the additional factor of being more degrading for her since Kunarac had "...rejoiced at the idea of being her 'first'." (Foca: 724) Echoes of linking rape with the issue of one's honor, as found in the 1949 Geneva Conventions, emanate from this statement. By making this comparison, the Chamber has re-placed rape within the restrictive ideas of honor and even of shame. This incident should have been assessed in the Judgement, and the Chamber should in turn have considered the implications of not emphasizing that rape needs to be removed from notions such as 'shame' and 'honor'. When an individual is tortured, the burden of such constricting concepts are not

[68] Parentheses added by this author. Nigel Rodley, 1999: 14.

placed onto the victim. It is necessary, therefore, for international law to move beyond an understanding of rape that is rooted in such misconceived and outdated conceptions. Fourth, and lastly, although the Trial Chamber correctly insisted that rape is a violation of sexual autonomy it also associated the repeated rapes of certain witnesses as "...perpetuating the attack upon the Muslim civilian population." (Ibid: 592) The question, to be considered in the next two Chapters, is if conceptualizing rape as a violation against sexual autonomy while also linking it to genocide which is a violation against a group (in this case the Muslim civilian population) leads to theoretical tensions.

Some Theoretical Implications to Pursue

From the Akayesu case and the Foca case two theoretical concerns have been identified by this book for further analysis. First, as mentioned in the Foca Judgement, rape is a 'violation against sexual autonomy'. I am not interested in the 'sexual' component of this view, *per se,* but rather with the notion of autonomy. Specifically, I shall need to return to the concept of human rights with its emphasis on the individual and apply it to rape as a violation of autonomy. To ensure a richer analysis I will need to consider rape as a form of torture due to the more established association of torture, under international human rights and humanitarian law, as a violation committed against the individual. A further point to use rape as a form of torture for this assessment is that torture, for various reasons, is often perpetrated against individuals who are politically active. It is this connection, between violations committed against the individual and what is meant by 'the political', along with its theoretical implications that I wish to explore. Second, both the Akeyesu Judgement and the Foca Judgement also placed rape within violations committed against the group. In Akayesu, rape was understood as genocide committed against the Tutsi ethnic group. In the Foca Judgement, rape was condemned as part of the attack against the Muslim civilian population (as a crime against humanity). Analyzing rape as part of a crime that emphasizes the group will be essential to this book, along with unlocking any implications of this conceptualization for rape, for torture, and for rape as a form of torture. Thus, Chapter five will analyze the theoretical implications of associating rape as a 'violation of autonomy', while Chapter six will examine the implications of associating rape with a crime that emphasizes violations committed against the group.

Chapter 4

SETTING THE THEORETICAL FRAMEWORK: SUBSUMING RAPE INTO ESTABLISHED INTERNATIONAL CRIMES (TORTURE AND GENOCIDE)

"Illusions: We accept the false values
which appear to us and when we
think we are acting we are in
reality motionless, for we are
still confined in the same
system of values."
Simone Weil
Gravity and Grace

OVERVIEW

As outlined in the Overall Introduction, the approach taken is an analytical one driven by the resources of political theory, while touching upon international law (human rights and humanitarian). The reason for adopting this interdisciplinary format is to effectively examine some of the theoretical arguments that underpin claims to human rights, and to assess the ways in which the crime of rape has been conceptualized, placed and treated within international law. Undertaking this broader approach offers a more comprehensive discourse; theory and law should not be viewed as necessarily mutually exclusive and more importantly, each discipline can assist the other.

This chapter sets out the broad theoretical framework underpinning the work. The aim is to highlight some of the critical themes such as how the status, role, and rights of the individual have changed and adapted over time to be able to fit within the current concept of human rights and how an emphasis on the individual exists within current understandings of human rights. In turn, the chapter discusses the public/private dimensions of human rights along with an overview of the State, the individual, human rights and the concept of harm as linked to rape. This section argues how these concepts, such as the emphasis on the individual or the framing of human rights within the public sphere, can affect how rape is conceptualized, placed and treated under international law. The final aspect outlines a process whereby under certain circumstances rape can be subsumed into the established international crimes of torture and genocide. This will provide the grounding, which will enable the exploration of the two theoretical implications identified: what can occur when rape is linked to torture and what can occur when rape is associated with genocide. It is the individual and the group elements of torture and genocide that will affect this analysis.

A Theoretical Process

Critically, any discrepancies between the theory and the practice of human rights must also be considered. For instance in relation to human rights violations and the role of international law, J. Shand Watson writes:

> "It is curious for a legal system, especially a customary one, to exhibit simultaneously both a growing body of prohibitive norms and a parallel body of thoroughly inconsistent practice by the participants. Yet this is undeniably the case with the protection of human rights in international law." (J. Shand Watson, 1999: 13)

In the aftermath of World War II, the formulation of international human rights norms was at the fore of international relations. From this discourse, the Universal Declaration of Human Rights (UDHR) was developed and passed as part of a resolution by the General Assembly of the newly formed United Nations (UN) in 1948.[1] In its Preamble, the UDHR sets out certain principles for the respect of a series of human rights and fundamental freedoms.[2] Since 1948 the claim, as outlined in the Preamble, Article 1, etc. of the UDHR, is that these human rights are universal has been supported but also contested. Much of the resistance to the UDHR rests in the perception that it is rooted in modern and western ideals and thereby excludes many of the traditions, histories and cultures of the world.

These issues are important and will highlight the development of the current concept of human rights, while linking some of the relevant conditions affecting rape, torture and genocide. For instance, natural rights – which are the precursor to modern human rights – emerged from classical liberal theory. An important aspect of this particular type of liberal thought was the emphasis on the individual and a distinction between public and private spheres. Understanding the development of and changes in the individual's role, in relation to first of all natural rights and later with the concept of human rights, is essential. It is the theoretical implications from recent international criminal tribunals that will be linked to and influenced by notions found within the current concept of human rights that may have an impact on rape. As such, I shall briefly note the progression of the individual and link this overview with the State.

---

1 The resolution (GA res.217 A (III), 10 December 1948) was accepted without a dissenting vote and with few abstentions – 48 Member States of the UN voted in favor and there were eight abstentions.

2 Universal Declaration of Human Rights. 1948. That is, generally Declarations may carry moral weight and are thus considered to be part of 'soft law', while Conventions are binding on States that sign/ratify them, and are referred to as 'hard law'. In turn, there is the concept of customary law, which will be mentioned where appropriate.

The State, the Individual and Human Rights

We can at first glance, see an important connection between liberalism and the concept of human rights, the emphasis on the individual. Again, one can debate to what degree the concept of human rights allows for notions such as the collective, group rights, and the community. In essence, there are three main features that link the political ideology of liberalism with human rights:

Individualism universalism all individuals as being 'morally equal'

These features, it can be argued, evoke a certain level of controversy. Yet, if one looks at Article 1 of the UDHR (1948), echoes of this liberalism emerge:

> "All human beings are born free and equal in dignity and rights. They are endowed with reason and conscience and should act towards one another in a spirit of brotherhood." (P.R. Ghandhi, 2000: 22 [3]

The seeds leading to the development of the concept of human rights are not only found in liberalism. Furthermore, other traditions may understand and present human rights differently. The implications of this may or may not adversely affect the overall concept of human rights. So, for the sake of clarity I will understand the current concept of human rights as emphasizing the individual. However, this individual can to varying degrees also have a place, role, and duties and receive benefits within his or her respective community. This approach will, hopefully, allow for more flexibility in the theoretical discussions to follow. [4]

During the 17th and 18th centuries changes occurred in the relationship between the 'state' and the individual where it was understood that the former existed for the individual and not the inverse. (Noberto Bobbio, 1995: 41) Regardless, due to how the current international system has been developed and continues to function, the role of the State in vis à vis the individual and his or her human rights continues to be paramount. First, and with reference to the UN, its Charter and how it operates is State-centered. Human rights are indeed mentioned in the UN Charter. However, these passages must be considered alongside Article 2(7), which addresses State sovereignty and domestic jurisdiction matters, since these are still relevant despite the plethora of human rights instruments and mechanisms subsequently developed within UN structures. [5]

Second, and in a twist of irony, despite the fact that human rights are to be used as a buffer in the face of abusive State power and violence it is these very entities that are charged with upholding lofty human rights norms. Taken to the extreme, this set-up is similar to a scenario whereby the fox is charged with protecting the chickens it also feeds upon.

As Article 2(1) of the International Covenant on Civil and Political Rights (1966) reads

[3] Beyond liberalism, the UDHR also echoes the broader notion of natural rights. As Johannes Morsink points out "Thus the similarity of language between the Universal Declaration and the eighteenth-century declarations of rights should not be taken too lightly." Morsink, however, adds, "Thus it is clear that although natural rights philosophy does inform the Universal Declaration, it does not inform all parts equally." Johannes Morsink, 1984: 311 and 334.

[4] For details on additional themes associated with human rights such as theories of rights (choice and benefit, etc.); the justification of human rights; and universality *v.* cultural relativism please refer to the relevant sections of Jack Donnelly (1989), Michael Freeman (2002) and Peter Jones (1994).

[5] To elaborate: "International relations is structured around the principle of sovereignty, which grants a state exclusive jurisdiction over its own territory and resources, including its population. Sovereignty in turn implies non-intervention in the internal affairs of other states." Jack Donnelly, 2nd Edition, 2003:157.

> "Each State Party to the present Covenant undertakes to respect and ensure to all individuals within its territory and subject to its jurisdiction the rights recognized in the present Covenant." (P. R. Ghandhi, 2000: 64)

Bringing complaints of human rights violations to international and regional human rights mechanisms are considered options of last resort. The State that violates the human rights of individuals within its jurisdiction, either through acts or omissions must, in theory at least, also rectify the situation. [6]

One explanation for such violations would be that States operating within a 'realist' model of international relations must protect their vested interests. [7] At times, due to real or even perceived threats emanating from within and without its borders, States commit human rights violations. Such 'threats' can range from peaceful political protests, attempts to overthrow a government, efforts to nationalize/privatize industries, to criticizing individual members of the government. In response, the human rights violations can include arbitrary detention, torture, and not delivering food-aid to certain regions of a State. It is not the case that States always fail to intervene in the face of human violations. States do rectify, or attempt to rectify, violations within their territories. Furthermore, States do intervene in matters concerning the domestic jurisdiction of other States. An example of the latter would be the efforts by the international community in the face of South Africa's past apartheid laws. Granted these interventions, which can range from diplomacy, to economic sanctions, and to armed interventions do not appear under all circumstances. Issues related to State interests, risks and advantages involved, indifference, and denial do factor into the equation. The effective and consistent enforcement of human rights norms is its Achilles heel. This tension was evident with the struggles to ensure that rape and other acts of sexual violence were prosecuted by the international criminal tribunals for Rwanda and the Former Yugoslavia. Without the efforts of non-governmental organizations and other elements from the international community, the innovative and important cases mentioned in this book would not have been possible.

The Individual/Group Schism

The current concept of human rights, as incorporated by national, regional, and international human rights mechanisms, places an emphasis on the individual. Theoretically, as argued by authors such as Jack Donnelly, these rights exist outside the reality of the modern State. Human rights are not given to human beings by the State. Individuals, by the

---

[6] A States' involvement within the jurisdiction of another State can also be called into question. The International Court of Justice (ICJ), in its examination of the United States' activities during Nicaragua's civil war, concluded – in relation to international humanitarian law - "...violations of common article 3, including torture and ill-treatment, are violations of the 'laws and customs of war' relevant to any armed conflict." Nigel Rodley, 1999 P. 72 (in reference to *Military and Paramilitary Activities in and against Nicaragua (Nicaragua v. United States of America), Merits,* ICJ Rep. (1986), para. 218.

[7] The realist model, which has dominated international relations, concludes that States are "...motivated by self-interest and not by ethical concerns such as human rights." Michael Freeman, 2002: 94.Freeman also adds some States allow cultural practices that in turn create human rights violations. He also touches upon why States 'repress' such as the nature of the threat faced by the state. Id. P. 132 and pp. 138-139.

One example of such a 'cultural practice' would be States where so-called honor killings are not considered criminal and prosecuted. 'Honor killings' are "...murders of women who commit adultery or seek divorce (etc.); they are perpetrated by their male relatives who seek to avenge the family honour." – brackets added by myself. Aaron Xavier Fellmeth, 2000: 694.

mere fact that they are human beings, already exist with certain rights. The process that entrenches human rights into law is separate. Yet, the individual still has a place and a role within larger frameworks such as society or the State. Individual human rights and notions such as the group and the State do not always co-exist without conflict. For instance, a group of immigrants living in a Canadian city attempted to change their district's by-laws to install permanent separate swimming areas between men and women at the municipal pool. In this case, the group, other individual bathers who did not support the need for separate swimming areas at the public pool, and the local council had to negotiate according to their respective needs, rights, and constraints. The process was protracted and complex. In the end, the request from the immigrant group was not granted since, according to the council, it did not match the overall culture of the local community and the rights of other individual swimmers. This example demonstrates how at times and depending on the human rights violation under scrutiny, the individual has to navigate a narrower and more precarious path. Within torture and rape as torture, the individual victim has a distinctive and well-established place. Within genocide and rape as genocide, the place for the individual is less defined and more complicated due to the nature of a crime rooted in the protection of human groups. The individual has to operate within the reality of the group. The degree of this accommodation would vary from case to case.

The Public/Private Dimensions of Human Rights

As introduced in the Chapter 2, feminist thinkers and writers have emphatically placed the idea that the development of and the enforcement of human rights has been constrained by the existence of a public/private schism. [8] One important argument is that the shape of a human rights violation tends to have gender undertones. (OMCT, 1999: 30) The violations may occur, be reported and analyzed in the same manner for men and women, but important social, cultural and even political factors related to women specifically may exist. For instance, the "Roles, attitudes and relationships of men and women adversely influence the rights of women…" (Ibid: 30-31) One example of this unequal reflection between human rights violations specific to women has been the struggle at the international level to recognize and effectively address gender-based (in this case, against women and girls) violence. As mentioned earlier, it was not until the 1985 UN conference at Nairobi that gender-based violence was addressed in a meaningful way. One reason this has occurred is that within the classification of human rights, civil and political rights have been given most of the attention by the international community. One 'justification' given is that civil and political rights are less expensive and less complicated to implement than economic, social and cultural rights. Another 'justification' would be that economic, social and cultural rights are best left for individual States to implement according to their respective needs and limitations. However, most human rights violations suffered by women tend to be economic, social and cultural rights. (Id: 31) Yet as the organization working against torture, OMCT, correctly points out the connection between all five categories of human rights affect women:

---

[8] A related critique of human rights can be found in what Broadbent refers to as 'male bias' in how human rights are formulated and addressed. Broadbent argues: "We must make the language of human rights relevant to women's lives."

Ed Broadbent in Joanna Kerr (ed.). *Ours by Right: Women's Rights as Human Rights*. P. 12.

> "Thus, in ensuring women's civil and political rights, including the right to be free from violence, the state must be held to an affirmative duty to ensure the eradication of those social and economical conditions that maintain and perpetuate subordination." (Id)

The roots of this hierarchy are varied [9] but due to the elements covered such as the implications of rape committed in public or with socio-political connections under situations of armed conflict, I have chosen to address the Public/Private dimensions of human rights.

The dichotomy between public and private spheres of actions, such as was argued within liberal discourses, has found its way within recent examinations of international law and human rights law. A precise understanding of public/private dichotomy within the context of human rights can be outlined as follows:

> "The public/private dichotomy distinguishes and attaches more importance and value to the 'public-ness' of roles and actions than to the private domain of the home." (Id: 31)

Even in domestic law, this priority of addressing violations committed within the public sphere as opposed to acts within the private or family sphere has unfolded. For instance, difficulties in bringing the issue of domestic violence on the legislative agenda and before national courts, has been and continues to be difficult. (Id: 32)

This important point, regarding violence against women, is made by Rhonda Copelon:

> "Women were thus challenged to confront this public/private dichotomy, which exists in both domestic and international law and which helps to shield those who commit violence against women." (Rhonda Copelan, 1995: 64)

Some of the roots of the public/private dichotomy can be found in Enlightenment constructions of the political and even within natural rights. Rousseau, Locke and Hobbes development the 'model citizen' or civil government with attributes reflected in the male ideal of the rational and public involvement. (Anne J. Cahill, 2001: 55-56) For Anne Cahill the result was detrimental for women in that:

> "The body justified the exclusion of women from the realm of the subject and thus, in modern political theory, from the realm of the political." (Ibid: 55)

Cahill goes on to argue that the *main* reason women were excluded from the public or from the political is not merely due to perceived shortcomings in women's mental capacities but more importantly due to modern political theory's project to promote equality without dealing with differences such as gender.

Linking with my earlier reference to Catherine A. Mackinnon's attempt to explain the tensions found in human rights violations affecting women or men in that these are either too specific for women or to generic for 'humans'. (Catherine A Mackinnon, 1994: 6) Cahill notes:

---

[9] OMCT lists the following factors (not exhaustive) as possible explanations for such a hierarchy within human rights discourse: "public/private distinction, State responsibility arising out of acts of individuals, universality versus the right to its own culture." Pp. 31-36.

> "They must accept the masculine imaginary as their own in order to become the subjects that have always inhabited the body politic. They must become generically human; they must become men." (Anne J. Cahill, 2001: 94)

In Chapter 5, I will argue the importance of the need to address the theoretical implications that emerge from an emphasis on the political, within the context of rape as torture. In other words, if the political links or political backgrounds of individuals who have been subjected to torture or to rape as a method of torture is often projected in literature or by human rights enforcement mechanisms this thesis argues that a theoretical analysis of this process must take place. Questions such as 'what is the political?', 'who is politically active?' and 'what are some of the implications of bringing forth the political connections of victims of torture or rape as a method of torture?' have been identified as critical. This process will be complex since clearly distinguishing between what constitutes a public or private act is not clear-cut. (Katharine Fortin, 2008: 3; Jill Marshall, 2008; 3; Hannah Pearce, 2002: 537) As Christine Chinkin points out in relation to law and government policy:

> "Since there is no constant, objective basis for labeling an activity or actor as 'private', the judiciary regularly resorts to this as a device to avoid ruling on political issues. This in turn obscures the ways in which government policy regulates the so-called private sphere." (Christine Chinkin, 1999: 389)

For the authors Charlesworth and Chinkin, international law tends to ignore the position of women since the former is concerned with official activities of the State (the public sphere), while the latter tend to operate within the private sphere which is considered outside the boundaries of international or even national law. (Hilary Charlesworth and Christine Chinkin, 1993: 69) According to Charlesworth and Chinkin, despite the break from tradition that international human rights law seemed to offer, namely eradicating the distinction between what the official State can do to its private citizens or to individuals within its jurisdiction, this body of law continues to uphold components of the public/private spheres within its construct. For instance, international human rights law – especially as formulated in the West - has emphasized the importance of civil and political rights. These rights tend to be the domain where men participate within the public sphere.

In contrast, economic, social and cultural rights most often affect women as they usually operate within the private sphere. (Ibid) Prioritizing civil and political rights above economic, social, and cultural rights did take place especially during the establishment and subsequent development of international organizations such as the United Nations. In fact, several non-western States abstained from passing the General Assembly resolution containing the Universal Declaration of Human Rights in 1948 since these believed that too much emphasis was placed on civil and political rights at the expense of economic rights. At the beginning of their existence, some human rights non-governmental organizations (NGOs) such as Amnesty International focused on a narrow vision of civil and political rights. Yet, it should be noted that during the 1980s and 1990s an important shift occurred whereby not only was more effort placed on addressing economic, social, and cultural rights, but on the interconnectedness between all five categories of human rights resulting in a better understanding of these rights. Organizations such as Amnesty International broadened their mandate (for instance focusing on the arms trade and its effects on human rights violations), and more NGOs with mandates covering economic, social, and cultural rights emerged and were given a voice at the United Nations. A further area of international law, and linked to human rights, affected by the public/private dichotomy is the development of norms such as *jus cogens*. A norm of *jus cogens* is non-derogable. These norms also incur obligations *erga omnes*, which according to the International Court of Justice (ICJ) in the *Barcelona Traction* case, are

> "By their very nature...the concern of all States. In view of the importance of the rights involved, all States can be held to have a legal interest in their protection; they are obligations *erga omnes*." (ICJ Report, 1970: 3)

To complicate matters, not every obligation *erga omnes* is a rule of *jus cogens* and not every rule of *jus cogens* constitutes a crime under international law. [10] There is no agreed list of such norms. It is generally accepted that genocide, crimes against humanity, war crimes, piracy, slavery, torture, etc. are considered norms of *jus cogens*. (De Than and Shorts, 2003: 9-10)

As can be seen, rape is not explicitly listed as such a norm, but torture is. According to De Than and Short, these norms have

> "...attained their *jus cogens* status because they threaten the security, peace or essential values of society as a whole and thus stand to be redressed by the international community as a matter of urgency." (Ibid: 10)

Criticism of norms of *jus cogens* exists. One critique asks how it is possible to include racial discrimination and not gender discrimination. (Charlesworth and Chinkin, 1993: 68) Another, and deeper, critique examines the process by which such norms are developed. The authors Charlesworth and Chinkin argue that norms of *jus cogens* reflect the preponderance of men in international law and thus mirror 'male values'. (Ibid: 68-69) One reason given for this discrepancy is the emphasis in international law placed on 'public' over 'private' activities. In other words, historically men tended to operate within the public sphere (politics, government, etc.), while women tended to remain in the private sphere (the family, the home, etc.). Human rights norms, including *jus cogens* norms that touch upon human rights, also mirror this focus. (Id: 69-70)

Charlesworth and Chinkin comment

> "The doctrine of *jus cogens*, with its claims to reflect central, fundamental aspirations of the international community, has not responded at all to massive evidence of injustice and aggression against women. (Id: 72)

As noted earlier, not all acts committed against women or men are human rights violations. These other acts would not go unpunished, but would be viewed as crimes that should be dealt with under national legal bodies. The distinctions between torture as a crime and torture as a human rights violation would be one such example. (Daniela De Vito, 2001: 20) This means that under current formulations domestic violence could be prosecuted as a crime, but not as a human rights violation. (Ibid: 20-21) There is, however, the matter of a State's acts or omissions. If, for instance, a perpetrator of domestic violence is not brought to justice due to a lack of will on the part of the police then a human rights violation may have taken place. [11]

This is not the place to construct a detailed argument as to whether or not domestic violence should or should not be considered a human rights violation. There are other acts, beyond those with a special resonance for women, which do not make it onto the human rights platform. While I do not disagree with Charlesworth and Chinkin's overall assessment that there exists a hierarchy within international law, it must also be placed within the understanding that rightly or wrongly a process takes place whereby 'new' human rights violations are added to such lists while other acts are still omitted. For example, the idea that excessive alternative service or prison terms used against individuals objecting to compulsory military service as 'conscientious objectors' is considered a human rights violation is a new and ongoing development.

I have written about this meandering and incomplete process:

> "In sum, perhaps (this process has) always been part of the overall human rights discourse. With so many stakeholders and complex issues involved it is easy to understand how this has happened...some may say that this has occurred deliberately, others may argue that it has not. I would suggest that both assertions are justifiable." (Daniela De Vito, 2001: 21) [12]

With specific reference to civil and political rights and the public/private dichotomy, the international crime of torture as defined in the UN Convention (1984) has been criticized due to the fact that for an act to qualify as torture it must take place within the public sphere since it must be committed by a public official or by someone acting in an official capacity. 13 An example of a contemporary distinction between the public sphere and the private sphere (albeit pre-UN Torture Convention 1984) can be found in the Cyprus v. Turkey Opinion, whereby the European Commission of Human Rights argued that the rape of Greek Cypriot women by Turkish forces had occurred on a 'large scale'. These acts of rape were only considered to be 'inhuman treatment', and not as the more serious international crime of torture. One criticism of this decision was that the European Commission did not investigate why some of the rapes had taken place in public. I have demonstrated earlier the social,

[10] I am grateful to Nigel Rodley for insisting on this point.

[11] In *Velasquez Rodriguez v. Honduras* the Inter-American Court of Human Rights stated "An illegal act which violates human rights and which is initially not directly imputable to a State (for example, because it is the act of a private person...) can lead to international responsibility of the State...because of the lack of due diligence to prevent the violation or to respond to it...This duty to prevent includes all those means of a legal, political, administrative and cultural nature that promote the protection of human rights and ensure that any violations are considered and treated as illegal acts." Inter-American (Human Rights Series C, No. 4). *Velasquez Rodriguez v. Honduras*. Judgement of July 29 1988 (1989). ILM 291.

[12] Brackets added by this author.

[13] Although the Rome Statute establishing the International Criminal Court (ICC) does remove the need for a connection to an official or to someone acting in an official capacity for torture to have occurred, the ICC is underway with ongoing cases at the time of writing. As such, and at the time of writing, no case law is available. Also, there is the point of flexibility required and present within international humanitarian law.

cultural, and political undertones and impact that rape committed during armed conflicts and specifically in public (and this would include in front of family members) can have. Within the definition of torture available at the time, this fact could have brought the rapes within the realities of this crime. The concern here is that by not acknowledging that some of the rapes had taken place within the public realm, rape was confined as a private matter and thus not as serious as torture that has a public sphere connection. [14]

The final section of this Chapter will link the broad themes thus far outlined. Specifically, I shall focus on the association between rape, torture, and the attachment of political considerations placed onto individual victims of torture. This section will also present a process whereby rape is formulated within the very public context of torture. This will assist in understanding the implications of linking rape as a form of torture with the political, which will be analyzed in the next Chapter. This will be augmented by exploring further the notion of harm as associated with rape and autonomy. Lastly, rape as genocide will be introduced.

The Nature of Harm in Rape [15]

The nature of harm in rape is an important and due to the areas covered is a complex notion. This is not to diminish harm caused by rape committed under circumstances beyond those mentioned here namely armed conflicts (international and non-international) and international crimes such as torture and genocide. Another way to understand this notion is with the term 'trauma'. [16] Also, I do not propose to cover all notions of harm and I cannot assume that the harms covered subsequently can be linked to every situation of rape. (Clare McGlynn, 2008: 78)

As Anne J. Cahill correctly points out:

> "That is, we must resist the urge to recognize only those harms that are present in each and every case of rape as the 'real' wrongs inherent in the crime. The multiplicity of rape as an embodied experience indicates that such ethical universalism is not only illusory but dangerous in that it could serve to define some rapes as less harmful, or perhaps not harmful at all, if they fail to incorporate those particular harms." (Anne J. Cahill, 2001: 197)

It is in the spirit of this quote that I proceed…

> In a recent and challenging article, David Archard distinguishes between *hurt*, and *harm* and *wrong*. These are in turn associated with rape and what a victim may or may not experience. Hurt is "…experienced pain, displeasure, discomfort" while harm is "a setback to another's interests" and wrong is "an indefensible setback to another's interests". (David Archard, 2007: 378) Archard goes on to argue that under certain circumstances rape could be experienced as hurtful, or not, but that in his words "…a woman who is raped is wronged." (Ibid: 379)

---

[14] For more details on this case, please refer to Chapter 2 (Literature on Torture).

[15] I am grateful to Joanne Conaghan for pointing out the importance of the issue and the formulation of this phrase.

[16] Please see:
Lisa Scharlach, 2000: 91 *and*
Kirsten Campbell, 2004: 333.

This may seem to be an impossible observation and Archard goes on to state that an individual can be harmed and wronged by the action of another but that this individual may not necessarily be hurt by the said action. In the case of rape, it may be that a woman is not aware that she has been raped (the example given is a woman in a 'permanent comatose state'). For Archard, the importance here is that the act of rape is wrongful since it violates a

woman's 'sexual integrity'. (Id: 378-379) In short, the wrong is independent of any hurt the individual may or may have not suffered. In his words:

> "On my typology, the rape is not harmless, since it sets back her legitimate interest in her sexual integrity; but it is nevertheless a hurtless rape." (Id: 379)

Although Archard admits to the controversial aspects of his typology, two points must be made. First, I would argue that all three aspects outlined by Archard, namely hurt, harm and wrong are interwoven within the context of rape. To be blunt, even if it could be determined that an individual has not suffered pain (physical or psychological) after a rape it would be impossible to find anyone who would not at least experience displeasure – as per his definition of hurt. Second and this may seem obvious, but with the example given of the woman in a 'permanent comatose state' one cannot make an assumption that even in this condition she could not experience pain. She may not be able to communicate this experience, but it may be that at some level she has experienced pain. Beyond sexual integrity or autonomy, rape also harms the individual in that it is a 'violation of personal dignity.' (Kelly Dawn Askin, 2005: 1010 at note 8)

I would like to return to the issue of the complexity involved in determining the nature of harm in rape within the realities covered. Two main areas have been identified as being especially relevant: understanding the nature of harm within the context of international crimes such as torture and genocide and the consequences of rapes that occur during armed conflicts.

First, it must be noted that when rape is subsumed within international crimes such as torture and genocide its nature of harm reflects the particulars of these respective crimes. For instance, when working with a definition of torture such as the one utilized within this book the harm of rape as a form of torture must be placed alongside the elements of torture. Specifically, the harm of rape as torture (be it physical or mental pain) must be of a level deemed to be severe. Repeating one of the three main elements that make up the definition of torture outlined earlier:

> '1. The act must cause severe pain or suffering, whether physical or mental…'

By insisting on a level of severity to distinguish acts of rape as torture, it is evident that a two-tiered understanding of harm develops. That is, rape that does not fit the definition of torture would not necessarily result in a level of harm that could be considered as severe. This may in fact occur with certain rapes but it is not a necessary component. In contrast, with rape as a form of torture the nature of harm to the individual in relation to physical or mental pain must attain the level of severe. For the purpose of this section, I propose that harm to the individual constitutes physical or mental pain. The next section involves a broader understanding of harm in that it also considers the group and society. This is not to say that the harm of rape as torture does not also affect groups or society. Instead, this section is framed as such to bring forth the necessary connections of harm within the definition of torture – severe pain (physical or mental). Regardless, others harms such as inter alia harm to the sexual autonomy and to the personal dignity of the individual who has been raped cannot be dismissed.

In relation to rape as genocide, an important consideration is not only the harm done to individuals but also harm done to the group. As a World Vision report on violence against women and with specific reference to genocide notes:

> "The group impact of rape is described by Nowrojee: 'The humiliation, pain and terror inflicted by the rapist is meant to degrade not just the individual woman but also to strip the humanity from the larger group of which she is a part. The rape of one person is translated into an assault upon the community through the emphasis placed in every culture on women's sexual virtue: the shame of the rape humiliates the family and all those associated with the survivor'." (Don Brandt, 2003: 77)

Furthermore, there is the legal definition of genocide under Article 2(b) of the Genocide Convention, which means that an act must "...cause serious bodily or mental harm to members of a protected group." (Kelly Dawn Askin, 2005: 1016) Once again, and with resonance to the section on torture, rape as genocide must attain a level of harm – in this case serious. Both torture and genocide are international crimes which involve specific elements and require a higher threshold of harm. For torture, this is deemed as severe pain (mental or physical) [17] and for genocide, this is serious bodily or mental harm. As such, the nature of harm in rape (if it subsumed within these two international crimes) must be placed alongside these requirements.

The second main area identified has to do with the realities of armed conflict. [18] Rape during armed conflict is not, in the words of Christine Chinkin, "...merely a matter of chance, of women victims being in the wrong place at the wrong time." (Christine Chinkin, 1994: 3) Rape during armed conflict is extremely destructive. Harms such as displacement, targeting and shaming a group, damaging communities or family links emanate from rape committed during such situations. Specifically, I am considering rapes that occur in public. To borrow a term used in an article on the genocide in Rwanda by Llezlie L. Green, rapes that happen in public result in a 'dual harm'. (Llezlie L. Green, 2002: Section 2) [19] For the individual victim of rape in public the following harms may be amplified – shame, social exclusion, physical and psychological harm, etc. [20.]

As Mary R. Fabri has observed in her work with victims of rape and torture:

[17] To reiterate, the definition of torture within the Inter-American system does not include the word *severe* and the European Convention on Torture does not include a definition of torture. I am merely following the definition of torture developed earlier and utilized throughout.

[18] Although genocide or torture does not require a nexus to armed conflict, the international criminal cases utilized did take place within the context of armed conflicts. In Rwanda, the armed conflict was of a non-international nature while in the Former Yugoslavia the armed conflict was international. As such, the harms outlined in this section could be applicable to rape that has taken place outside situations of armed conflict.

[19] This list of harms also relates to rape that does not take place in public or during times of armed conflict. It is the possibility of an amplification of harm, due to rapes occurring in public, which may develop. Green uses this term 'dual harm' in connection to 'physical mutilation and violence'.

[20] This list is taken from Llezlie L. Green.

> "Across cultures and classes women are taught to value relationships, to assume roles such as daughters, wives, and mothers that are defined within a family, within a community, within a culture, and within a larger society. Women, therefore, often experience the definition of their self in relation to the others in their life...The shame inherent in rape enhances these feelings of broken affiliations. This is of particular importance in understanding the persistent and pervasive brokenness that many women describe." (Mary R. Fabri, 1999)

Thus, the individual who is raped in public suffers harms linked to the rape(s). [21] They are also harmed in that the public aspect of the rapes may exacerbate the expectations placed on women within respective societies and negatively alter how an individual victim/survivor is perceived. As a survivor of rape during the genocide in Rwanda explains:

> "...after rape, you don't have value in the community." (Llezlie L. Green, 2002: 2. Effects of Sexual Violence)

How then do these multiple understandings of the nature of harm in rape affect its conceptualization, placement and treatment under international law? If an act is deemed to be harmful to the individual, in the case of rape this could be linked to violations of sexual integrity/autonomy or as a violation of dignity or as other harms mentioned, then it could be argued that this is one way to justify intervention. In other words, if an act such as rape is understood as harmful then pressure is placed on international law bodies such as the international criminal tribunals and on the International Criminal Court resulting in the need to address the issue in a more meaningful and effective way. I would argue that the focus placed on the rapes that took place during the genocide in Rwanda and during the conflict in the former Yugoslavia, and especially the emphasis placed on the effects or harms of the rapes contributed to the shift in how international law has addressed rape within recent years. For example, pressure placed on the International Criminal Tribunals for Rwanda and for the former Yugoslavia by NGOs, the media, academics and individual victims contributed to indictments of rape and to significant jurisprudence contributions and innovations. In addition, acknowledging and reporting on the nature of the rapes – especially those that occurred in public – have added to a legitimacy of action by international law and by the international community in that the harms not only affected individual victims but also wider communities. This observation has not been made to place the harms suffered by communities above those of the individual victim. Nor am I necessarily accepting without debate perceptions and expectations placed onto women and as developed by respective communities. Instead, and in the spirit of not creating *exact lists* of harms applicable to every situation of rape, I make this observation as an acknowledgement of the complexities involved in any attempt to understand the nature of harm in rape.

[21] For instance, during the genocide in Rwanda many women were gang raped.
Llezlie L. Green, 2002.
Donatilla Mukamana and Anthony Collins, 2006: 150.
See also:
Katie Thomas, 2007: 15-16.

Conceptualizing Rape

Prior to reviewing the implications incurred when the individual victim of rape as a form of torture has been attached with the label of 'political', which follows in Chapter five, it is necessary to understand the process of placing rape within the very public context of torture. The current concept of human rights has tended to operate within a framework that elevated certain rights above others. In particular, civil and political rights which were nurtured within the public realm of activities such as free speech and the right to vote. These were deemed to have more of a priority than their counterparts of economic, social and cultural rights, which tended to be placed within the private sphere such as social security and family rights. Part of this emphasis is the opinion in some segments, especially in western states, that civil and political rights are more likely to be attained due to *inter alia* cost factors. than economic, social and cultural rights which are conceived as more progressive and long-term in nature. Despite these initial parameters recent work at the United Nations, within regional human rights bodies and other components of the international human rights discourse have come to a more realistic understanding that all five categories of human rights are important and interlinked. However, the matter of placing, accurately or not, certain human rights within the public or private realms has not, to this point, been completely settled. It is for this reason that the process of accepting rape as a form of torture – a human rights violation committed against the individual and traditionally associated with the public sphere – must be examined.

Catherine A. Mackinnon has proposed that rape committed within the confines of the private sphere, such as in homes, on the street, etc. should be considered both as a human rights violation and as a form of torture. (Catherine A. MacKinnon, 1993: 25) Under current international law, this perspective has not been accepted. For MacKinnon, though, this reality erroneously omits 'torture' committed against women within domestic boundaries. MacKinnon asks why acts such as rape, violence, and pornography, when committed against women in a setting outside 'official' sanction such as a prison, are not considered torture and thus a human rights violation. (Ibid: 25)

In turn, and related to this Chapter, Mackinnon questions why these circumstances of rape are not 'political' in nature? She focuses on the fact that women are specifically targeted and that these acts reflect "…the distribution of power in society." (Id: 26) She also notes that what tends to be considered political are situations whereby men commit violent acts against other men.

The pinnacle of this political link is if men are upholding some political ideology and if they are being victimized for this. (Id) In Mackinnon's words:

> "So their suffering has the dignity of politics and is called torture. The point is that the definition of the political is an unequal one, determined on the basis of sex such that atrocities to women are denied." (Id)

More will be said on this critical point in the next section.

MacKinnon also challenges the idea that the State is not involved in these acts of violence against women. For her, the State is 'complicit' in the experiences of women outlined in her article because it did not always assist the victims of domestic violence. (Id) Mackinnon does agree that to keep the rapes described within the private sphere, beyond State involvement, is not correct and does not adequately address the issues in hand. (Id: 27)

Two issues arise from MacKinnon's arguments.

First, not all acts can and should be considered human rights violations. An assault committed by one individual against another outside a pub on a Friday night, is a crime that should be dealt with by the police and the judicial system. It would be a crime, with various categories such a grievous bodily harm under respective national statutes. The assault would not be a human rights violation per se. What are the possible implications of this formulation? [22] It is true that within the human rights discourse, not all acts perpetrated against an individual or a group of individuals qualifies as a human rights violation, with the possibility of placing such acts under the rubric of international law. These other acts would not go unpunished but would be viewed as a crime that should be dealt with under national legal bodies. The distinction between torture as a crime and torture as a human rights violation would be one such example. Nigel S. Rodley, 1999: 300-301) Furthermore, and despite the understanding that crimes and human rights violations can be distinct, this formulation has the effect of placing human rights within an interconnected and cumulative model. [23] In order to determine the implications of this I shall map out the model and relate it to violence against women.

The Interconnected and Cumulative Human Rights Model:

The model that will be outlined was inspired by the manner in which human rights have been understood during the United Nations meetings and documents surrounding the *Beijing Plus Five* process. This involved a review that took place in the year 2000, of the document produced from the UN Beijing Conference (1995) entitled the *Beijing Platform for Action* in relation to advancing the equality of women and girls throughout the world. [24] Violence against women and girls has been linked to the notion that it can constitute a *violation of human rights*, a *human rights issue/concern*, a *crime*, or a violation/impairment or nullification of the *enjoyment of human rights and fundamental* freedoms, wether it takes place in public or in private situations. (Daniela De Vito, 2001: 3-8) The model is a subjective interpretation and does not presume to represent an all-inclusive picture of how human rights can be perceived and developed. Even in this limited state, it has been formulated in order to better understand some of the possible implications of this process as it relates to women and to human rights.

In order for an act of violence against women and girls to be considered a human rights violation *per se*, four interconnected stages must be passed. These stages are not hierarchical in nature, but these do build upon one another and are therefore cumulative. For the purpose of this exercise, the act of domestic violence will be incorporated. The first stage involves the *conceptualization of a human right* that includes "...attempts to first formulate concepts of (its) specific content." (Nigel S. Rodley, 1999: 300-301) This is followed by the second stage whereby *the human right is recognized and respected.* (Women, Law and Development International, 1997: 314) This recognition and respect would *inter alia* involve placing a human right that has been conceptualized into an international or regional instrument and ensuring that States parties uphold this instrument. (Ibid) The third stage pertains to the

[22] The following section is taken from a publication by this author produced through the Human Rights Centre at the University of Essex.Daniela De Vito. *Beijing Plus Five: An Assessment*. 2001.

[23] I am grateful to Pauline Ngan for her comments during an informal discussion while this model was being developed.

[24] For more details on this process, please see:

enjoyment of this human right. This includes both positive attributes that would enable the enjoyment and negative aspects such as obstacles that would hinder the enjoyment.

> The penultimate element reflects the point at which an act is considered a *human rights_violation*. Finally, one could arrive at the *potential criminalization of a human rights violation*. In the words of Cherif M. Bassiouni, this process focuses at "…the extent to which human rights violations can or should be internationally criminalized…" (Cherif M. Bassiouni, 1996: 185)

Not all human rights violations enter into this process. Once at this stage, or even in the previous one, there is no reason why a particular human right could not pass through certain stages again since, for instance, its content could evolve/change over time. Also, there is no reason why one *model* could not be interconnected with another where human rights are passing through the five stages mentioned.

As such, the *interconnected and cumulative human rights model* can be understood by the following schema:

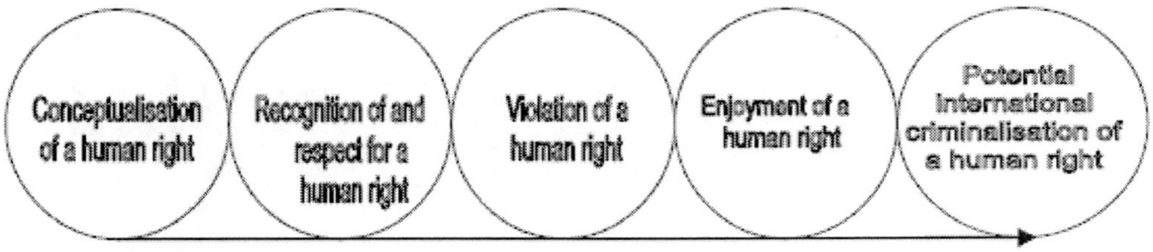

Currently, and as noted during the Beijing Plus Five Process, the act of domestic violence against women and girls would not be considered a human rights violation.[25] Despite the fact that domestic violence could be placed within the *interconnected and cumulative human rights model*, since it is viewed as a *human rights issue* and it is linked to the *enjoyment of human_rights*, it could never reach, on its own, the final stage as a *human rights violation* and beyond.[26]

Daniela De Vito. P. 1.

[25] This statement has not been made to initiate a debate as to whether or not this consideration should in fact take place. Instead, I have merely used the act of domestic violence to illustrate some of the implications involved in how the concept of human rights can be understood.

[26] Emanating from the Beijing Plus Five process:

"It is widely accepted that violence against women and girls, whether occurring in public or private life, is a human rights issue. It is accepted that violence against women where perpetrated or condoned by the State or its agents constitutes a human rights violation...There is increased awareness and commitment to preventing and combating violence against women and girls, including domestic violence, which violates and impairs or nullifies the enjoyment of their human rights and fundamental freedoms."

UN document. *Further actions and initiatives to implement the Beijing Declaration and Platform for Action*. Paragraph 13.

See also: The Inter-American Convention on the Prevention, Punishment and Eradication of Violence Against Women (1994), including its references to public/private dimensions, rape and links to established and enumerated human rights. Preamble and Articles 1-6.

A continuing obstacle is the fact that domestic violence is an act committed within the private sphere and not directly carried out by the State or its agents or those acting in an official capacity. In other words, freedom from being subjected to domestic violence does not exist as a human right. As such, the act of domestic violence could not involve a human rights violation on its own. Why would this matter? A parallel can be drawn with the UN Declaration on the Elimination of Violence Against Women in that

> "...by stating that violence merely impairs the enjoyment of human rights, the Declaration on Violence allowed governments to continue to characterize violence as a common crime, not as a violation of international human rights." (Felice D. Gaer, 1998: 23)

The repercussions of this approach includes the fact that certain international law remedies, such as *inter alia* the recently adopted Optional Protocol to the Convention on the Elimination of All Forms of Discrimination Against Women (CEDAW) which allows for individual complaints against States parties, can only be accessed if a human rights violation is claimed to have occurred. (UN document. Further Actions and Initiatives, 2000: 26.)

Thus, as outlined in this section, a victim of domestic violence could not access these particular remedies since the act is viewed as a human rights issue and as an obstacle to the enjoyment of human rights, but not as a human right that has been violated. However, and as developed in documents such as the Inter-American Convention (1994), since other established human rights are violated in connection to domestic violence, then it could be possible for these remedies to be accessed by individuals. This process also ensures that domestic violence does not remain within the confines of the private sphere. Like rape within the context of international law, domestic violence has been associated with established human rights.

Finally, does the fact that an act such as domestic violence cannot enter the final two stages of the *model* result in a setback for human rights in general? Two answers are possible. First, the human rights discourse is not stagnant. New concepts are developed or existing ones are re-worked to reflect changes in attitudes or the understanding of issues. New international human rights and humanitarian law instruments are produced. Innovative interpretations of these instruments are engaged. International and regional mechanisms are developed or adapted, and national remedies are addressed to reflect all of these changes. These factors, along with many others that have not been enumerated, contribute to the ongoing formulation of what should be undertaken in order to ensure gender equality and the promotion and protection of human rights. As such, the question could be answered in the negative. Second, it should be appreciated that the understanding of human rights just presented does leave room for roadblocks – such as the one faced by the act of domestic violence – to appear. The next step would involve overcoming these obstacles thereby enabling a particular act to enter the fourth and possibly the fifth stages of the *model*. It could be argued that this creates a setback for human rights since some acts that could involve a human rights violation are not addressed as such, until this 'extra' step has been initiated and completed.

The second point emanating from Catherine MacKinnon's arguments is that the acts described could indeed involve a separate layer of human rights violation with specific reference to the State. If a State, via its police and judicial system, does not arrest or prosecute someone who has committed violence against his/her spouse/partner then a human rights violation has taken place. The State, through its omissions has committed the human rights violation. However, the crime of domestic violence would not be the human rights violation. The human rights violation would emanate from the State not acting upon the crime. This means, that under certain situations, States have obligations in relation to such acts whether these are perpetrated by public or private actors. MacKinnon acknowledges this possibility. However, she also asks, "...why is torture on the basis of sex in the form of rape, domestic battering, and pornography is not seen as a violation of human rights?" (Catherine A. Mackinnon, 1993: [29]) Perhaps, at a certain level, international law is moving towards a broader understanding of torture and under what circumstances it can take place. For instance, under the Rome Statute of the recently established International Criminal Court (ICC), the definition of torture removes a necessary connection to officials or to those operating in an official capacity. Nor is there a requirement in terms of the 'purpose' behind the torture. [27] This is in contrast to the UN Convention (1984) definition of torture. Although it remains to be worked through, this author is not convinced that these changes will automatically lead to domestic violence committed by a private individual being accepted as a form of torture and therefore as a human rights violation.

In sum, at a certain level, conceptualizing rape as a form of torture can bring it out of the private sphere and into the fold of acts committed within the public realm. Torture, especially when it is attached with political undertones, operates within an understanding of human rights strongly associated with the public sphere. Unlike the proposal made by Catherine MacKinnon whereby rape committed by individuals not associated with the State or acting in an official capacity, and critically, within the private realm such as a home, this author is not convinced that this act should be considered a form of torture. Rape under these circumstances should remain a crime, unless the State is unable or unwilling to prosecute whereupon this would entail a human rights violation. Creating more human rights violations without fully analyzing the implications, benefits and even disadvantages will not necessarily clarify the consideration of torture that relates to violations committed against women. Merely adding layers to the established international crime of torture does not inevitably result in advancement within the complex discourse of human rights.

The problem, at this point in the development of international law, is not solely focused on the process of transferring rape from the private realm to the public realm. Much work has been done, and continues to progress, on this issue including challenging for example to how the Geneva Conventions (1949) have linked rape to a woman's honor. The concern at this juncture is more textured in that attaching rape to the international crime of torture also involves a series of steps so that rape can fit into an accepted definition of torture. Such a definition may change or adapt over time, as is evident with the Rome Statute establishing the recently enacted International Criminal Court's understanding of torture (with its lack of an explicit 'official' connection.[28]), but to consider rape as a form of torture certain criteria must be met. This reality does present restrictions in terms of under which particular circumstances rape can be accepted as a form of torture. As demonstrated with the *Interconnected and Cumulative Human Rights Model*, not all acts can be understood as human rights violations

---

[27] Article 7 (2) (e): "(e) 'Torture' means the intentional infliction of severe pain or suffering, whether physical or mental, upon a person in the custody or under the control of the accused; except that torture shall not include pain or suffering arising only from, inherent in or incidental to, lawful sanctions;" W. Van Der Wolf and J. Oppenheim (eds.). *International Courts and Tribunals*. P. 219.

[28] Rome Statute (1998). Article 7 (2)(e). Despite this, it will be interesting to see the limits of this varied understanding of torture with reference to a seeming lack of 'official' connection.

and not all acts of rape can or should be considered as a form of torture. Some acts of rape will remain a crime, but this does not in turn mean that rape is considered an act that only takes place within the private sphere and therefore should be treated differently. This incorrect consideration of rape exists not due to the fact that is not associated with torture, but because of how particular legal systems, societies, or cultures perceive rape. Automatically linking rape that takes place within the private realm as torture will not solve these mistaken perceptions of rape. It is for these reasons that Catherine Mackinnon's approach, as it has been set out, would not benefit the consideration of rape as a form of torture. Rape still needs to operate within the restrictions offered by the international crime of torture.

Rape, Torture, and the Political

Returning to rape, whether occurring under national jurisdictions or international mechanisms, rape is committed against the individual. National courts and international entities address the individual victim. [29] Similarly, the international crime of torture is a violation against the individual. When rape is committed in situations that could fall within the criteria of torture, it is also committed against an individual. For example, if a prisoner is raped by a prison official, and the rape occurred in an attempt to elicit information from this individual, the act could be deemed 'rape as a form of torture'. The act of rape as torture would be a violation of that individual's human rights. In this case, the emphasis is on the individual and on his/her individual human rights. Therefore, and following the framework within the current concept of human rights and as applied under international law, the individual as a victim of rape (be it as a form of torture or as genocide) should be the focus of the theoretical analysis.

An additional and critical layer of complexity emerges when rape is considered as a form of torture. Individual victims of torture, recognized under international law, tend to have been politically active or have political connections. Both men and women suffer rape under conditions covered by human rights and humanitarian law. An important consideration, highlighted by Sandesh Sivakumaran, is the underreporting of male rape by various entities such as non-governmental organizations (NGOs). (Sivakumaran, 2005) In the author's words, "...the subject of male/male rape is a cause without a voice." (Ibid: 1275) Yet women are more likely to be subjected to rape both in situations of armed conflict and in situations outside of armed conflict, than men are. In a study (1990) comparing 56 politically active men and women who had been tortured in Latin America, it was found that 12 of the 28 women and 5 of the 28 men had been raped while in custody. (F. Allodi and S. Stiasny, 1990: 144-146) The results confirmed the hypothesis that for women "...torture was more frequently sexual (in nature), and its consequences more often affected the women's sexual adaptation." [30]

Furthermore, for acts falling short of rape, the report states "...men...were, as often as women, subjected to sexual humiliation and abuse." (Ibid: 147) The report also added that both men and women who were politically active suffered higher levels of 'persecution and

[29] Although rape as a criminal offence is formulated under a trial system with the perpetrator and the State as participants, for the purpose of this Chapter that rape is a crime (or under international law and within the rubric of human rights violation) committed against the individual victim. I am grateful to Sam Ashenden for insisting on this clarification.

[30] "Women reported...much higher incidence of sexual dysfunction, namely sexual anxiety and avoidance." Ibid: 146-147. Parenthesis added by this author.

torture'. (Id) A later study conducted by TAT [non-governmental association against torture] of men (47) and women (17) from the Basque region of Spain who had been arrested during 1992-1993 found "...significantly more women than men being subject to such abuse ('sexually tortured') (94% vs. 66%)."(The Lancet, 1993: 1307) The two studies just quoted examine the numbers of men and women who have been raped and focused on those who had been politically active in their respective countries. Does this emphasis on political involvement provide an accurate description of all torture victims? Moreover, and critically for this discussion, what is meant by the 'political' and can this include a broad notion of the concept? Lastly, is this the best option? Similar questions will be posed in conjunction with rape as genocide, in light of what constitutes the current concept of human rights – the individual v. the group dynamics.

At the United Nations (UN) level, this focus has been addressed with the acknowledgement that in reality the majority of individuals who have been tortured were not politically active or associated with persons who had been political. Specifically, the UN Special Rapporteur on Torture has outlined:

> "It is true that many of the more high-profile cases of torture that come to international attention concern people involved in political activities of various sorts. Such victims of torture may well be of a class or connected with organizations that have international contacts." (UN doc. A/55/290: 8)

Beyond such a perception of who is a victim of torture, the Special Rapporteur on Torture instead asserts: "...the overwhelming majority of those subjected to torture and ill-treatment are ordinary common criminals from the lowest strata of society." [31] Even in terms of considering rape as a form of torture, proponents have also at times presented their case with an emphasis on the political. For instance, Evelyn Mary Aswad has argued that rape may be considered as a form of torture if for example "...government officials rape for political purposes..." (Evelyn Mary Aswad, 1996: 1930) More recently, such an association has been presented by the Medical Foundation for the Care of Victims of Torture:

> "For example, how is raped used politically and what impact does it have when perpetrated in the context of torture...Political beliefs and political identity as a context." (Michael Peel, 2005: 23)

The Medical Foundation, from their own files (from 2000-2003), examined one hundred cases whereby women had been raped (as torture). Of the 100 cases, 39 women said they were raped due to their direct political involvement and 21 stated they were raped due to a political association via a family member or partner. (Ibid: 45-47) It is interesting to note that the Medical Foundation does not consider the second category (21 cases) as falling into the active 'political' camp. (Id: 47)

What could be the link between torture and the political? The traditional view behind the use of torture may be an important indicator. For example, according to Nigel Rodley, torture has historically been used as a way of arriving at the 'truth'. (Nigel Rodley, 1999: 7) In ancient Greece and Rome, torture occurred to extract the truth in relation to serious crimes. In

---

[31] It should be noted that these two comments were made in reference to a link between torture and poverty.

Roman times, torture was also used in cases of treason. (Ibid: 7-8) By the middle ages in Europe, the use of torture had become more formalized within a rationalized approach to getting at the truth via proof. The need for a confession and arriving at what was then known as 'the queen of proofs' seems to have resulted in the use of torture within the legal process. Technically, there were strict rules in place as to when torture could be used, for example as a last resort. However, religious inquisitions in Europe led to the abuse of these so-called safeguards. Despite attempts to end its use during the Enlightenment period, torture did not vanish throughout the world. In Europe its use by the Nazis, especially against individuals suspected of participating in the resistance, is well documented. Even with the Universal Declaration of Human Rights (1948), and subsequent international and regional conventions prohibiting the use of torture, the practice is in use extensively throughout the world. The purposes behind the use of torture tend to be limited in scope. Most often, the torture attempts to extract information from the victim in relation to either his/her activities or the activities of others associated with the victim. Such activities may be political or criminal in nature. The torturer may also want to intimidate the victim or others. The torturer may want a confession. (Id: 8-11)

The purposes behind the use of torture, some of which have been identified, do not adequately explain why political activities tend to be associated with individual victims of torture. Therefore, it must be as the UN Special Rapporteur on Torture and authors such as Nigel Rodley have proposed, victims of torture with political involvement are more likely to report the violations to relevant human rights mechanisms and/or organizations. The reasons for this includes, *inter alia*, the victims may be better educated and more aware of existing reporting mechanisms and organizations, or these individuals may be less likely to remain silent about their experiences. (Id: 10) It may also have been due to the mandate of some of the human rights organizations operating within this field. For instance, in its early days Amnesty International focused heavily on releasing Prisoners of Conscience and to ensure that these individuals were not subjected to torture. Imprisoned or 'disappeared' for their beliefs and opinions (without advocating or using violence), many of these individuals were politically active or were associated with those who were involved in political, trade union, or other movements. This may have contributed to a perception that most victims of torture also had a political 'connection'. There is, however, no clear demarcation as to why the focus of recognized cases of torture has been on the political. This fact does not reflect the nature of torture *per se*. It also does not have to do with how torture has been defined under international law. Instead, this reality leads to two key theoretical questions: what is the political and what are the implications of referring to torture or to rape as a form of torture within the political activities of the victims or of those associated with the victims?

Finally, what is the justification for linking the individual component of the current concept of human rights (in this case torture or rape as a form of torture) with the political? On the surface, it may seem that the best way to address the emphasis placed on the individual within the concept of human rights is to examine in detail what is an individual and what is the individual's place within the development of the concept of human rights. Although important, there is another layer of analysis utilized that will complement and contribute to the process of understanding the implications of considering rape as a form of torture – a crime committed against the individual. As such, the interest lies in working

Ibid.

through the type of individual who has been subjected to torture, including rape as a form of torture. Since reported cases tend to include a political element, the task will be to assess what is meant by the political involvement or association of the individual victim of torture. The focus still remains on the individual, a key component within the concept of human rights, but the approach undertaken will bring into the discussion 'what makes up this individual'? In the case of torture and rape as a form of torture, this includes examining and understanding 'the political'.

Rape as Genocide

In 1998, the International Criminal Tribunal for Rwanda (ICTR) in the Akayesu Judgement determined that rape could constitute genocide. According to the Trial Chamber, Tutsi women were raped because of their membership in an ethnic group. This was genocide since these were acts that contributed "...to bring about its (the Tutsi ethnic group) physical destruction in whole or in part." (1948, Article II c) Genocide, according to the UN Convention on Prevention and Punishment of Genocide (1948), is a crime against a group be it a national, ethnical, racial, or religious group. A theoretical complexity emerges once rape, which is constructed as a violation against the individual, is subsumed into a crime such as genocide that is focused on protecting the group. Subsequently there will be an analysis of the theoretical implications for rape when it attempts to operate both as a construct for the individual and within the confines of a crime developed for the group. What will develop is an understanding that rape can benefit from being subsumed into the crime of genocide and that it must find space for both the individual and the group. Due to how genocide has been presented within international law, this space will be unequal and may change how rape is conceived, placed and treated.

With the advent of human rights, what then, happens to the individual and to the individual in relation to the group? Prior to World War II, the term 'human rights' was not specifically referenced within international law. Issues such as the international movement to abolish slavery and to protect minorities – through the defunct League of Nations - and trade union rights did exist during the 19th and early 20th centuries. In 1919 the International Labor Organization (ILO) was established by the Treaty of Versailles. The ILO's work included, for instance, initiating international provisions to protect freedom of association. In 1926, the Slavery Convention came into being. There were also steps in relation to protecting non-combatants during war and constraints on the conduct of war. (Nigel Rodley, 1999: 1-2) Despite this slow evolution, the individual did not possess a prime position. The State was the critical player. International relations and even international law as it was understood depended on State to State relations, needs and interests. This is evident with human rights before the 1940s whereby such matters tended to be considered within the "*domaine réservé*, or domestic jurisdiction, of states." (Ibid: 2) To elaborate, during this period "...for most purposes governments could do what they wished with those under their jurisdiction and international law had no opinion on the matter, much less any means to act." (Id)

After World War II, the international community understood that what a State does in its own back garden was indeed the business of others. (Id) It was not enough to be simply concerned with how a State acted in response to another State. Individuals, in relation to the protection of their human rights, needed not only their respective States to comply with norms but also other States have to be involved. How deeply and under which circumstances this involvement should occur was not only a concern during the early days of the UN and the first human rights instruments, but these tensions continue to be problematic today. Yet, and taking into account counteracting opinions and interpretations mentioned throughout this book, what emerges over the past sixty years is indeed a remarkable picture. The individual has a set of human rights outside any references of the State. The individual does not receive his/her human rights from the State. This set of rights may change over time and the rights may not universally be replicated exactly. Regardless, States have a responsibility to uphold these rights. Within later human rights conventions that include such provisions, which unlike the UDHR are legally binding for States parties, the individual has a right to seek redress for violations of their human rights. The emphasis is for this redress to take place within the State in question, but if this process is not possible or fails then international and regional mechanisms are in place.

In a dissenting voice to this overview, J. Shand Watson argues:

> "The traditional position on the status of the individual is thus a practical and efficacious one. First, there must be state consent for the creation of rights because this is the only way to ensure tangible results. Second, only states can be the subjects of rights because only states have the political power to create and enforce them. Since individuals lack such power, they are dependent on representation by states and are thus the objects rather than the subjects of rights." (J. Shand Watson, 1999: 295)

Although I concur with Watson's understanding of the reality that States still wield an enormous amount of power, the position of the individual has changed over the centuries. There continues to be variations, to the overview mentioned above, that understand the individual as primarily existing within the group and within the 'state'. Watson, in his book, correctly points out the inconsistencies within human rights theory and State practice. However, theoretical developments are important and should be considered as part of a more complete picture. The system is not perfect and individuals are still limited in their capacities. Human rights violations committed by the State through its acts or omissions take place. Redress is not always possible, sometimes it takes several years, or the outcome may not be beneficial. What must, however, be emphasized is that the relationship between the State and the individual who possesses human rights has transformed. This changed relationship continues even with the difficulties or inconsistencies that exist within the concept of human rights and within the system evolved to uphold these norms. In theory, at the very least, the individual now has a place at the table.

The implications of this means that when rape is considered as a form of torture or as genocide the degree to which the individual is addressed within the constraints of these varied human rights violations must be factored. In other words, although the individual has gained a firm place within the human rights discourse, variations still exist due to the specific nature of particular violations such as torture and genocide. In the former, the individual will have a stronger role while in the latter the individual will have to make room for the 'group'. Rape and rape as a form of torture are violations against the individual. Rape as genocide is a crime against a particular group. As noted, the current concept of human rights promotes the individual and yet makes room under certain conditions for the group. A similar schism had developed between the individual and society.

However, the differences between the individual and the group/society and the current concept of human may not always be at odds or in conflict. For instance, it may be necessary to create space for a Tutsi woman who has been raped because of her membership within this ethnic group, to view the act of rape as a violation committed against the Tutsi group and not as a violation against her as an individual. [32] This may be the solution if the aim is to bring closer together the schism created by the individual/group dilemma found within the current concept of human rights. How, then, can these differently constructed crimes (rape as a form of torture and rape as genocide) be compatible? In addition, how does each notion fit into the current concept of human rights? These critical theoretical questions will be now be discussed.

[32] I am grateful to Sam Ashenden for pointing out this possibility.

Chapter 5

RAPE AS TORTURE: ARRIVING AT AN UNDERSTANDING OF THE 'POLITICAL'

"The crucible of humanity has become the torture chamber."
Joanna Bourke
The Times, 10 February 2006

OVERVIEW

As argued prior, the concept of human rights, as developed through the United Nations and other components of the human rights regime, [1] tends to emphasize the human rights of individuals and human rights violations committed against individuals. Within the confines of international human rights and humanitarian law, rape, torture, and the consideration of rape as a form of torture are violations committed against the individual. With specific reference to rape, this conceptualization is evident with the International Criminal Tribunal for the Former Yugoslavia (ICTY) case – Foca. According to the Trial Chamber in its Judgement, rape reflects a 'serious violation of sexual autonomy'. (Foca case, 2001: 441) It also understood that sexual autonomy "...is violated whenever the person subjected to the act has not freely agreed to it or is otherwise not a voluntary participant." (Ibid: 457) As with torture, rape therefore constitutes a violation against the individual. A similar approach can be taken with the consideration of rape as a form of torture.

Beyond presenting the individual as a victim/survivor [2], torture and the consideration of rape as a form of torture bring out an additional layer of complexity – an association of the individual with 'the political'. Even in terms of considering rape as a form of torture, proponents have also at times presented their case with an emphasis on the political.

---

[1] A variety of components make up the human rights regime including *inter alia* the United Nations, regional bodies such as the European Commission on Human Rights, international and regional instruments such as the Universal Declaration on Human Rights (1948), and non-governmental organizations.

[2] The distinction between victims and survivors is used in order to denote those who have been tortured and died – either as a result of injuries inflicted during the torture, or in connection with any circumstances surrounding the torture - and those who did not. It is not, however, used to distinguish between levels of suffering.

Evelyn Mary Aswad maintains that rape may be considered as a form of torture if for example "government officials rape for political purposes…" (Evelyn Mary Aswad, 1996: 1930)

Despite the fact that this is a critical issue, I am not at this point interested in examining 'why?' victims/survivors of torture have been perceived as being associated with the 'political'. Briefly, this formulation has taken place in connection to his/her own activities, his/her association with others such as family members, and/or the 'purpose' behind the torture. [3] Rather, I wish to unpack the political and determine some of the implications for the individual if the political is emphasized when considering rape as a form of torture. As will be demonstrated, this process involves several components and cannot be settled with a singular approach. That is, to determine what can be understood as the 'political' and how this could affect the individual it is necessary to include an examination of the following two elements.

First, what are the possible contexts or circumstances under which the label 'political' is attached to an individual victim of torture or rape as torture? For example, is it only an individual who is a member of a trade union or an opposition political party member who can be given the label of political activist? Second, since the issue of torture will be the underlying theme of this overview of the political and the definition of torture developed earlier will be utilized, it was extremely important to also incorporate the notion of the 'purpose' behind an act of torture to determine what the 'political' can entail. That is, an individual who is in prison may not be involved with a trade union or may not be a member of an opposition political party but this individual may have been tortured to *inter alia* intimidate fellow prisoners. Also, since this section focuses on the constituent elements of torture as outlined in the UN Convention (1984), for an act of rape to qualify as a form of torture it must also meet the three-part criteria developed in this definition of torture. That is, rape as a form of torture must have involved severe pain or suffering; must have been committed for a prohibited purpose; and must have been carried out by a public official or by an individual(s) acting in an official capacity. [4]

Once again, influencing this study is the current concept of human rights with its focus on the individual. As such, individuals who have suffered torture and the reality that an emphasis is placed on survivors/victims who have been politically active or were linked to others who are politically active, along with an examination of what constitutes 'the political' will form the basis of this examination. Thus, the purpose is to understand some of the theoretical implications emanating when the label of 'political' is attached to individuals who have been tortured or who have been raped under situations that can be considered as torture. In turn, determining whether a broader or a narrower notion of this concept is more useful when examining which ideas, issues, and acts could be considered as political is critical to this discussion. Does the label of 'political victim' expand or restrict the category of victim of torture or victim of rape as a form of torture? Controversially, does the label of political make the individual victim more acceptable within the international human rights discourse thereby affecting how the group is perceived?

[3] I am grateful to Stanley Cohen, from his comments on an earlier version of this Chapter, for identifying a third possible contextual element to the political dimension of torture – the relationship between the offender and victim. However, as I will develop the focus of the inquiry will be on what constitutes the political and how an emphasis on the political can affect the individual victim of torture.

[4] Once again, the 'official link' or 'specific purpose' may not be a requirement for all definitions of torture such as with the International Criminal Court (ICC) in its Elements of Crimes.

WORKING THROUGH WHAT IS 'THE POLITICAL'?

Any attempt to grasp an essentially contested concept, such as the political, is fraught with interesting challenges. However, this is not to say that these challenges are insurmountable. Much depends on the endeavor(s) and the approach(es) undertaken. In order to arrive at a more solid understanding of the political the use of two avenues is foreseen, which when combined will enable the emergence of a broader or a narrower notion of this concept. On the one hand it is necessary to determine the 'nuts and bolts' involved in any understanding of the political. Questions such as 'what is it?' and 'which issues can be placed in the political?' are some of the considerations involved in this phase. My aim is not to attempt the formulation of an all-encompassing definition, but to present and assess a range of perceptions that can subsequently be used, adapted, or even discarded. At the outset, it may seem as if by using this approach I will be in fact be moving away from a more solid view of the political. On the contrary, it is by exploring a variety of options that one can appreciate the critical nuances that make up the overall process of working through the political. On the other hand, it is also important to gage 'where the political is applicable'. This second avenue will involve outlining realms such as the public, the social, and the private since any definition of the political will need a depository – or perhaps even a number of depositories. Alternatively, these avenues can be understood as developing the "nature and boundaries of the political."(Judith Squire, 1999: I) [5]

In combination, a broader or a narrower notion of the political can emerge. [6] With reference to rape as a form of torture, it will be argued that even if a broader understanding of the political is used - when it is attached to individual victims – the end result will still restrict which individuals are considered to have suffered rape as a form of torture. Key, instead, will be to move beyond insisting on the focus of a correlation between the individual and political activities or associations without fully expanding on its meanings.

What is the Political?

Introducing the political as a part of the State and its institutions offers an initial albeit limited understanding of the concept. Although several options are available in order to move beyond this juncture only institutional/instrumentalist understandings of the political will be briefly outlined. However, framing the political as I will develop into a more expansive perspective will be the focus. [7] Judith Squires writes about approaches utilized to work through definitions of the political. During the 1950s/1960s it was the "positivist perspective (endorsing objectivity)" which prevailed, while during the 1970s/1980s the focus was on

[5] Also:
Adriano Cavaro in Stephen K. White (Ed.) and Donald J. Moon (Ed.), 2004.

[6] Although I shall be outlining each avenue separately and then combining them to see how a broader or a narrower notion of the political can emerge, the entire process will not unfold in a clearly demarcated manner. Instead, this exercise could be understood as each 'stage' having the potential to flow into another. Much like the image of sharing a certain amount of water between three glasses.

[7] The inspiration for this term comes from an article by Jean Bethke Elshtain entitled "Displacement of Politics" where she mentions "...boundary shifts in our understanding of 'the political'..." in Weintraub and Kumar (Eds.), 1997: 169.

"socially constructed and historically variable forces". (Judith Squires, 1999: 7) During the last decade of the twentieth century, this second approach also referred to as contextualist, witnessed the development of deconstructionist methodologies. (Ibid: 8) More recently, the positivist and contextualist approaches were joined by a "third perspective" which argues "Definitions of the political…are neither empirically true nor simply reflections of underlying social relations, but rather active means to shape the 'real' world." Despite these varied perspectives Squires sees that an overall split has emerged in political studies between institutional and instrumental standpoints. (Id)

Therefore, an institutional understanding of the political means that politics occurs in government institutions, whereas an instrumental understanding asserts that politics is concerned with power and decision-making. It should be noted that although the issue of power and relationships of power are extremely important when attempting any formulation of the political, due to the scope of this book the concept will be left to one side. Yet, as Noel Wood succinctly remarks "...every exercise of power usually contains some element of the political." (Neil Wood, 2002: 27 and Noel O'Sullivan, 2000)

What are some of the concerns with this so-called divide? William E. Connolly points out that politics becomes "bifurcated … between principle and instrumentality". In the former camp, one finds individualists such as rights and justice theorists, and in the latter camp are 'utilitarians, pragmatists' who focus on instrumentality over principle. (William E. Connolly, 1983: 8) One result of this bifurcation is that two separate notions emerge in terms of how to distinguish between the political and the rest of society, one based on principle and the other on instrumentalism. Another worry for Connolly is that both understandings insist on the individual as opposed to groups. (Ibid: 9)

What does this mean? It is possible that what is linked to one or the other understanding of the political – such as rights and justice or power and policy - can also be found in its opposite viewpoint. To elaborate, in an attempt to understand the political A. W. Sparkes has developed a 'model' which I would argue includes the potential for such overlaps. (A.W. Sparkes, 1994: 61-69) It is for this reason that Sparkes' model has been used, as a starting point for the development of my understanding of the political as a more expansive perspective and for its potential transfer to the issue of rape as a form of torture. Rather than calling this model a definition of the political per se, Sparkes refers to it as "a list of ten political-making characteristics." (Ibid) For the sake of brevity, I shall not replicate the model nor shall I delve into how/why the author arrived at its ten components. However, it should be noted that at its crux the model is divided between the 'Quasi-Polis' and the Politician which he calls "poles". [8]

Using this model as a backdrop the divide between institutionalism and instrumentalism begins to loose its absoluteness. This occurs not because these two understandings of the political are outlined in an unclear manner but, rather, due to the fact that overlaps can exist. Although Sparkes does emphasize 'the polity', his model of the political does not read in terms of an institutional/instrumental divide. This can be understood with reference to characteristic (vi) "…the social structure of power and its uses…" – which straddles the

[8] Sparkes argues, "I am quite sure that *primarily* the concept of the political refers to the polity, so that its applicability to the governance and internal affairs of other groups depends on certain significant resemblances between them and the polity". With reference to quasi-polis he adds "I shall use the word 'quasi-polis' to refer to the polity and other groups." Sparkes, 1994: 65.

quasi-polis and the politician planes [9] – and to characteristic (x) "politics of a collective… law and order…"

Taking a momentary step back from what Sparkes is attempting to do with this model, and without presuming that this was his intention, I would suggest that point (vi) "power…" is an instrumental component and point (x) "politics of a collective … law and order…" is an institutional one. [10] In other words, the former involves 'instrumental issues', whilst the latter involves 'juridical' considerations and matters of principle. If both can operate in the consideration of 'Quasi-polis and its Governance', then they can also overlap. This is what I mean by the 'so-called' divide between institutionalism and instrumental understandings of the political. Beyond introducing the possibility of overlaps in institutionalism / instrumentalism, Sparkes' model also brings into play the notion of framing the political as a more expansive perspective.

What then does a more expansive perspective of the political entail? Critically, it should not be understood solely as how Sparkes has presented his ideas. That is, there are several additional understandings of the political which attempt to break through supposedly set boundaries. One such example would be Jean Bethke Elshtain who advocates the existence of "boundary shifts in our understanding of the political but that a limit needs to be present. (Jean Bethke Elshtain, 1981: 169) In other words, "But minimally, a political perspective requires that some activity called 'politics' be differentiated from other activities, relationships, and patterns of action." (Ibid: 170)

Thus, and in simple terms, a more expansive perspective of the political should include the following three basic points. [11] First, this perspective should approach formulating both 'what is the political?' and 'where should the political be placed?' flexibly. For example, it would not be adequate to say that the political only pertains to the State and its institutions. Second, an understanding of the political should accept that due to the topic(s) in hand it operates on an open-ended plane.

Third, although a more expansive perspective of the political is at its essence more open to accepting varied issues and institutions, this does not mean that everything could be placed in the political or that the political can be found everywhere. To consider the act of playing 'fetch' with one's dog - in a dog-friendly park - as political would be contestable. Whereas the act of stealing a loaf of bread, if one were hungry and if one's government refused to provide programs which could help alleviate poverty, would be easier to include in an understanding of the political. [12] In relation to rape as a form of torture, and its links with the political involvement or association of individual victims, it is necessary to understand where 'the political' can be found. Is it only within government institutions; within political activities such as trade union membership; or is the political also found in broader social relationships such as neighborhood watch schemes.

This last point brings up an interesting consideration – that of politicization. In other words, when is an issue, act, or thought political? In a sense, the answer to this question is

[9] Sparkes refers to this area as the "Equator". Ibid: 65 and 68.

[10] Sparkes presents law as "something imposed on those subject to it. But a respect for persons, a commitment to autonomy…requires that, so far as possible, it should not be *pure* imposition…"Sparkes, 1994: 195.

[11] I am not claiming that these points are all encompassing. Neither am I assuming that only these three are relevant. Instead, they have been included as an introduction to the idea that the political can be understood in this manner.

[12] Although I have used 'acts' in these two examples the political can also involve other aspects such as thought.

twofold. Initially it is necessary to bring into the discussion the possibility that something can indeed be non-political. At a certain level, this could be upheld. For instance, one way to understand hedonism is to view it as "the doctrine that only bodily sensations are real, is but the most radical form of a non-political, totally private way of life, the true fulfillment of Epicurus' … ('live in hiding and do not care about the world')." (Hannah Arendt, 1994: 112-113) [13] However, someone like Sparkes would counter this idea by insisting that "while there are things which are essentially political and things which are not essentially political, there are no things which are essentially non-political." (A. W. Sparkes, 1994:70) It may seem that in using Sparkes' quote I have in fact contradicted myself on two counts. One in relation to the playing 'fetch' with a dog example and the other with regards to the third point for a more expansive perspective of the political. In the former, my focus was solely on the act of, for instance, throwing a ball for the dog to chase. However, a link could in turn be made to the political process that resulted in the park being converted into a dog friendly area or under what conditions and where the ball was manufactured. This is how I understand Sparkes' idea that "there are no things which are essentially non-political." So, and in this case, an individual throwing a ball for their dog is "not essentially political" but how the dog friendly park came about is "essentially political". The latter count is more difficult to resolve. One way would be to insist that the understandings of the political that have been presented all include certain limits. The main consideration would therefore be the degrees involved. As linked to a more expansive perspective of the political, Sparkes limits his model to the quasi-polis and to the politician. In contrast, Elshtain goes beyond this and asserts "By the political here I refer to a specific version of what is public: that which is, in principle, held and considered in common and which is, in principle, open to public scrutiny." (Jean Bethke Elshtain, 1981: 170) So, for Elshtain the political would go beyond the limits of the quasi-polis – as framed by Sparkes – but remain within the public realm. In other words, Elshtain does not uncritically accept the notion that "The personal is political". [14] Why should such limitations be included? One concern has to do with the possibility of creating an understanding of the political "that is so wide as to lose its specificity and usefulness." (A. W. Squires, 1994: 9) Alternatively this can be understood as something which has become "…one of those 'sponge' concepts that C. Wright Mills mocked as it sweeps together and liquidates indifferently whatever crosses its path." [15] A comparison can, at this point, be made to torture. References to the term have also been used to elucidate situations that are outside formal definitions. Despite the idea that a built-in caveat concerning limits has also been included in a more expansive perspective of the political, individual or group perceptions of what should be considered political and in which realm(s) should it be deposited - which may

---

[13] Arendt distinguishes between "ancient and modern varieties" of hedonism, 310.

[14] This phrase is associated with feminism and the move to expand where the political could be found. One way to understand this idea is to state that the personal "is legally constructed, culturally defined, and the site of power relations." Jean L. Cohen in Weintraub and Kumar, 1997: 136.Advocates of a strict notion of 'the personal is political' would insist "the claim… (is)… not that the personal and political are interrelated in important and fascinating ways…but that the personal *is* political." Elshtain, 1981: 171. To elaborate, Elshtain does think that considering political issues which were previously "hidden behind a gloss of professed concern for the sanctity of the 'private' realm" may be laudable, but she goes on to point out several concerns including the idea that "Nothing 'personal' was exempt from political definition…"Elshtain, 1981: 171-172.

[15] The concept being examined in this quote is 'revolution'. However, in this chapter the quote has been used in relation to 'the political' and to 'torture'.
Dick Howard, 1988: 110.

go beyond the above-mentioned limitations - cannot be placed to one side and completely ignored.

Therefore, a more expansive perspective of the political can include limits in terms of content and applicability, but these 'other' perceptions may in turn be looking in and at times may need to enter into the fold. A secondary, and complementary, way to answer 'when is an issue political?' involves an examination of the process by which particular issues or acts gain the mantle of 'the political'. In other words, "There is, in fact, nothing more political than the constant attempts to exclude certain types of issues from politics." [16]

Depositing the Political

Determining where to deposit the political should not take place in isolation from the process of working out what makes up the political. Both tasks are intertwined and are crucial in any attempt to understanding the political. In this part of the book I will examine the realms of the public, private and social, and their connection to the political.

Traditionally, political discourse has included a distinction between the public and private realms. Even the ancient Greeks dealt with this split. In contrast to later developments Aristotle thought that economics and family matters took place in the 'private' realm (or oikos – household), and that the "political community" was to be found in the public realm. (Weintraub and Kumar, 1997: 13 and 25) [17] More recently, however, there have been attempts to work through this 'dichotomy'. The essays in Public and Private in Thought and Practice offer one such alternative in that they include "not a single paired opposition, but a complex family of them, neither mutually reducible nor wholly unrelated." (Ibid, 1997: xii) With reference to rape conceptualizing and placing this violation beyond notions that it should remain within the private realm has been and continues to be discussed. Whether rape is committed as a crime or as a human rights violation, a process still exists (despite recent advances in this area) in changing perceptions and legal practices to ensure that it is not left within the private sphere and thus not adequately addressed as a matter for State or international mechanisms involvement. Even if rape is subsumed into the international crime of torture, a long established human rights violation often linked to activities or associations that take place within the public realm there must be an understanding of how rape can operate within the formulation of rape as a form of torture. This is especially critical when the label of 'political' is associated with an individual victim of torture or of rape as a form of torture, since this firmly places the activity/association within the public sphere. It is with this spirit in mind that I approach this part of the discussion. Within these realms it has been assumed – and at times challenged - that the public contains the political and the private contains the non-political. However, even this idea is not so straightforward. In other words, depending on which understanding of the political is utilized within these parameters the public realm can also be transformed. For example, Jeff Weintraub outlines two perspectives of the "public as political" where one "means the administrative state" and the other "means a

---

16 Leftwich and Held quoted in Squires, 1994: 9.

17 For an interesting overview of how 'economics'/'private realm' links were dealt with by "seventeenth –century Natural Law theorists" and subsequent developments please see Gobetti, Daniela in Weintraub and Kumar, 1997: 108-111.

world of discussion, debate, deliberation, collective decision making and action in concert." (Wintraub and Kumar, 1997: 10-11) In turn, the political theorist Carole Pateman in The Sexual Contract challenges accepted liberal discourse that the private and public realms are so clearly demarcated. For Pateman, understanding how each sphere operates and affects both how politics function and how individuals carry out their private lives is critical. The goal is not to merge the two realms, but to examine their respective effects within each sphere. (Carole Pateman, 1988)

Accepting the possibility of multiple publics, or even varied alternatives including ones that aim to articulate what is involved in a single public realm, raises the question of whether this means that the private realm is completely emptied of its contents? Two points are relevant to this inquiry. First, leaving some issues within the private realm may be necessary and a positive aspect of this discourse. As Hannah Arendt outlines

> "The distinction between the private and public realms, seen from the viewpoint of privacy rather than of the body politic, equals the distinction between things that should be shown and things that should be hidden." (Hannah Arendt, 1998: 73)

In a textured analysis of the political Hannah Arendt contributes to the discussion by outlining the social realm. [18] Arendt begins by considering the Latin roots of 'social' (*societas*) which "originally had a clear, though limited, political meaning; it indicated an alliance between people for a specific purpose, as when men (*sic*) organize in order to rule others or to commit a crime.... Such an alliance could also be concluded for business purposes." [19] Later in history "the term 'social' begins to acquire the general meaning of a fundamental human condition." (Ibid: 23 at note 3 and 24) Arendt considers that the social realm proper and not the

private/public worlds which according to her is a more recent development. (Id: 28) This is due to the idea that from 'families', a greater entity emerged – that of society which in turn became the 'nation'. (Id: 29)

For Arendt this social realm is a "characterization of modern civil society." [20] Arendt is concerned with the development of this "curiously hybrid realm where private interests assume public significance that we call 'society'." (Hannah Arendt, 1998: 35)

Before proceeding to the final section I would like to develop a schema which includes the understandings of the political and the depositories for the political which have been discussed. Schema 1 includes the following realms: Public = **P1**, Social = **S** and Private = **P2** along the line. These are not plotted in an exact manner but are placed to simply signify which one(s) a particular understanding of the political fulfills. Of course, this does not mean that some viewpoints could not also include elements from the 'social'. In addition, both

---

[18] Nicolas Rex outlines what he has termed the "...invention of the social" at the beginning of the 20th Century. Nicolas Rex, 1999: 112.

[19] Briefly, for Arendt "the political realm rises directly out of acting together, the 'sharing of words and deeds'." As such, "The distinction between a private and a public sphere of life corresponds to the household and the political realms..."Arendt, 1998: 28 and 198.

[20] Jeff Weintraub offers this assessment and links it to how he uses the term civil society in his essay: "I will use 'civil society' to refer to the social world of self-interested individualism, competition, impersonality, and contractual relationships – centered on the market – which as thinkers in the early modern West slowly came to recognize, seemed somehow able to run itself." In turn, Liberalism is associated with civil society in that "its tendency is to reduce society to civil society." Weintraub and Kumar, 1997: 13 and 35.

endpoints would relate to all three realms. These areas have been presented as extremes and their plausibility in real life would require additional analysis. Moving away from them means re-adjusting how the political could be understood and potentially which realms are applicable. To summarize this section, if I was urged to express my own viewpoint it would rest within a *more expansive perspective* of the political – including the limits outlined; it would be closer to the endpoint 'everything as political' to signify a broader notion of the political; and it would involve all three realms, in a potentially overlapping manner, as possible depositories for the political.

I have not articulated an exact map of which issues or acts could be considered as political, or, how each of the three realms could appear. The reason, as noted at the beginning of this section, is that the aim was to work through how the political could be understood and not to develop a particular formulation of this concept. This area on Schema 1 has been marked with an '*'.

Schema 1

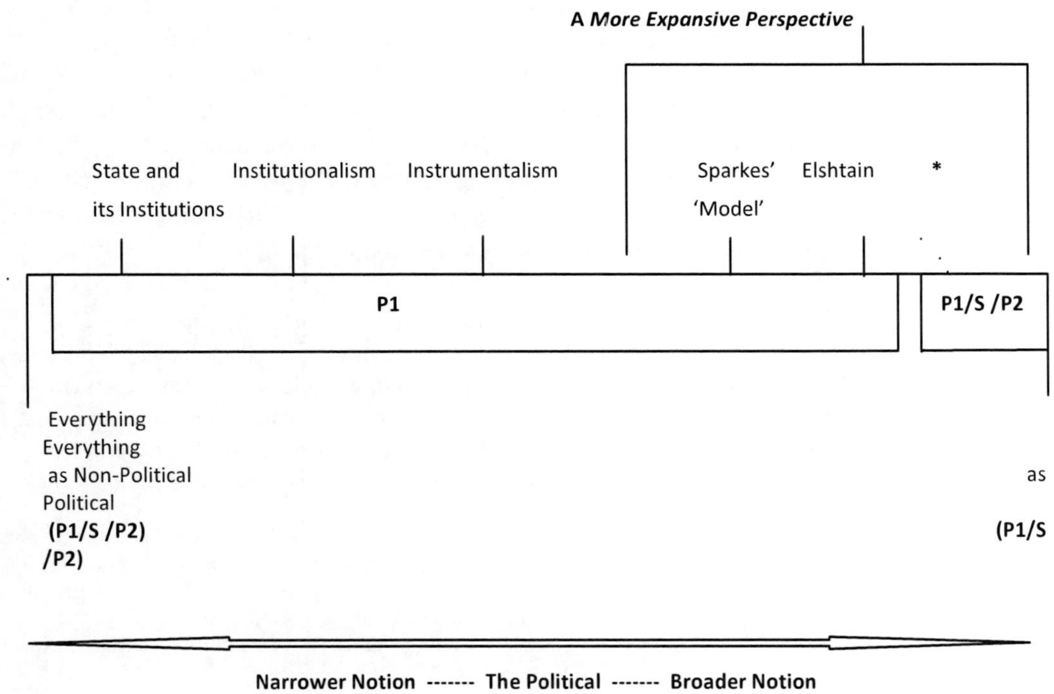

Public = **P1**, Social = **S** and Private = **P2**

ASSOCIATING THE POLITICAL WITH RAPE AS A FORM OF TORTURE

In the overview of this chapter, I pointed out two elements that could be examined in connection to the political and its association with torture. One was rooted in the contexts or circumstances under which individuals had been subjected to torture, and the other was linked with the purpose for the torture. [21] In this section both aspects will be applicable to the consideration of rape as a form of torture, and some of the possible implications of this association will be examined.

Even if rape is considered as a form of torture, can its conceptualization be problematic? In short, the answer is yes for several reasons. That is, at times, when proponents for the consideration of rape as a form of torture present their arguments one criterion discussed involves the existence of a political component to the act. For example, Evelyn Mary Aswad presents if "government officials rape for political purposes, those rapes should be classified as torture if they inflict severe pain." (Evelyn Mary Aswad, 1996: 1930)

In this instance the link to the political falls within one of the three components of the definition of torture namely the purpose behind an action.

Two points must be made about this emphasis on the political. First, it could be argued that the political should be broadly interpreted. Or, to borrow from Schema 1, a more expansive notion of the political should be applied. Certain components of the human rights regime have tried to work through an understanding of the political. [22] In 1997 an Expert Group Meeting under the auspices of the UN Division for the Advancement of Women (DAW) took place. The overall topic of the meeting related to "Gender-based persecution", but in a section pertaining to the UN's 1951 Convention Relating to the Status of Refugees (hereinafter the Refugee Convention) the meeting addressed political opinion:

> "The meeting agreed that feminism constitutes 'political opinion' for the purpose of defining who is a refugee in the context of the Refugee Convention. It considered that political opinion or imputed political opinion may be determined from behavior as well as expressed opinion. It noted that behavior by a woman that does not conform to cultural or social norms with respect to gender roles may be construed as political opinion with respect to gender roles or the political opinion, feminism. The meeting also pointed out that peaceful activities by

[21] A connection to *political actions* could occur if an individual is related to or associated with someone who was politically active. That is, the victim/survivor of torture would not necessarily have had to participate in a political activity, etc. for this association between the political and torture to exist. *In addition:*

"Rape, particularly when used as a political weapon, meets the definitional criteria for torture under international law." Deborah Anker, 1995: 784.

"At the same time, the political motivations of the perpetrator or torturer in selecting rape as a method of abuse are largely ignored." Deborah Blatt, 1994: 846.

Also:

"Politically and socially active women are particularly vulnerable to rape under these circumstances." and in terms of refugee women "Public officials with authority over a woman's fate, such as border guards, soldiers, and refugee camp administrators, extort sexual favors in exchange for food, services, or a positive determination of the woman's refugee status…Sexual extortion of refugee women constitutes a method of torture under Article 1 of the torture convention." It should be noted, however, that in the example given concerning refugee women, sexual extortion is not mentioned as rape but as a distinct form of torture.

Ibid, 859 and 862.

[22] Attention to the following example came from a section in:

Triffterer, Otto (ed.), 1999: 148-149.

> women in the course of armed conflict may be construed by opposing groups to impute political opinion. Political opinion may also be imputed to women as a result of the political opinion of male family members." (UN doc. EGM/GBP/1997/Report: 10)

The key aspects of this meeting's understanding of the concept – albeit in terms of the Refugee Convention - are that it could involve several layers beyond simply the act of expressing one's political opinion, and that the political can also be linked to cultural, social, or gender factors.

Another attempt to understand the political is in relation to the Rome Statute of the International Criminal Court (1998) which establishes the permanent International Criminal Court (ICC). The ICC has jurisdiction over "the most serious crimes of concern to the international community as a whole" and the list includes genocide, crimes against humanity, war crimes and aggression. [23] Commenting on Article 7 of the Rome Statute (crimes against humanity), and in particular how to understand one of the 'grounds' for persecution listed – persecution on political grounds, M. Boot and C. Hall speculate that it could be related to the "…'State or its government, or public affairs generally and its institutions'…" but also that it "might not be limited to grounds that concern membership of a particular political party or adherence to a particular ideology." (M. Boot and C. Hallin Triffterer (ed.), 1999: 148) In turn, "the word 'political' might be understood as including public affairs issues such as environment and health; a political ground for persecution would then cover at least the existence of a difference of opinion concerning these issues as a reason for committing the acts concerned." (Ibid) The authors go on to add, "Remarkably, social grounds have not been expressly included" in the Rome Statute. (Id: 150) In terms of rape as a form of torture, it could be argued that the political should be broadly interpreted.

Therefore, a more expansive notion of the political would not only include the scenario whereby a government official subjects an individual to torture in order to gain information about a political opposition party, but it could also include the situation whereby a woman is tortured because she works for an organization that is demanding better social services for women from the government. Even if a more expansive notion of the political is accepted a secondary point reveals itself. Emphasizing the political – broadly or narrowly – limits which particular acts of rape can be considered as a form of torture. Furthermore, I would argue the political in this context, as for instance part of a 'purpose', has the effect of constraining the definition of torture. If a prison guard rapes a woman who has been convicted of stealing money from her employer, would this not be considered a form of torture? Alternatively, Article 1 of the Torture Convention (1984) includes the following:

> "…for such purposes as obtaining from him or a third person information or a confession, punishing him for an act he or a third person has committed or is suspected of having committed, or intimidating or coercing him or a third person, or for any reason based on discrimination of any kind."

This understanding of what constitutes a 'purpose' is quite broad. By promoting the political even this can become lost. If a woman has been raped not while being interrogated to gain information about a political organization or because of her involvement with a social

[23] The crime of aggression still needs to be worked out.

organization, but because the prison guard uses this method in order to keep the female prisoners *in-line,* would this also not constitute torture? The answer to both questions is yes, if all three elements of torture are present. So, if a prison guard rapes the woman who stole money from her employer in order to intimidate her and her fellow inmates, and she suffered severe pain (physical or mental) then she would have been subjected to torture. I am not asserting that authors such as Anker, Aswad and Blatt are deliberately excluding such possibilities, and these may not be applicable in terms of rape that occurs during situations of armed conflict. However, by emphasizing the political - either in relation to the victim/survivor or to the purpose for torture - the net result is a restraint in terms of which acts of rape should be considered as a form of torture. Having said that, the political must not be completely disregarded either.

As such, a more appropriate understanding can be found with the UN Special Rapporteur on Violence against Women:

> "Rape committed as a part of political oppression is prohibited under international law as torture or cruel, inhuman or degrading treatment" and "Numerous international authorities have also recognized rape as a form of torture when rape is used to punish, coerce or intimidate, and is performed by State agents or with their acquiescence." (UN doc. E/CN.4/1999/68/Add.4, 6.)

Key is to understand the implications of associating individuals who have been raped within the context of torture with the label of 'political'. It is not adequate to merely state that such individuals have been politically active or have had a political association. One must also develop what is meant by this concept. Furthermore, the reality that most victims/survivors of torture have not been politically active or have a political link is critical . Otherwise, and I return to the controversial questions posed in the introduction to this chapter, the net effect of this pattern may be that such a political connection does indeed make the victim/survivor of rape as a form of torture more acceptable. The individual has a special place within the human rights discourse. Most of the human rights violations listed in a multiplicity of regional and international human rights documents relate to the individual and to his/her rights. The right not to be subjected to torture as well as rape as a form of torture are both formulated for and addressed to individuals. Furthermore, and as noted from the ICTY Foca case, rape is a violation against one's sexual autonomy. I did not delve into what makes up an individual in relation to the current concept of human rights or what it means to violate the human rights of an individual. Rather, I was interested in addressing the complex fact that many individuals who have been tortured or raped under circumstances that can be considered as torture have also been constrained with the additional layer of political involvement or association. I was also concerned about individuals who had not been deemed to have this political label. As such, I have explored how the political as an essentially contested concept can be understood and where it can be deposited. A less restrictive approach was promoted which resulted in a *more expansive perspective* of the political. This in turn meant that a broader notion of the political could emerge. Regardless, I argued that insisting on the political, when considering rape as a form of torture, is too restrictive. The political would not be swept away. Yet, it is also critical to recognize that the overall realities in which rape as a form of torture occurs is multi-dimensional. In turn, these factors must be considered even while acknowledging *contexts or circumstances* whereby the individual victim does indeed have a political affiliation or whereby the *purpose* behind the act of torture or rape as torture is political. Thus, rape as torture fits more comfortably within the current concept of human rights with its emphasis on the individual. Rape and torture respectively are acts committed against the individual. In addition, this section has demonstrated that torture via its frequent but incomplete perception affects the individual who is placed within and confined by the parameters of the political – even if it is a broader understanding of the political. Rape as torture is also committed against the individual and in turn must negotiate these complex realities. It was therefore necessary to elaborate on this tripartite relationship of the individual influenced by the current concept of human rights, of rape as torture, and of the political in order to appreciate what can occur to rape when it is placed within such constructs. The next step is to outline the theoretical implications for the group when rape is subsumed within the international crime of genocide and to determine what happens to the individual.

Chapter 6

RAPE AS GENOCIDE: THEORETICAL IMPLICATIONS FOR THE GROUP [1]

"Then, too, there is no general agreement on a scale of values (norms or human rights), and situations juxtapose different values in new relationships, raising problems of their ordering… The scale of values regulates the salience of different human rights issues and the significance to be accorded their violation."
Leo Kuper, Genocide

OVERVIEW

This section examines the second theoretical implication to emerge from the international cases mentioned earlier. Specifically, acknowledging the possible implications of considering rape – a crime committed against the individual – as genocide, which has been constructed as a crime against the group, will unfold. [2]

From this analysis, two interesting questions emerge:

a) Does compatibility exist when rape is subsumed within the category of a group violation (genocide), if rape is constructed as a violation of an individual's sexual autonomy? [3]

---

[1] I am grateful to Gary B. Herbert, editor of the *Human Rights Review,* and an anonymous reviewer from the same journal for their extremely helpful and insightful comments on an earlier adaptation of this chapter. The adaptation concerned appears in *Human Rights Review*, Volume 9, Number 3, September 2008, 361-378.

An alternative version of this chapter also appears in: Daniela De Vito, Aisha Gill and Damien Short. "Rape Characterised as Genocide." *SUR International Journal on Human Rights*, Year 6, Number 10, June 2009, 28-50

[2] Since this chapter is firmly grounded within recent international human rights and humanitarian law developments in relation to rape, the author acknowledges earlier definitions and a cultural perspective found in national definitions of rape, but has not addressed these in an expansive manner. For more on these issues, such as the emphasis on either consent or coercion elements please refer to Catherine A. Mackinnon, 2006: 940.

[3] The Trial Chamber from the International Criminal Tribunal for the former Yugoslavia (ICTY) argued that rape constitutes a violation of an individual's sexual autonomy. More on this subsequently International Criminal

b) Is the link between rape and genocide necessarily problematic within this notion of autonomy for the individual victim of rape?

Once again, this process unfolds within an analytical political theory approach that touches upon the current concept of human rights with its focus on the individual. Although the key element is the individual, the concept of human rights also creates a space, albeit limited and at times controversial, for the group. The analysis brings out some of the theoretical implications when rape is subsumed within the international crime of genocide, which is defined as a violation committed against particular groups. Rape as genocide is a recent occurrence within international law. As Catherine A. Mackinnon observes "Each time a rape law is created or applied, or a rape case is tried, communities rethink what rape is." (Catherine A. MacKinnon, 2006: 941) Rape as a crime or as a human rights violation is conceptualized and treated as an act committed against the individual. [4] In contrast, genocide under the Convention on the Prevention and Punishment of the Crime of Genocide (1948), includes a series of acts "...committed with intent to destroy, in whole or in part, a national, ethnical, racial or religious groups, as such..." (P. R. Ghandhi, 2000: 19) In other words, genocide has been conceived, placed and treated as a denial of the right to life of certain human groups.

The Trial Chamber for the International Criminal Tribunal for Rwanda (ICTR) delivered its innovative judgement in the case of the Prosecutor *v.* Jean-Paul Akayesu. (Akayesu case, 1998) Jean-Paul Akayesu was a local official (*bourgemestre*) when the genocide against the Tutsi group in Rwanda began. Although he did not commit the particular acts of genocide - such as the rapes and killings – himself, he was found guilty of genocide due to the authority he wielded in the region. The Akayesu case was the first time that an international criminal body considered the possibility of rape as genocide. In its Judgement, the Trial Chamber argued that women were raped because they were members of the Tutsi ethnic group. Because genocide had been deemed by the Trial Chamber to have occurred in Rwanda during 1994, rape in relation to this case constituted genocide. Individual victims of rape testified within the context of the trial against Jean-Paul Akayesu. It was these individuals who were raped, and they were in turn members of the Tutsi ethnic group.

One possible way to approach the questions posed earlier is to consider that in some situations it may be more beneficial to subsume rape within the international crime of genocide. Genocide is often characterized as the most heinous of all human rights violations. [5] Its long history (pre-1940s and during more recent events such as in Rwanda), its devastating impact on groups and societies contribute to this conclusion. By recognizing rape as part of genocide, it could be argued that the result is to elevate rape above other international crimes and human rights violations. Since rape is absent in much of international

---

Tribunal for the Former Yugoslavia (ICTY), *Prosecutor v. Dragoljub Kunarac (et al)*, (IT-96-23-T and IT-96-23/1-T, Judgement, 22 February 2001): 457.

[4] As noted, and when brought to trial at the national or international level, the Prosecutor faces the defendant in a rape case it is also the individual victim's story that is considered. Furthermore, and if appropriate, it is the individual victim who testifies before the court.

[5] For instance, the opening sections of the Convention on Prevention and Punishment of Genocide (1948) reads "*Recognising* that at all periods of history genocide has inflicted great losses on humanity; and *Being convinced* that, in order to liberate mankind from such an odious scourge, international co-operation is required:" P. R. Ghandi, 2000: 19.

human rights law or as noted is distorted within international humanitarian law, this approach may be helpful as one option to counter these imbalances.

On the other hand, some women who have been raped during genocidal events may deem for themselves that an association between rape and genocide is of greater consequence than to solely focus on the individual component of rape. It may be that the need to ensure a record of this association, for instance Tutsi women were raped because they were part of the Tutsi ethnic group, is more important than to keep the violations within the parameters of an act solely committed against the individual. In addition, the issue of harm as associated with rape can affect this discourse. An approach so imbedded in theoretical discussions cannot forget these components. Furthermore, emphasizing the importance of placing rape within the crime of genocide has been criticized since the effect may be to lessen the importance of other types of rape. As Rhonda Copelon argues "By treating genocidal rape differently, one is in effect saying that all these terrible abuses of women can go forward without comparable sanction." (Rhonda Copelon, 1995: 67) Although this caveat is an important consideration, depending on the circumstances, it may also be argued that it is crucial for rape to be considered as genocide for the victims and/or to more precisely reflect the context of a particular genocide.

If an area of accommodation, which includes both the individual and the group, can be created within the crime of genocide, then rape as genocide can operate both as a violation against the group and as a violation against the individual. This area of accommodation can never involve an equal share of the space, for genocide will always need to occupy the majority of the surface area since its key concern is the survival of human groups. When rape is subsumed into genocide, which is conceived, placed and treated as a crime against enumerated groups, its dynamic changes. Rape is no longer just a violation against the individual. Rape becomes part of a notion developed to protect the group. Once again, this process relates to what can occur on a theoretical level when rape is subsumed within the international crime of genocide. Therefore, the determination from an analytical political theory perspective is that there is still a place for the individual victim of genocide or the individual victim of rape as genocide. However, as with the current concept of human rights, this space is unequal and not always comfortable. Crucially, even with innovative jurisprudence such as the ICTR case (Jean-Paul Akayesu, 1998) and literature on this issue, there is a need to assess this complex relationship between rape, which affects the individual, and rape as genocide, which is placed within the group dynamic.

The Group and the Contention of Group Rights

Which areas of international law, and even general theoretical traditions, have influenced the deliberation and the creation of a definition of the crime of genocide? Raphael Lemkin focused on the life of the group and in particular on national groups.

According to Lemkin, genocide could be understood as:

> "...the criminal intent to destroy or to cripple permanently a human group. The acts are directed against groups, as such, and individuals are selected for destruction only because they belong to these groups." (Raphael Lemkin, 1947: 146)

With this quote, one begins to see that both the group and the individual function within the concept of genocide. However, individuals are targeted due to their membership within a particular group. The implications of this for rape as genocide will be explored later.

In 1946, the newly formed UN General Assembly passed resolution (96-I) which stated:

> "Genocide is a denial of the right of existence of entire human groups, as homicide is the denial of the right to live of individual human beings..." [6]

Within the United Nations, three types of law were interwoven into a concept of genocide – international criminal law (for individual criminal responsibility), human rights law, and humanitarian law. (William A. Schabas, 2000: 5) From international human rights law, a critical connection emerges. The right to life, outlined in the Universal Declaration of Human Rights (1948) and in the International Covenant on Civil and Political Rights (1966), is a human right accorded to individuals. The right to life is not an absolute right, since in times of war and under certain circumstances this right may be breached. There is also capital punishment, which technically is not prohibited under international human rights law, but whose eventual cessation is encouraged in human rights instruments. Although the right to life is *imprinted* within the Genocide Convention (1948), it is the right to life of 'human groups' that is in fact protected. In particular, it is the right of these human groups to exist (the right to existence) that should be protected. (Ibid: 6) Furthermore, the prohibition against genocide is pivotal since it is a crime "...directed against the entire international community rather than the individual." However, genocide has also been described by William A. Schabas as "...a violent crime against the person." (Id) It is this two-pronged interplay, a violation against the group and a violation against the individual, which makes genocide and rape as genocide, such textured concepts.

What then is a 'group'? In simple terms, 'groups consist of individuals'. (Id: 106) At the UN level, the term 'group' or 'groups' is noted in several instruments. For instance, the Universal Declaration of Human Rights (UDHR, 1948) mentions the family as a 'fundamental group unit of society' and that education will "...promote understanding, tolerance and friendship among all nations, racial or religious groups." [7] The UDHR in Article 30 speaks of 'any State, group or person', which means that a group consists of more than one individual. (William A. Schabas, 2000: 106) Other instruments, such as the International Covenant on Civil and Political Rights (ICCPR, 1966) and the International Convention for the Elimination of All Forms of Racial Discrimination (ICERD, 1966), speak of 'peoples' having the right to self-determination and of 'racial or ethnic groups' respectively. [8] In the latter Convention (1966), Article 14 addresses the right of petition for individuals or for groups of individuals whom have suffered racial discrimination.

A more formal understanding, within the framework of international law, has been proposed by Natan Lerner:

"In international law, the notion of group requires the presence of those already mentioned unifying, spontaneous (as opposed to artificial or planned) and permanent factors

[6] UN General Assembly Resolution, 96-I, 11 December 1946.

[7] P.R. Ghandi, 2000: especially Articles 16(3), 26(2) and Article 30, 21-25.

[8] P.R. Ghandhi, 2000: Article 1(1). P. 64. Article 1(4), 56.

that are, as a rule, beyond the control of the members of the group." (William A. Schabas, 2000: 107 and Natan Lerner, 2003: 84)

Critically, what emerges from this proposal is that groups consist of individuals and that groups protected under international law involve a degree of permanence such as race or ethnicity. It may be more difficult to place religious groups, since some may argue that religious beliefs can change, within Lerner's understanding of a 'group'. The Genocide Convention (1948), including the reference to religious groups, was framed with the notion of focusing on the 'permanence' of groups thereby excluding other groups. [9] However, Lerner's wording does allow for some flexibility because he includes the words 'permanent factors that are, as a rule, beyond the control of members.' Furthermore, and specifically with reference to minority rights "…the right extends to 'persons belonging to such minorities,' and not the minority as a group." (Bill Bowring, 1999: 3-4) Key is the individual members of a minority group.

How can this understanding of individuals, being part of a minority group, relate to genocide? The groups outlined in the Genocide Convention (1948) – national, ethnical, racial or religious – are not framed solely within a minority standing. That is, these groups can be in the minority or these groups can make up the majority population in a State, or they can lack power within the State. There are no restrictions within the Convention. Genocide is an international crime aimed at national, ethnical, racial or religious groups. An additional component is attached since individuals, as members of said groups, are the particular victims of genocide. With reference to when rape is considered as genocide, individuals are victims of this crime due to their membership in one or more of the enumerated groups. This may contradict the UN's vision with reference to this crime. Specifically, in its 1946 Resolution,[10] a distinction was made between the right to life of human groups and of individuals. Leo Kuper's work on this subject is a characteristic of a contrasting view to this approach. For Kuper argued that genocide "…is a crime against a collectivity, it implies an identifiable group as victim." (Leo Kuper, 1981: 53) However, as this section will argue, there must be the possibility within any understanding of genocide to include an examination of not only what occurs to the group as a whole but also to individual victims of genocide within the group. This overall conclusion may, or may not, seem to follow the ICTR Judgment in the Jean-Paul Akayesu case. Within the Akayesu Judgment, genocide was understood to involve an act (taken from the list of five which are enumerated in the Genocide Convention 1948) that is committed "…with the specific intent to destroy, in whole or in part, a particular group targeted as such." (Akayesu case, 1998: 731)

It is necessary to briefly re-visit the dichotomy between individual human rights and the suggestion of group rights. For *if* rape as genocide is conceptualized as a violation against an individual who is part of a group, and not as a violation exclusively committed against the group as a whole and without considering the individual, then the implications of formulating this crime within the accepted understanding of the current concept of human rights must be assessed. This will involve a brief re-visit of the current concept of human rights, with its

---

[9] There was and continues to be concern with the Genocide Convention's limited enumeration of groups that can be targeted. The exclusion of 'political' groups is one such example. There have also been calls to consider the category of 'female' as a group that can suffer genocide. For more on these issues please refer to: Lisa Sharlach, 2000: 91-92.

[10] *Supra* note 6.

emphasis on the individual and its acknowledgement of the 'group', and an introduction to the debate of whether human rights are applicable to groups as a whole and not just for individual members of a group.

It was not until the Second World War and with the rise of Nazism that the current concept of human rights emerged. After the end of World War II, the newly formed United Nations (UN) set about articulating the idea of human rights. This process can be found *inter alia* in the UN Charter (1945) and in the Universal Declaration of Human Rights (UDHR, 1948). The current concept of human rights addresses the rights and freedoms of the individual. However, this individual can to varying degrees also have a place, a role, and duties and receive benefits within his or her respective community. As Jack Donnelly sets out in *Universal Human Rights in Theory and Practice*, theoretically human rights exist outside the reality of the modern State. Human rights are not given to human beings by the State. Individuals, by the mere fact that they are human beings, already exist with certain rights. The process that entrenches these rights into law is separate. (Jack Donnelly, 2nd edition, 2003: 12) Yet, the individual still has a place and a role within larger frameworks such as society or the State. Furthermore, the current concept of human rights does acknowledge the 'group' under certain circumstances. There is Article 16(1) of the UDHR (1948) which mentions 'family' and in the Preamble to the ICCPR (1966) 'peoples' are said to have the right to self-determination. (Michael Freeman, 2002: 75) Critically, at the UN level, and for instruments that have such mechanisms, it is the individual who petitions the relevant bodies such as the Committee against Torture. Furthermore, human rights violations are determined with the individual in mind. (Koen de Feyter in De Feyter and Pavlakos, 2008: 22) This leads to an important debate within the human rights discourse. Does a group have human rights? Or, as Jack Donnelly and others insist, is it only individuals as members of particular groups that bring human rights to the table? Koen De Feyter mentions the construction of some human rights instruments that address *categories of human beings* such as women or children but in turn he acknowledges the difficulty in recognizing collective rights per se. (Ibid: 19)

Returning to genocide and to rape as genocide, the implications of considering these acts as violations, either committed against the group, or against the individual as part of the group, are critical. As stated earlier, if an individual is raped within the context of genocide it may be the case that placing this act within a crime carried out against the group is more important for the victim than if it were to remain as a crime against the individual. In turn, the implications of this approach may be to remove the 'individuality' of rape and of rape as genocide.[11]

This section will address minority and group rights to bring out a clearer understanding of the challenges that still exist within the current concept of human rights between the individual and the group. The purpose will be to understand how the individual and the individual as part of a group is able to function, and to determine if compatibility between the individual and the group exists within differently constructed violations such as rape and rape as genocide. [12] Finally, although a distinction exists between group rights (such as the right of

[11] The inspiration for this the term 'individuality', in conjunction with genocide, comes from Leo Kuper's phrase "As a crime against a collectivity, it (genocide) sets aside the whole question of individual responsibility; it is a denial of individuality." Leo Kuper, 1981: 86.

[12] The aim of this section is not to outline or to resolve all the various positions within the human rights discourse related to 'who is the bearer of rights – the individual; the individual as a member of a group; or the group as a

'peoples' to self-determination) and minority rights, the emphasis is to clarify the notion of the individual as opposed to the group within the framework of 'rights'. With reference to the right of 'peoples' to self-determination, there is continued debate as to its exact place within international law in general. The only established parameter for this right has been in relation to peoples extracting themselves from situations of colonialism. Once colonialism has been removed, then this right has been interpreted to mean States. Recent and ongoing efforts, with reference to the rights of indigenous peoples, seem to be moving more in the direction of groups of 'peoples' having rights. Yet, this is far from being a settled and accepted approach. (Nigel Rodley, 1999: 61) [13]

However, as Jack Donnelly notes:

> "What is one to conclude? Is there an internationally recognized collective human right of peoples to self-determination? It is hard to say. Maybe. Sort of. Not exactly. Therefore, I propose to set this right aside. But even if there is such a right, the fact that there is (at most) precisely one internationally recognized human right of peoples can be seen largely as confirmation of the rule that human rights are the rights of individuals." (Jack Donnelly, 2003: 132-133)

International law [14] and theory in general, have had a difficult time in accepting that human rights could be applicable to groups. Another term for this concept is 'collective rights'. (Bill Bowring, 1999: xiii) [15] One concern, if group rights are subsumed into the category of human rights, is that all the initiatives and accomplishments since the Enlightenment period, which led to the current concept of human rights with a prime place given to the role and placement of the individual, would be negated.

As Jack Donnelly argues:

> "I must insist that there *are* collective rights, just not collective *human* rights, and that a number of human rights are exercised by individuals as *members of a collective group*." (Jack Donnelly, 1993: 149-150)

For Donnelly, to change the idea that collective rights should be considered as another branch of human rights would significantly alter the concept of human rights, which developed to protect individuals. (Ibid: 145) This viewpoint, whereby individuals as members of groups can exercise human rights, tends to reflect the current approach within international law. (Neus Torbisco Casals, 2006: 44 and David Ingram, 2000: 242) However, discourse has taken place whereby the rights of groups are considered an essential component or addition to

whole?' As such, the position used will remain within the notion that human rights are individual rights but that the group based on factors such as race, ethnicity, gender, etc. also has an important role.

13 The recently passed (2008) UN Declaration on the Rights of Indigenous Peoples (1994/95) speaks of 'indigenous peoples' in its articles. It is, however, a declaration and the document remained as a draft for over a decade due to its contentious content.

14 As Jack Donnelly, in reference to minority rights, observes: "I am not, let me repeat, challenging the idea of minority rights as they are already established in the major international human rights instruments (i.e., as individual rights that provide special protections to members of minority groups)." Jack Donnelly in Gene M. Lyons and James Mayall (eds.), 2003: 37.Danilo Turk in De Feyter and Pavlakos, 2008: 4.

15 Gerrit-Bartus Dielissen, within the context of his article, offers a more narrow definition of groups rights to mean the rights of any minorities. Gerrit-Bartus Dielissen in De Feyter and Pavlakos, 2008: 41.

the concept of human rights. As Lyons and Mayall predict "The question is whether the existing regime can be expanded to include group rights or whether a new set of obligations need to be added." (Lyons and Mayall, 2003: 6) One approach is to develop group rights as a branch of human rights. Another standpoint is to leave human rights with its focus on the individual as rights bearer. (Neus Torbisco Casals, 2006: 37) In turn, there may even be a possibility to create a new category of group rights that are separate to but influenced by the current human rights regime. [16] K. De Foeter has written about this issue in terms of the 'collective rights of groups'. In addition, these 'rights' would not be about the duties of the State but would in fact challenge the authority of the State. As correctly noted, when framed in such a manner, the collective rights of groups are extremely contentious and have not found much support within the established international community. (Koen De Feyter in De Feyter and Pavlakos, 2008) These are but a few examples of how the discourse surrounding the issue of group rights has emerged. As noted, the aim is not to outline in a detailed manner the varied approaches, nor is its purpose to reconcile group rights with the concept of human rights. Rather, it should be noted that this section and its theoretical analysis of rape as genocide is situated within the realities of current international law whereby human rights norms and regimes tend to elevate the individual but also acknowledge possible complex notions vis à vis the 'group'. [17]

John Rawls, in 'The Idea of Public Reason Revisited', attempts to bring the individual and the group together. In this article, Rawls writes about the place and role of citizens when dealing with the State and its institutions. In one section, he tries to link the family with the idea that equal justice can be applied to men and women within these entities. However, even Rawls is clear that any rights or responsibilities found within the family unit are very much attached to its individual members as part of the group and not to the group as a whole. As Rawls argues:

> "Now consider the family. Here the idea is the same: political principles do not apply directly to its internal life, but they do impose essential constraints on the family…and so guarantee the basic rights and liberties…of all its members. (John Rawls, 1999: 595-597)

At the UN level, Donnelly and Rawls' arguments are evident. Article 27 of the International Covenant of Civil and Political Rights (ICCPR, 1966) outlines the rights of individuals as part of a listed minority group(s) – "In those States in which ethnic, religious or linguistic minorities exists, persons belonging to such minorities…" This article, however, does not set out rights for the minority group as a whole. (Bill Bowring, 1999: 4)

---

[16] This possibility has been articulated in relation to certain minority groups. Jennifer Jackson-Preece in Lyons and Mayall (eds.), 2003: 68.In general, the line of inquiry can be understood as attempts to "…distinguish between, on the one hand, rights that depend on an individual's belonging to a group or community, and, on the other, individual rights common to all human beings. "Neus Torbisco Casals, 2006: 57.

[17] As Hurst Hannum, with reference to indigenous rights, succinctly expresses: "This Chapter does not attempt to resolve the philosophical clashes over individual versus collective rights or majority versus minority rights." Hurst Hannum in Lyons and Mayall (eds.), 2003: 94.Furthermore, and as a caution against placing women as a group within human rights, Eva Brems argues "In years to come, the collective dimension of women's rights may come to the forefront, for example, as a framework for addressing the root causes of gender discrimination. However, from an inclusive perspective, this would be a step in the wrong direction, as the same structural problems usually also affect men, and remedies created in response to women's group claims risk excluding them." Eva Brems in Lyons and Mayall (eds.), 2003: 121.

Even in a more recent UN instrument, Declaration on the Rights of Persons Belonging to National or Ethnic, Religious and Linguistic Minorities (1992), the emphasis is on 'persons' belonging to such groups. (P. R. Ghandhi, 2000: 132-134) In other words, as currently framed, "...minority rights are individual rights." (Bill Bowring, 1999: 14) However, Bill Bowring argues that international human rights law must move beyond this narrow interpretation and that it should recognize group and minority rights as such. (Ibid)

An attempt to expand on this formulation has been proposed by Will Kymlicka in *Mutlicultural Citizenship: A Liberal Theory of Minority Rights*. His focus is on the possibility of developing minority rights. Human rights, it was argued by liberal thinkers after World War II, would protect and thus solve the problems faced by, for instance, ethnic and national minorities. (Will Kymlicka, 1997: 2-3) In the face of discrimination, the newly developed international human rights instruments would protect individual members of minority groups. There would be no need to include 'minority group rights'. In fact, with this background in mind, the UN removed any reference to ethnic and national minorities in the Universal Declaration of Human Rights (1948). (Ibid: 3) In other words, "...post-war liberals around the world have repeatedly opposed the idea that specific ethnic or national groups should be given a permanent political identity or constitutional status." (Id: 4) For Kymlicka, the concept of human rights alone is not adequate to address the needs of minority groups. For example, the individual right of free speech does not outline what sort of minority language policy a State should enact. It is for this reason that he proposes to enhance human rights with a 'theory of minority rights'. (Id: 5)

In his words, 'group-differentiated rights' whereby

> "...members of certain groups have rights regarding land, language, representation, etc that the members of other groups do not have." (Id: 34)

In a similar vein, Charles Taylor's *Multiculturalism and "The Politics of Recognition"* examines this interplay between the individual and the group. Writing about the importance of recognizing the needs, identities, etc. of individuals, Taylor presents the idea that individuals define their respective identities with the help of others:

> "We define our identity always in dialogue with, sometimes in struggle against, the things our significant others want to see in us. Thus, the contribution of significant others...continues indefinitely. (Charles Taylor, 1992: 33)

Individuals, for the most part, operate both on their own stage and within the constraints and advantages of the larger community or group such as the family. Once again, for Taylor, the group is addressed in terms of its individual members along with the potential 'collective goals' linked to 'members of the community'. [18] The contribution that Kymlicka's book can offer towards understanding the implications of genocide and of rape as genocide is that he makes a connection between individual and group rights – a theme hinted at within the international crime of genocide. Kymlicka acknowledges that 'group-differentiated rights' may seem to counter efforts to emphasize the individual in that his theory focuses on the group. (Will Kymlicka, 1997: 34) Yet, Kymlicka argues that there can be compatibility

[18] Taylor is speaking about the collective goals of French speaking Québecois. Charles Taylor, 1992: 39 and 53-58.

between individual rights and group-differentiated rights. For instance, minority language rights are an area whereby a right is attached to an individual member of a group and to the group as a whole. In Canada, as his example follows, the right of francophones to use French in courts is one enacted on by individuals. The right may be aimed at the entire francophone group, but it is exercised by individual *francophones*.[19] Other rights in Canada, such as fishing/hunting rights for indigenous peoples, are accorded to groups. Working with both the individual and group elements of the issues, Kymlicka points out:

> "Just as certain individual rights flow from each individual's interest in personal liberty, so certain community rights flow from each community's interest in self-preservation. These community rights must then be weighed against the rights of the individuals who compose the community." (Will Kymlicka, 1997: 47)

Hence, the preservation of the group, which is deemed critical, can operate alongside the rights and needs of individual members of the community or group. There may be conflict such as if groups impose restrictions on its members, but Kymlicka differentiates between *internal* ('claims of a group against its own members') and *external* ('claims of a group against the larger society') protections, both of which have limitations such as fitting within human rights or to balance opportunities, etc. between groups. (Ibid: 35)

Returning to genocide, acts associated with this crime are aimed at destroying in whole or in part a national, ethnical, racial or religious group. In turn, it is individual members of said groups who are killed, harmed, etc. The two components of Kymlicka's vision, the group and the individual within the group, are able to co-exist within this formulation. This does not exclude the current concept of human rights with its emphasis on the individual and his/her human rights. This part of Kymlicka's approach does not, as warned by Jack Donnelly, completely subsume the category of group rights within human rights thereby negating a place for the individual. Rather an area of accommodation has been created whereby both the group is protected, and where the individual within the group is also protected, and in turn, acknowledged and can play an active role. The next question becomes, if rape as genocide can also be placed within this area of accommodation.

Rape as Genocide

The international crime of genocide emerges first and foremost as the destruction in whole or in part of a national, ethnical, racial or religious group. Yet, by delving further into this violation and by incorporating certain elements from Kymlicka's work, one is able to find a space for individual members of said groups since the acts of genocide enumerated in the Genocide Convention are committed against individuals.

As Jack Donnelly notes with direct reference to genocide:

> "Therefore, it is individual members of threatened groups who must exercise the right." (Jack Donnelly in Catherine Brolman et al (eds.), 1993: 131-132)

---

[19] Kymlicka insists that French Canadians are a national minority thereby ensuring they can be accorded group-differentiated rights. Will Kymlicka, 1997: 45- 46.

Is it acceptable, therefore, for rape as genocide to be placed within Kymlicka's formulation? Any response to this question should simultaneously consider some of the implications emanating from the two International Criminal Tribunal Judgements mentioned in the introduction to this book. The reason is that these Judgements offer quite distinct presentations of rape.

In the International Criminal Tribunal for the former Yugoslavia Judgement (Kunarac *et al* - Foca case, ICTY – 2001: 441), the Trial Chamber considered that rape could be understood as 'a serious violation of sexual autonomy'. (Catherine A. MacKinnon, 2006: 950) In its overview of several common and civil law jurisdictions in relation to definitions of rape, the Trial Chamber concluded that the main principle linking these systems "…is that serious violations of sexual autonomy are to be penalized." In turn, "Sexual autonomy is violated wherever the person subjected to the act has not freely agreed to it or is otherwise not a voluntary participant." (Foca case, 2001: 457) As with the international crime of torture, this conclusion states that rape should be conceptualized as a crime committed against the individual. As such, rape is an act perpetuated against the individual and it specifically violates the sexual components of the individual. [20]

As Catherine Mackinnon observes within the context of consent definitions of rape, "This crime (rape) basically occurs in individual psychic space."

Sexual Autonomy can be understood as having three components:

> "The first two are mental – an internal capacity to make reasonably mature and rational choices, and an external freedom from impermissible pressures and constraints. The third dimension is equally important. The core concept of the person…the bodily integrity of the individual." (Stephen J. Schulhofer, 1998: 111)

Although this definition of sexual autonomy crucially includes both mental and physical aspects, there is concern with the notion of making choices. A similar link can be made with theories of human rights whereby the capacity to claim human rights implies the ability to hold human rights. One concern, if taken to the extreme, would be to contemplate if an individual in a coma truly has human rights? [21] In his examination of sexual autonomy, Stephen J. Schulhofer goes on to add that determining if a violation of sexual autonomy constitutes rape is an additional step and one that can be linked to cultural factors or social conditions.

As Schulhofer clarifies:

> "In sexual crimes, however, the labeling decision may be very important. A persistent pitfall of rape reform has been the tenacity of common culture and its influence over the interpretation of ambitious reforms." (Ibid: 104)

In contrast, the International Criminal Tribunal for Rwanda (ICTR) in its pivotal Judgement (Prosecutor v. Jean-Paul Akayesu, 1998), for the first time international law

---

[20] As Catherine A. Mackinnon states "Force abrogates autonomy just as denial of self-determination is coercive." Catherine A. Mackinnon , 2006: 941.

[21] For more on this topic, please refer to Peter Jones, 1994: 67-71.

conceptualizes rape under certain circumstances as genocide. The women who were raped [22] during the genocide of 1994 were, according to the Trial Chamber, targeted for rape because they were members of the Tutsi ethnic group.

The rapes were therefore considered as genocide within this context since, in the words of the Chamber,

> "...the Chamber is satisfied that the acts of rape and sexual violence described above, were committed solely against Tutsi women...and specifically contributing to their destruction and to the destruction of the Tutsi group as a whole." (Akayesu case, 1998: 731) [23]

The chamber added,

> "These rapes resulted in physical and psychological destruction of Tutsi women, their families and their communities." (Ibid)

One way in which the rapes contributed to the destruction of the Tutsi group, was because many of the Tutsi women and girls who were raped were killed afterwards or died from their injuries. (Angela M. Banks, 2005: 9-10) Another critical point, in relation to how rape was deemed as genocide, relates to the reality that Tutsi women were considered as 'sexual objects' and as the Trial Chamber in the Akayesu case observed "...sexual violence was a step in the process of destruction of the Tutsi group – destruction of the spirit, of the will to live, and of life itself." (Kelly Dawn Askin, 2005: 1010) The rapes of Tutsi women, within this context, could be placed "...under the legal definition of genocide because they represent the enemy's intent to destroy." (Lisa Sharlach, 2000: 93) In addition, rape as genocide can be understood as a 'particularly effective tool of genocide' [24] and a way to inflict serious bodily or mental harm onto a group.

As the Akayesu Trial Chamber observed,

> "Indeed, rape and sexual violence certainly constitute infliction of serious bodily and mental harm on the victims and are even, according to the Chamber, one of the worst ways of inflicting harm on the victim as he or she suffers both bodily and mental harm." (Akayesu case, 1998: 731)

Some of the after effects of the rapes that took place within the context of genocide in Rwanda included survivors becoming socially outcast and excluded. (Lisa Sharlach, 2000: 91) That is to say, an additional layer of complexity emerges linked to cultural opinions and sensitivities.

---

[22] Jean-Paul Akayesu did not rape the women directly. Instead, the charges of rape in his case stem from the fact that he had administrative control and authority in the region where the rapes occurred.
Akayesu case (ICTR-96-4-T, Judgment, 2 September 1998): Indictment.

[23] It should be noted, in the Akayesu Judgement, that rape and other sexual violence within the parameters of genocide was "...defined by whatever causes serious bodily or mental harm." This is due to how the Genocide Convention (1948) has been formulated. Catherine A. Mackinnon, 2006: 941.

[24] This reference relates to "The devastation that follows rape makes it a particularly effective tool of genocide because it destroys the morale of a woman, her family, and perhaps her entire community." Lisa Scharlach.

As Lisa Sharlach argues in her overview of genocide in Rwanda, Bangladesh and the former Yugoslavia, in general rape as genocide stigmatizes the survivor and that,

> "In such communities, women in their roles as mothers of the nation and as transmitters of culture symbolize the honor of the ethnic group. When a woman's honor is tarnished through rape, the ethnic group is also dishonored." (Ibid: 90)

If both cases (Kunarac and Akayesu) are considered together, does the innovative link between rape and genocide as presented in the Akayesu case result in rape losing its understanding as a violation of autonomy? Upon closer examination of the Akayesu Trial Chamber comments quoted above, it would appear that the compatibility found within genocide as discussed earlier between the individual and the group can be located in this case. Yes, the Trial Chamber focuses on the fact that individual victims were targeted due to their membership in the Tutsi ethnic group. However, the Trial Chamber also acknowledges that both the Tutsi group and the individual victims of rape were targeted for genocide.

Recalling the words of the Chamber: "…and specifically contributing to their destruction and to the destruction of the Tutsi group as a whole." Therefore, in this particular case, the crime of rape as genocide is conceived as both an act committed against an individual and as an act committed against the group. As such, rape as genocide has retained its understanding as a violation against one's autonomy, but also as a violation against the group as a whole. The ICTR Trial Chamber in this particular Judgement has created an area of accommodation whereby the group (Tutsi ethnic group) and the individual (Tutsi women) are acknowledged with the aim of hopefully protecting both in the future. Even with this compatibility, between the group and the individual, the Trial Chamber insisted that the women who were raped were victims because they were Tutsi. The attachment to the group is not completely removed despite the fact that the Chamber has also acknowledged space for the individual. This means that the individual victims of rape were not targeted because they were individual women, but because they were Tutsi women. This approach may further deny the 'individuality' of the victims since they have been placed by the Trial Chamber within the category of Tutsi women and not within the general category of 'women'. The construct of the Genocide Convention (1948), which the ICTR Trial Chamber must follow, would explain the restriction of only focusing on the Tutsi ethnic group.

Does this insistence on a strong connection with the 'group' diminish the so-called compatibility between rape (autonomy) and genocide (group)? I would argue it does not since a key component found within the definition of genocide is the protection of groups. As noted by the United Nations Commission of Experts (for the Former Yugoslavia), with reference to this author's argument that the relationship between rape and genocide is a compatible one but inevitably—due to how genocide has been constructed in international law—an unequal relationship:

> "…the crimes against a number of individuals must be directed at them in their collectivity or at them in their collective character or capacity." (UN Document S/1994/674, 'Final Report of the Commission of Experts', (1992): 524

However, if deemed necessary, this compatibility should also be arrived at via a decision made by those who have suffered these crimes.

As mentioned, it may be beneficial for such a label to exist if the individual victims of rape as genocide consider this proposition to be so. These victims must also have a voice in the process that constructs and interprets such international law judgements. As such, some of the theoretical implications have been examined emanating from a situation whereby international law has placed rape simultaneously as a violation against the individual and as a violation against the group.

In contrast to rape as a form of torture with its association to the individual, it has determined that rape, as genocide has to operate within the confines of genocide with its links to the group. Although genocide has been conceived as a denial of the right to life of human groups, it also includes scope for the individual. In other words, genocide is an attack against a national, ethnic, racial, or religious group, but it is also an attack against individual persons within these groups. This complex interplay, found within genocide, between the group and the individual, affects how rape as genocide is understood. This means that individuals are victims of rape as genocide due to their membership in one or more of the enumerated groups in the Genocide Convention (1948), and within circumstances found under the definition of genocide.

Therefore, this author has presented that there must be an opportunity to consider rape as genocide to be conceived as a violation against an individual because they are part of a group, and not as a violation solely committed against the group as a whole. If this formulation is not possible, within international law cases addressing such issues, then the result will be an exclusion of the construction of rape as a violation of an individual's sexual autonomy.

Despite the definition of genocide under international law, it cannot completely remove the notion that rape is a violation committed against the individual. Victims of rape who appeared before the ICTR in the case of the *Prosecutor v. Jean-Paul Akayesu*, albeit within limits set out by the Tribunal and the Trial Chamber—such as time limits and the rigors of cross-examination (PBS, 2004)—do have an opportunity to recount what happened to them as individuals during the 1994 genocide in Rwanda. The context of the genocide in Rwanda, namely that it was committed with the purpose to destroy in whole or in part the Tutsi ethnic group, was in turn a necessary component attached to the Akayesu (1998) Judgement. As such, the Trial Chamber in this case did acknowledge that the women were raped because they were members of the Tutsi ethnic group but also that they were individual Tutsi victims.

As developed in this book, the definition of genocide—outlined in the Genocide Convention (1948) and as utilized by the international criminal tribunals—can offer a compatible space for rape. Although constrained by this definition, the group elements of this international crime can create room for the individual components of rape. For example, insisting on this connection with the group, an individual's sexual autonomy does at a certain level become enmeshed within the group. Does this change the nature of rape? To a certain degree the answer is "yes" since rape is not solely associated with the sexual autonomy of an individual. Yet, the construction of rape as a violation committed against the individual does not completely disappear. An unequal space is indeed created whereby the group elements of genocide and the individual aspects of rape operate once rape is considered as genocide. The point is not to shift and to re-configure this unequal space, but rather to accept that this is the reality and the consequences of innovative international jurisprudence, once rape is subsumed into genocide, such as with the Akayesu Judgement (1998). In turn, victims of rape as genocide must also have the opportunity to decide for themselves how it is beneficial to consider rape as genocide. Linked to this, they must also be able to determine which aspects are held onto in terms of if the violation affects the individual, the group, or a combination of the two. As argued in relation to both rape as torture and rape as genocide, such theoretical implications and perhaps others must also be considered when assessing juridical innovations.

Theoretical challenges for group theory emerge when assessing a violation such as rape and within the context of international human rights or humanitarian law. Rape is generally constructed as an act committed against the individual. Currently rape is not an enumerated international crime and must be subsumed into an established crime to be prosecuted. In this instance, the focus was on rape as torture and rape as genocide. As such, any discussion of the group or of group rights must also consider the theoretical implications of what can occur to rape since it must navigate through constructs that focus on the individual, on the group or at times on both parameters. Thus, the consideration of rape as torture and of rape as genocide is not an insurmountable challenge for group theory but one that must address both the individual and the group due to how rape is understood. As noted, the harm of rape for both the individual and at times the group was an important example of this juxtaposition. This is why seemingly unrelated concepts such as human rights, the individual, and the political were in turn associated with group theory and in particular group rights. If the *outsider* [25] of group rights is to develop a firmer place within current theoretical and legal discourse then the implications of such concepts must be fully explored.

[25] This term has been utilized simply due to the current difficulties still present within international law that prevent a fuller acceptance of group rights.

Chapter 7

OVERALL CONCLUSIONS

OVERVIEW

The purpose of this Chapter is to offer a synthesis of the discussions and arguments developed throughout the book. The aim will be to consolidate some of the theoretical implications once rape is subsumed either into the international crime of torture or genocide.

A Synthesis

Overall

The conceptualization, placement and treatment of rape within international human rights and humanitarian law present both inconsistencies, and in recent times, innovative conclusions. In terms of the former category, inconsistencies, this book has demonstrated that within international human rights law – at the level of universal and legally binding conventions – does not explicitly address rape. Within the United Nations (UN) system – and beyond the Rome Statute for the International Criminal Court, which is just underway as an institution - the Declaration on the Elimination of Violence Against Women (1993), which is not a legally binding instrument, and Security Council Resolution 1325 explicitly addresses rape. With reference to the latter type of international law, humanitarian, problems surface since at times rape must be interpreted into documents pertaining to armed conflict such as with the Grave breaches provisions of the Geneva Conventions (1949). Alternatively, if rape is explicitly mentioned, it is associated with a woman's honor and not as a crime of violence or it is linked with the protection of women and not with the prohibition of rape. The two examples contradict how the international crime of torture has been conceptualized in that it is a crime of violence and its prohibition is paramount.

The net effect of this absent, skewed, or even late establishment of rape within both types of international law has been a fragmented reality in terms of reporting, understanding, and working towards the eradication of rape under the auspices of international human rights and humanitarian law. Rape, on its own, is at times absent from documents, or is associated with a woman's honor as opposed to an act of violence, or it has only been addressed in a meaningful way very recently. A significant by-product of this process is that no single authoritative law or provision exists at the universal level to define rape. The process instead involves a variety of shifting and not always consistent understandings that function within numerous sections of UN mechanisms. One cannot point to a single overarching definition of rape that can be utilized within this context. However, this book has also made clear that precisely and inflexibly defining acts such as rape and torture is not beneficial since it may constrain how these acts are addressed at the international law level. [1]

Furthermore, beyond being subsumed into an established international crime such as torture, genocide, grave breaches provisions of the Geneva Conventions (1949), or crimes against humanity, rape currently does not stand on its own as an enumerated international crime. Rape is indeed prohibited under international law, but it has not been viewed as a stand alone international crime. It is this author's view that subsuming rape into an established international crime such as torture and genocide has been innovative, and yet this process must not be understood as offering rape an elevated status. If rape, under specific circumstances, fits into the categories of torture, genocide, etc. then this would be a positive step and would reflect reality. This should, however, not mean that rape becomes an important or serious violation because it has been subsumed into these crimes. Yet, even with innovative international law cases and literature acknowledging that rape can be placed within these crimes, this author suggests that rape should in turn be understood as an international crime. Acceptance within this category would not only reflect the seriousness of the violation but this would also assist in eradicating its historically fragmented reality in relation to reporting, understanding and working towards the prohibition of rape under international human rights and humanitarian law. International crimes, such as those listed in the Rome Statute establishing the International Criminal Court (ICC) are those that are of the greatest importance to the international community. Rape has been subsumed into categories such as torture and genocide. Nevertheless, its consideration as a stand-alone international crime should also be undertaken. Furthermore, in the future *and* if it is beneficial, it may be possible for rape to be incorporated within the category of a norm of *jus cogens* and even that it may incur obligations *erga omnes*. One can hope!

As such, understanding on a theoretical level what can happen to rape once it is subsumed into such categories is essential for developing a clearer framework to address this violation. When considering rape within one of these international crimes, torture, it has to operate not only within the realities of international law but also more specifically within the confines of the current concept of human rights. Even when torture occurs within international humanitarian law, the influence of the concept of human rights is evident. The right of an individual not to be subjected to torture has its roots in a concept developed over several centuries and culminating with the Universal Declaration of Human Rights (UDHR, 1948) and subsequent international, regional, and national human rights instruments. What occurs when rape is subsumed into the second international crime covered in this book – genocide – is more complex and this process will be reviewed shortly. Thus, this book has contributed to the understanding of rape in general by identifying and assessing some of the theoretical implications emanating from its current conceptualization, placement and treatment within international human rights and humanitarian law.

[1] Please see Nigel Rodley, The Treatment of Prisoners under International Law, page 77 on this issue.

The Current Concept of Human Rights

When rape is placed within the discourse of human rights, from its conceptualization as a crime under national legal mechanisms, its construction does not completely change. Beyond varied definitions of rape found in national jurisdictions, rape as a crime is committed against the individual. As mentioned earlier, if the case proceeds to trial, although it is the prosecutor who technically presents the case (on behalf of the community) against the accused, when possible it is the individual victim's story that is told before the judge and jury. The crime of rape is conceptualized and treated as an act committed against the individual. Torture, as a human rights violation, is also conceptualized and treated as a violation against the individual. Once rape is subsumed into the human rights violation of torture, it also relates to violations committed against the individual.

The current concept of human rights very much emphasizes the individual. The notion, within political theory, that individuals have certain inalienable rights that were also distinct from the State and any positive laws enacted by these entities or due to the position in society of the individual is a relatively recent innovation. The roots of this notion can be traced to the Enlightenment period, in Europe, during the seventeenth to the nineteenth centuries. The antecedent of human rights, were natural rights. This book demonstrated the importance, in relation to the later development of the concept of human rights, of this stage in the development of the individual. Changes to how the individual, albeit within the existing and yet shifting constraints of the State, religion, and society was understood and given a more prominent place were critical to this process. The individual placed more demands on the State and other entities with reference to rights and possible roles outside pre-determined factors.

For the purpose of this book, two main areas of influence on the development of natural rights were examined in detail since these affected the later concept of human rights – the rise of the individual and the influence of liberalism.

The development of and the changes in the role of an individual, in relation to natural rights and later within the concept of human rights, was essential to the book. Within the concept of human rights, torture is a violation committed against an individual and rape as a form of torture is committed against the individual. These two violations follow the focus found within the concept of human rights, that is, an emphasis on the individual and his/her rights. In contrast, rape as genocide is a violation against a determined group. The interplay between these two formulations has an impact on how rape is understood once it is subsumed within torture and genocide.

Critical for the development of the individual was a shift whereby its relationship with the State was less and less determined by pre-conceived and pre-determined constraints such as social position and wealth. Even with the growing emphasis towards the individual, political theory then – as now – has wrestled with the placement of the individual and with considerations of society. In other words, the tensions between the natural rights of individuals and the requirements of society influenced thinkers during the Enlightenment period in many ways. The current concept of human rights has also needed to address these matters.

Alongside these radical ideas, in relation to the place and role of the individual and the emergence of natural rights, was the political ideology of liberalism. Key was the emergence of the individual and its distinct perception within liberalism. Furthermore, relating which human rights are placed within the public sphere and within the private have been given a stronghold within the human rights discourse. Echoes of liberalism still operate within the framework of human rights. This is evident in how both liberalism and the concept of human rights need to work through the relationship between the rights of individuals and the collective good of society. At its root, liberalism promotes individual liberty and a free society that is more open and tolerant. The critical proviso is that an individual can choose how he/she wants to live as long as these choices do not interfere with the liberty of others. This process places much weight on equality in terms of having an equal chance to succeed and not on the notion that we are all the same.

A further consideration for liberals is the dichotomy of the public and private spheres. This distinction also resonates for human rights since the categories of rights such as civil and political ones have been understood as being part of the public sphere, while several of the (until very recently) less prevalent economic, social and cultural rights - such as rights of the family-have been placed within the private sphere. In its earlier manifestations, liberalism was concerned with breaking through the limits found within authority and tradition that rulers held over individuals. Understanding the distinctions between the public and the private also affected the determination of the proper boundaries between the State and the individual. Another difficulty was deciding which particular individuals could operate within each sphere. For instance, in which sphere could women and non-citizens be found?

The tension was therefore a matter of State authority and its relation to the individual striving for freedom via the channels of autonomy. A strong association existed between classical liberalism and the distinction of the public and private worlds. For women, especially, attributes found within the private sphere were attached and their place within this sphere was entrenched.

Emanating from natural rights, with its links to the rise of the individual and its changing relationship with the State and to liberalism with its attempts to work with society and to determine the difference between the public and private realms, is the concept of human rights. To re-iterate Jack Donnelly's words, *human rights* are "*...the rights one has simply because one is a human being.*" (Donnelly, 2nd edition, 2003: 10) Although controversy still exists at the international, regional and national levels as to the exact nature, application, applicability, levels of enforcement, etc. the concept of human rights is an important theoretical, legal, and institutional development.

At its crux, the concept of human rights addresses the rights and freedoms of individuals. As with liberalism, the concept of human rights does include some space for the group in terms of the family and the right of peoples to self-determination. However, this scope is limited. When the confines of human rights are blurred, such as in the case of rape as genocide which combines the individual/group schism found in the concept, theoretical implications emerge which must be examined. A further influence from liberalism, which has found its way into the current concept of human rights, is the public/private dimension. This can be seen with specific reference to international human rights law, whereby despite innovative steps dealing with the limitations placed on the State in its relationships with citizens or individuals in their respective jurisdictions this body of law continues to uphold components of the public/private spheres within its construct. For instance, international human rights law – especially as formulated in the West – has promoted the importance of civil and political rights. These rights tend to be the domain where men participate within the public sphere. In societies such as the United Kingdom, due to the difficulties in obtaining political party nominations much fewer women are considered as candidates for various democratic elections. In contrast, economic, social and cultural rights most often affect women, as they tend to operate within the private sphere. Although very recent efforts at the UN level to bring out the importance and interconnectedness of all five categories of human rights has been wide-reaching, a slight hangover from these distinctions still exists within international human rights law and within the mechanisms created.

Rape as Torture

The book then moved on to examining two real life international criminal tribunal cases. It was highlighted that applying the concept of human rights to rape as a form of torture and to rape as genocide is on the one hand innovative and important for how rape is conceived, placed and treated. Removing rape especially within the context of international humanitarian law, from constraints offered by considering rape as an attack on a woman's honor or as an issue requiring the protection of women, more accurately reflects the violent nature of rape and the need for its effective prohibition. On the other hand, and what has driven this book, theoretical questions emerged such as what are the implications for rape once it is subsumed into torture which focuses on the individual and once it is subsumed into genocide which is a crime conceived to protect human groups? In other words, understanding – be it positive or negative - what occurs once rape is placed into well-established international crimes must take place. The aim was not to consider which approach is best for rape but to delve deeper into the real life decisions. With this process in place, a contribution was made to the overall consideration of how rape is/will be conceived, placed and treated within international human rights and humanitarian law.

When rape is committed in situations that could fall within the criteria of torture, it is also committed against an individual. For instance, if a prisoner is raped by a prison official, and the rape occurred in an attempt to elicit information from this individual, the act could be deemed 'rape as a form of torture'. The act of rape as torture would be a violation of that individual's human rights. In this case, the emphasis is on the individual and on his/her individual human rights. This treatment of rape as a form of torture, with its emphasis on sexual autonomy, was evident in the International Criminal Tribunal for the Former Yugoslavia Judgement (ICTY), 'Foca case' of 2001 that was assessed.

An additional and critical layer of complexity was highlighted when rape is considered a form of torture. Individual victims of torture, recognized under international law, tend to have been politically active or have political connections. In reality, most of those who have been subjected to torture have not been politically active or do not have any political association. As such, this book posed the critical question of What does it mean to have the label of 'political' attached to an individual who has been raped within the context of torture? It was suggested, albeit controversially, that placing the label of the political onto individuals who have been tortured may make him/her more acceptable since political activities are deemed nobler than petty crimes. The importance of understanding what the political means, and this was proposed in an earlier Chapter of the book as a narrower or more expansive vision, cannot be underestimated since as argued it can result in either restricting or increasing the numbers of individuals considered to have been tortured. This exercise is especially significant for determining when individuals have been raped within situations of torture, as this is still a relatively new and not always consistently considered crime.[2] Furthermore, even when rape is promoted as strongly having a place in the international crime of torture it is framed within the political activities or associations of the individual. For rape as a form of torture, it was suggested by this author that the political should be broadly interpreted. Therefore, a *more expansive perspective* of the political would not only include the scenario whereby a government official subjects an individual to torture in order to gain information about a political opposition party, but it could also include the situation whereby a woman is tortured because she works for an organization that is demanding better social services for women from the government. However, even with a *more expansive perspective* of the political, by highlighting the political and placing this label onto individuals who have been tortured, the net result is the creation of a restraint in terms of which acts of rape should be considered a form of torture. The political, as a label attached to individuals who have been tortured or raped within situations of torture should not be swept away. Instead, as this author has proposed, it is also critical to recognize that the overall context in which rape as a form of torture occurs is multi-faceted.

Rape as a form of torture seems to fit comfortably into the concept of human rights since the emphasis is on the individual who has been subjected to torture. Yet, as discussed, there are serious implications in that these individuals are often placed within categories such as political involvement or association. Not only can this limit the numbers of those considered by the international community to have been tortured, but an added burden is placed onto individuals who have been tortured since the perception of victims who have been tortured for political reasons may be easier to accept than that of others outside this remit. Even after developing a *more expansive perspective* of the political, this book has concluded that attaching such labels does not benefit the overall issue of accepting that rape can and should be considered a form of torture when this act falls within the definition of torture. This is not to say that there should not be an acknowledgement of the fact that, at times, individuals who suffer rape as a form of torture do so within political circumstances. Rather, when writing about the issue or when deciding on such cases, it should also be consistently expressed and understood that these 'political' situations do not reflect the reality of the majority of cases when rape is used as a form of torture. Furthermore, what the political entails and where it can be deposited needs to be expressed when making such connections.

Rape as Genocide

In contrast to rape as a form of torture with its association to the individual, this book has determined that rape as genocide has to operate within the confines of genocide with its links to the group. Yet the book argued that although genocide has been conceived as a denial of the right to life of human groups, it also includes scope for the individual. In other words, genocide is an attack against a national, ethnic, racial, or religious groups but it is also an attack against individual persons within these groups. This complex interplay, found within genocide, between the group and the individual, affects how rape as genocide is understood. This means that individuals are victims of rape as genocide due to their membership in one or

[2] The circumstances within the International Criminal Tribunal for Rwanda in the Akayesu Judgement (1998), whereby the Trial Chamber acknowledged that some of the rapes could have been charged as torture but were not, is but one example. There are also the constraints of 'honor' and rape found within the Geneva Conventions (1949).

more of the enumerated groups in the Genocide Convention (1948), and within circumstances found under the definition of genocide. Therefore, this author has presented that there must be an opportunity to consider rape as genocide to be conceived as a violation against an individual because they are part of a group, and not as a violation solely committed against the group as a whole. If this formulation is not possible, within international law cases addressing such issues, then the result will be an exclusion of the construction of rape as a violation of an individual's sexual autonomy.

Despite the definition of genocide under international law, it cannot completely remove the notion that rape is a violation committed against the individual. Victims of rape who appeared before the ICTR in the case of the *Prosecutor v. Jean-Paul Akayesu* (1998), albeit within limits set out by the Tribunal and the Trial Chamber; do have an opportunity to recount what happened to them as individuals during the 1994 genocide in Rwanda. The context of the genocide in Rwanda, namely that it was committed with the purpose to destroy in whole or in part the Tutsi ethnic group, was in turn a necessary component attached to the Akayesu (1998) Judgement. As such, the Trial Chamber in this case did acknowledge that the women were raped because they were members of the Tutsi ethnic group but also that they were individual Tutsi victims.

The definition of genocide, as outlined in the Genocide Convention (1948) and as utilized by the international criminal tribunals, can offer a compatible space for rape. Although constrained by this definition, the group elements of this international crime can create room for the individual components of rape. For example, insisting on this connection with the group, an individual's sexual autonomy does at a certain level become enmeshed within the group. Does this change the nature of rape? To a certain degree the answer is yes since rape is not solely associated with the sexual autonomy of an individual. Yet, the construction of rape as a violation committed against the individual does not completely disappear. An unequal space is indeed created whereby the group elements of genocide and the individual aspects of rape operate once rape is considered as genocide. The point is not to shift and to re-configure this unequal space, but rather to accept that this is the reality and the consequence of innovative international jurisprudence, once rape is subsumed into genocide, such as with the Akayesu Judgement (1998). Finally, as noted in this book, victims of rape as genocide must also have the opportunity to decide for themselves how it is beneficial to consider rape as genocide. Linked to this, they must also be able to determine which aspects are held onto in terms of if the violation affects the individual, the group, or a combination of the two. Thus, as argued in relation to both rape as torture and rape as genocide, such theoretical implications and perhaps others must also be considered when assessing juridical innovations.

Upon Reflection

In its very early manifestation, this book proposed to assess the issue of rape as torture and as genocide with the lofty aim of formulating a new and better way in which rape would be conceived, placed and treated within international human rights and humanitarian law. Over the years it became evident to this author that the purpose of the book instead lies within an incremental stage found much earlier than the one originally pursued. Understanding some of the theoretical implications for rape once it has been subsumed into the international crimes of torture and genocide is critical and so offers a sound contribution to the eventual stage that will hopefully see a better way in which to deal with rape. This has been the path chosen for the book.

This has meant utilizing the complex current concept of human rights as a leveler for the examination of the two real life International Criminal Tribunal cases dealing with rape. Themes such as the individual, liberalism, the distinction between public and private realms, and the matter of groups, have influenced not only the concept of human rights but also how these rights have been treated within the human rights discourse. The reason for using this multidisciplinary approach was two-fold. First, the cases examined offered quite distinct views of rape. In the ICTY case (Foca, 2001) rape was considered a violation of sexual autonomy. Rape was also placed within the international crime of torture, which is a violation against the individual. In the ICTR case, (Jean-Paul Akayesu, 1998) rape was considered as genocide, which addresses the protection of human groups.

Second, searching beyond claims of innovative international jurisprudence, analysis with reference to rape must take place if this crime is to be better understood and treated within international human rights and humanitarian law. It is not adequate to merely say that 'judgement X' is the first time that rape has been considered in such a manner, nor is it adequate to simply say that since rape has been subsumed into the well established international crimes of torture and genocide it has gained in status. The consequences of these judgments, in the case of this book the theoretical consequences factored in the concept of human rights, must also emerge. This has been the contribution made to the extensive and existing knowledge in these varied areas of study.

As such, the book has arrived at several conclusions. First, it is not better or worse for rape to be placed within the individual or group camp. It is, however, critical to understand that different and sometimes conflicting theoretical implications emerge from these placements. This was brought out in this book by using the current concept of human rights as a base and its effects on the individual/group schism. Rape within the individual model and rape within the group model means that a variety of parameters, constraints, and results ensue. Sometimes the individual is supreme and sometimes the individual has to find an unequal space. Second, this process may indeed change how rape is to be conceptualized, treated, and even placed within international human rights and humanitarian law. More study will be required to work through these important questions. Third, the book flagged and analyzed these theoretical implications. It was pointed out that there is a need for future jurisprudence decisions and literature addressing rape as torture and rape as genocide (and other international crimes such as crimes against humanity) to incorporate some of these, and other, theoretical implications.

Perhaps the use of a metaphor would better encapsulate the process undertaken.

Imagine a staircase, constructed of organic materials, that leads from the shore and into a lake. On the first step, we find a plant growing known as innovative jurisprudence. It is clearly visible since the plant is above the water level. This represents recent innovative judgements associated with rape within international human rights and humanitarian law, including cases dealing with rape as a form of torture and rape as genocide. This plant demonstrates an association of rape with well-established and serious international crimes. It also ensures that future violations can be addressed using a stronger and more consistent base. Just below the surface of the water we can see another plant, which is floating, and which we shall call the current concept of human rights. The idea that human rights are rights individuals have because they are human beings is why this plant grows near innovative jurisprudence. Two branches emanate from the current concept of human rights: one growing into the second step, while the other grows into the third and deepest step. At this point, the water in the lake is quite murky.

The branch on the second steps pertains to the history of and to the influences that have shaped the current concept of human rights. Factors such as natural rights, the rise of the individual, liberalism, the public/private dichotomy, the group element, etc. are addressed on this branch. Deeper, and on the third step, is the branch that considers some of the theoretical implications for rape when it is associated with innovative jurisprudence and the current concept of human rights. This involves understanding what occurs when rape is subsumed into torture and when rape is subsumed into genocide. Looking down upon the staircase, it is critical to search for factors in the less clear and more complicated areas of the lake to assist in the process that will offer a better way in which rape is conceptualized, placed and treated within international human rights and humanitarian law.

The key area identified by this book was the need to analyze theoretical implications such as what occurs when rape is subsumed into a crime associated with the individual and with a crime affecting the group. In reference to the former, rape as a form of torture is a crime against the individual. Furthermore, individuals who have been tortured tend to be given the label of political involvement or association. It was argued by this author that the political must be understood and that even if a more expansive perspective of the political is utilized this can have the negative effect of restricting how rape as a form of torture is presented and who its individual victims actually are. In terms of the latter area, rape as genocide, this book concluded that rape has to work within the confines of a definition of genocide, which is an attack against the group but that unequal space for the individual also exists within the construction of genocide.

To conclude, it may seem indulgent to have placed a greater importance on the murkier theoretical questions than on the real life cases and on the experiences of the individuals who have been victims of rape, of rape as torture and of rape as genocide. I acknowledge that these voices have not been given the prime place in this book that is most definitely deserved. [3] However, it is because of these individuals that the study was initially undertaken and it is in the hope of contributing to a better and more innovative understanding of the realities faced by them that I offer this research and theoretical analysis.

[3] There is also the sensitive issue of, as outlined by Joanne Conaghan, "How, in other words, do we *make* knowledge claims about women and, yet, how do we not?" Joanne Conaghan. "Reassessing the Feminist Theoretical Project in Law. Journal of Law and Society. P. 370.

Cases Cited

1) Barcelona Traction Case. International Court of Justice (ICJ), 1970.
2) Declaration of Diana Ortiz. (Xuncax v. Gramajo, Nos. CIV. A. 91-11564-DPW, CIV.A. 91-11612- DPW, 1995 WL254818 (D. Mass., Apr. 12, 1995), 886 F. Supp. 162.
3) European Court of Human Rights. *Aydin v. Turkey*. Reports of Judgements and Decisions. 25 September 1997. No. 50.
4) European Human Rights Reports. *Cyprus v. Turkey Opinion*. V. 4. 1982. 537.
5) Inter-American Human Rights Series (C, No. 4). *Velasquez Rodriguez v. Honduras*. 29 July 1988. ILM 291.
6) ICTR. *Prosecutor v. Jean-Paul Akayesu*, ICTR-96-4-T, Judgement, 2 September 1998. (Akayesu Case)
7) ICTR. Prosecutor v. Alfred Musema, ICTR-96-13-A, Judgement, 27 January 2000.
8) ICTR. *Prosecutor v. Laurent Semanza*, ICTR-97-20-T, Judgement, 15 May 2003.
9) ICTY. *Prosecutor v. Dragolijub Kunarac, Radomir Kovac and Zoran Vukovic*, ICTY, IT-96-23-T and IT-96-23/1-T, Judgement, 22 February 2001. (Foca Case)
10) ICTY. *Prosecutor v. Zejnil Delali, Hazim Deli et al.* ICTY, IT-96-21-T, Judgement, 16 November 1998. (Celebici Case)
11) ICTY. *Prosecutor v. Anton Furundzija*, ICTY IT-95-17/1-T10, Judgement, 10 December 1998.
12) Yearbook of the European Convention on Human Rights. *The Greek Case*. V. 12. 1969. 504.

References

Afsharipour, Afra. "Empowering Ourselves: The Role of Women's NGOs in the Enforcement of the Women's Convention" Columbia Law Review, 99(1), 1999.

Allodi, F. and Stiasny S. "Women as Torture Victims." *Canadian Journal of Psychiatry*, Vol. 35: 144, March 1990.

Alston, Philip (ed.). *The United Nations and Human Rights: A Critical Appraisal*. Clarendon Paperbacks, Oxford, 1996.

Andreopoulos, George J. (ed.). *Genocide: Conceptual and Historical Dimensions*.
University of Pennsylvania Press, 1994.

Anker, Deborah. "Women Refugees: Forgotten No Longer?" *San Diego Law Review*, 32, 1995.

Archard, David. "The Wrong of Rape" *The Philosophical Quarterly*, Vol. 57, No. 228, July 2007.

Arendt, Hannah. *Eichmann à Jérusalem*. Quarto Gallimard, Paris, 2002.

Arendt, Hannah. The Human Condition (Second Edition). The University of Chicago Press, London, 1998.

Askin, Kelly Dawn. *War Crimes Against Women: Prosecution in International War Crimes Tribunals*. Kluwar Law International, The Hague, 1997.

Askin, Kelly Dawn. "Gender Crimes: Jurisprudence in the ICTR." *Journal of International and Comparative Law (JICJ)*, 3 (2005).

Aswad, Evelyn Mary. "Torture by Means of Rape." *The Georgetown Law Journal*, Vol. 84: 1913, 1996.

Baines, Erin K. "Body Politics and the Rwandan Crisis." Third World Quarterly, Vol 24, No 3, 2003.

Ball, Terance and Dagger, Richard. *Political Ideologies* and the Democratic Ideal. Pearson Longman, USA, 2006.

Banks, Angela. "Sexual Violence and International Criminal Law: An Analysis of the Ad Hoc Tribunal's Jurisprudence and the International Criminal Court's Elements of Crimes." (The Hague: Women's Initiatives for Gender Justice, September 2005), 9-10.

Bantekas, Ilias and Nash, Susan (eds.). *International Criminal Law*. Cavendish, London, 2001.

Bassiouni, M Cherif. *Crimes Against Humanity in International Criminal Law (2nd Edition)*. Kluwer Law International, The Hague, 1999.

Bassiouni, M. Cherif (ed.). *International Criminal Law (2nd Edition)*. Transnational Publications, N.Y., 1999.

Bassiouni, M. Cherif and Manicas, Peter. *The Law of the International Criminal Tribunal for the Former Yugoslavia*. Transnational Publications, N.Y., 1996.

Berman, Helen and Estella Rosa Irías Girón and Antonia Ponce Marroquí. "A Narrative of Refugee Women Who Have Experienced Violence in the Context of War." CJNR 2006, Vol. 38 No 4, 32-53.

Beswick, Stephanie. " 'If You Leave Your Country You Have no Life!' Rape, Suicide, and Violence: Sudanese Female Refugees in Kenyan Refugee Camps." Northeast African Studies, Vol. 8, No 3 (New Series), 2001, 69-98.

Blatt, Deborah. "Recognizing Rape as a Method of Torture." *New York University Review of Law and Social Change*, Vol. 5, 1994.

Bobbio, Norberto. *The Age of Rights*. Polity Press, Cambridge, 1995.

Bosmans, Marleen. "Challenges in Aid to Rape Victims: the Case of the Democratic Republic of the Congo." Essex Human Rights Review, Vol. 4 No. 1, February 2007, 1-12.

Bowring, Bill in Futtrell, Derdre and Bowring Bill (eds). *Minority and Group Rights in the New Millenium*. Martinus Nijhoff Publishers, The Hague, 1999.

Brandt, Don (ed.). *Violence Against Women: From Silence to Empowerment*. World Vision International, California, 2003.

Brecher, Bob. *Torture and the Ticking Bomb*. Blackwell Publishing, Victoria, Australia, 2007.

Brems, Eva in Lyons, Gene M. and Mayall, James. *International Human Rights in the 21st Century*. Rowman and Littlefield, Oxford, 2003.

Broadbent, Ed in Joanna Kerr (ed.). *Ours By Right: Women's Rights as Human Rights*. Zed Books, Guildford, 1993.

Brownlie, Ian. *Principles of Public International Law*. Clarendon Press, Oxford, 2003.

Brownlie, Ian and Goodwin-Gill, Guy S. *Basic Documents in International Law*. Oxford University Press, Oxford, 2002.

Brownmiller, Susan. *Against Our Will: Men, Women, and Rape*. Penguin Books, New York, 1975.

BRIDGE (development-gender). Amani El Jack. *Gender and Armed Conflict: Overview Report*. Institute of Development Studies, Sussex University, 2003.

Buss, Doris E. "Women at the Borders: Rape and Nationalism in International Law." *Feminist Legal Studies*, Vol. VI no. 2, 1998.

Cahill, Anne J. *Rethinking Rape*. Cornell University Press, London, 2001.

Campbell, Kirsten. "The Trauma of Justice: Sexual Violence, Crimes Against Humanity and the International Criminal Tribunal for the Former Yugoslavia." *Social and Legal Studies*, Vol. 13(3), 2004.

Card, Claudia. *The Atrocity Paradigm: A Theory of Evil*. Oxford University Press, Oxford, 2002.

Carpenter, Charli. "Surfacing Children: Limitations of Genocidal Rape Discourse." Human Rights Quarterly 22 (2000), 428-477.

Casals, Neus Torbisco. *Group Rights as Human Rights*, Springer, UK, 2006

Cassesse, Antonio. *Inhuman States: imprisonment, detention and torture in Europe Today.* Polity Press, Oxford, 1996.

Cavaro, Adriano in Stephen K. White (Ed.) and Donald J. Moon (Ed.), *What is Political Theory?* Sage Publications, London, 2004.

Cesereanu, Ruxandra. "An Overview of Political Torture in the Twentieth Century." JSRI No. 14, Summer 2006, 120-143

Charlesworth, Hilary and Chinkin, Christine. "The Gender of Jus Cogens." Human Rights Quarterly, Vol. 15: 1993.

Charlesworth, Hilary. "The Public/Private Distinction and the Right to Development in International Law." Australia yearbook of International Law, Vol. 12:190, 1992.

Chesterman, Simon. "Never Again…and Again: Law, Order, and the Gender of War Crimes in Bosnia and Beyond." *Yale Journal of International Law*, Vol. 22, Number 2: 299, summer 1997.

Chalk, Frank and Jonassohn, Kurt. *The History and Sociology of Genocide*. Yale University Press, London, 1990.

Chinkin, Christine. "A Critique of the Public/Private Dimension." *European Journal of International Law (EJIL)*, Vol. 10 No. 2, 1999.

Chinkin, Christine. "Rape and Sexual Abuse of Women in International Law." *European Journal of International Law (EJIL),* Vol. 5: 1-341, 1994.

Chiwengo, Ngwarsungu. "When Wounds and Corpses Fail to Speak: Narratives of Violence and Rape in Congo (DRC)." Comparative Studies of South Asia, Africa and the Middle East, Vol. 28, No. 1, 2008, 78-92.

Cohen, Roberta. " 'What's so Terrible about Rape?' and Other Attitudes at the United Nations." SAIS Review, Summer-Fall 2000, 73-77.

Cohen, Stanley. *States of Denial: Knowing about atrocities and suffering.* Polity Press, Cambridge, 2002.

Conaghan, Joanne. "Extending the Reach of Human Rights to Encompass Victims of Rape: MC *v.* Bulgaria." *Feminist Legal Studies*, 13, 2005.

Conaghan, Joanne. "Reassessing the Feminist Theoretical Project in Law." Journal of Law and Society, Vol. 27, Number 3: 351-85, September 2000.

Connolly, William E. *The Terms of Political Discourse* (Second Edition). Martin Robertson, Oxford, 1983.

Copelan, Rhonda. "Surfacing Gender: Reengraving the Crimes against Women in Humanitarian Law". In: N. Dombrowski (ed.) *Women and War in the Twentieth Century*, Garland Publishing, NY, 1999.

Copelon, Rhonda. "Women and War Crimes." St. John's Law Review, Vol. 69:37, 1995.

Crelinsten, Ronald D. *Politics of Pain*. COMT, Leiden, 1995.

De Feyter, Ken in De Feyter and Pavlakos (Editors), *The Tension Between Group Rights and Human Rights: A Multidisciplinary Approach*, Oxford and Portland, Oregon, 2008.

De Than, Claire and Shorts, Edwin. *International Criminal Law and Human Rights*. Sweet and Maxwell, London, 2003.

De Vito, Daniela. *Beijing Plus Five: An Assessment*. University of Essex, Human Rights Centre, 2001.

Dixon, Rosalind. "Rape as a Crime in International Humanitarian Law: Where to from Here?" *European Journal of International Law (EJIL)*, Vol. 13 No. 3, 2002.

Donnelly, Jack. *Universal Human Rights in Theory and Practice Second Edition*. Cornell University Press, NY, 2003.

Donnelly, Jack in Lyons, Gene M. and Mayall, James. *International Human Rights in the 21st Century*. Rowman and Littlefield, Oxford, 2003.

Donnelly, Jack in Brolmann, Catherine (ed.). *Peoples and Minorities in International Law*. Martinus Nijhoff, London, 1993.

Douzinas, Costas. *The End of Human Rights*. Hart, Oxford, 2000.

Duner, Bertil (ed.). *An End to Torture: Torture and Other Barbarous Practices*. Palgrave New Copy, London, 1998.

Durham, Helen. "Women and Civil Society: NGOs and International Criminal Law." In Kelly Dawn Askin and Doreen M. Koenig (eds.), *Women and International Human Rights Law*. Transnational, Ardsley, N.Y., 1999.

Eboe-Osuji, Chile. "Rape as Genocide: Some Questions Arising." *Journal of Genocide Research*, 9(2), June 2007.

Elshtain, Jean Beth. *Public man, private woman: Women in social and political thought.* Robertson, Oxford, 1981.

Engle, Karen. "Feminism and its (Dis)Contents: Criminalising Wartime Rape in Bosnia and Herzegovina." *American Journal of International Law*, Vol. 99, No. 4, October 2005.

Fortin, Katharine. "Rape as Torture: An Evaluation of the Committee Against Torture's Attitude to Sexual Violence." Utrecht Law review, Volume 4, Issue 3 (December) 2008, 145-162.

Gardam, Judith. "Women and the law of armed conflict: Why the silence?" International Comparative Law Quarterly, Vol. 46, 1997.

Gewirth, Alan. *Human Rights: Essays on Justification and Applications*. University of Chicago Press, Chicago, 1982.

Fabri, Mary R. "A Clinical Perspective of the Role of Gender in the Torture Experience." *Chicago Torture Conference March 4-7 1999*. Located at: http://humanities.uchicago.ed u/cis/torture/abstracts/maryfabri.html printed on 31/03/99).

Fallmeth, Aaron Xavier. "Feminism and International Law: Theory, Methodology and Substantive Reform." *Human Rights Quarterly*, Vol. 22: 694, 2000.

Fein, Helen. *Genocide: a sociological perspective*. Sage, London, 1993.

Forrest, Duncan (ed.). *Glimpse of Hell: reports on torture worldwide*. Amnesty International, London, 1991.

Freeman, Michael. *Human Rights: An Interdisciplinary Approach*. Polity, Cambridge, 2002.

Freeman, Michael. "The Theory and Prevention of Genocide." *Holocaust and Genocide Studies*, 6(2), 1991

Gaer, Felice D. "And Never the Twain Shall Meet? The Struggle to Establish Women's Rights as International Human Rights." American Bar Association, 1998.

Gardam, Judith and Jarvis, Michelle. *Women, Armed Conflict and International Law*. Kluwer Law International, The Hague, 2001

Ghandi, P.R. *Blackstone's International Human Rights Documents*. Blackstone Press, London, 2000.

Giffard, Camille. *The Torture Reporting Handbook: How to document and respond to allegations of torture within the international systems for the protection of human rights*. Human Rights Centre, University of Essex, 2000.

Giles, Wenona and Hyndman, Jennifer. *Sites of Violence: Gender and Conflicts Zones*. University of California Press, Berkeley, 2004.

Ginbar, Yuval. *Why not Torture Terrorists? Moral, Practical and legal Aspects of the 'Ticking Bomb' Justification for Torture.* Oxford University Press, oxford, 2008.

Glanville, Luke. "Is 'genocide' still a powerful word?" Journal of Genocide Research (2009), 11(4), December, 467-486.

Grayzel, Susan. *Women's Identities at War: Gender, Motherhood and Politics in Britain and France during First World War*. University of Carolina Press, Chapel Hill, 1999.

Green, Jennifer. "Uncovering Collective Rape: A Comparative Study of Political Sexual Violence." *International Journal of Sociology*, 34, 2004.

Green, Llezlie L. "Sexual Violence and Genocide Against Tutsi Women." *Columbia Human Rights Law Review*, Summer 2002.

Hannum, Hurst in Lyons, Gene M. and Mayall, James. *International Human Rights in the 21st Century*. Rowman and Littlefield, Oxford, 2003.

Healey, Sharon A. "Prosecuting Rape under the Statute of the War Crimes Tribunal for the Former Yugoslavia." Brooklyn Journal of International Law, Volume 21: 327, 1995.

Hilde, Thomas C. "Introduction: On Torture." South Central Review, 24, 1 (Spring 2007), 1-7.

Hinton, Alexander Laban (ed.). *Genocide: An Anthropological Reader*. Blackwell Publishing, Oxford, 2002.

Human Rights Watch. "Kosovo Backgrounder: Sexual Violence as an International Crime." May 1999.

Human Rights Watch. "Women's Human Rights: Step by Step", 1997.

Hobbes, Thomas. *Leviathan (Introduced by CB Macpherson)*. Penguin Classics, 1982.

Howard, Dick. *The Politics of Critique*. The Macmillan Press Ltd, London, 1988.

Ignatieff, Michael. *The Lesser Evil: Political Ethics in an Age of Terror*. Edinburgh University Press

Ingram, David. *Group Rights: Reconciling Equality and Difference*, University Press of Kansas, Kansas City, 2000.

International Expert Meeting. "International Humanitarian Law and Gender." Report Summary, 'Gender Perspectives on International Humanitarian Law.' Stockholm, Sweden, 4-5 October 2007.

Jackson, Jennifer in Lyons, Gene M. and Mayall, James. *International Human Rights in the 21st Century*. Rowman and Littlefield, Oxford, 2003.

Jansen, Golie G. *"Gender and War."* Affillia, Volume 21, No. 2, 2006, 134-145.

Jones, Adam. *Genocide: A Comprehensive Introduction*. Routledge, London, 2006.

Jones, Peter. *Rights*. Macmillan Press, London, 1994.

Kant, Immanuel. *The Metaphysics of Morals*. Cambridge University Press, Cambridge, 1993.

Kegly and Wittkopf. *World Political Trend and Transformation*. Wadsworth Publishing, London, 2003.

Kent, Gregory. *Framing War and Genocide: British Policy and news media reaction to the war in Bosnia*, Hampton Press Inc., Cresskill, NJ, 2006.

Kerr, Joanna (ed.). *Ours By Right: Women's Rights as Human Rights*. Zed Books, Guildford, 1993.

Kois, Lisa M. in Bertil Duner (ed.) *An End to Torture: Strategies for its Eradication*. Zed Books, London, 1998.

Kuper, Leo. *Genocide: Its Political use in the Twentieth Century*. Yale University Press, New Haven, 1982.

Kymlicka, Will. *Multicultural Citizenship*. Clarendon Press, Oxford, 1997.Lancet – letter to the editor. "Prevalence of Sexual Torture in Political Dissidents." Vol. 345: 1307, 20 May 1995.

Lauterpacht, H. *International Law and Human Rights*. Stevens, London, 1950.

Lemkin, Raphael. "Genocide as a Crime under International Law." *American Journal of International Law*, Vol. 41: 146, 1947.

Lerner, Natan. *The UN Convention on the Elimination of all Forms of Racial Discrimination*. Kluwer Law International, Boston, 2003.

Levinson, Sanford (ed.). *Torture: A Collection*. Oxford University Press, NY, 2004.

Locke, John. *Two Treatises of Government (Edited by Peter Laslett)*. Cambridge University Press, Cambridge, 1967.

Lusby, Katherine. "Hearing the Invisible Women of Political Rape." *University of Tulsa Law Review*. Vo. 25: 911, 1995.

Lyons, Gene M. and Mayall, James (eds.). *International Human Rights in the 21ST Century: Protecting the Rights of Groups*. Rowman and Littlefield, Oxford, 2003.

Mackie, Vera. "Sexual Violence, Silence and Human Rights Discourse." In Anne-Marie Hilsdon,

Martha MacIntyre and Maila Stivens (eds.). *Human Rights and Gender Politics: Asia Pacific Perspectives*. Routledge, London, 2000.

MacKinnon, Catherine. "Defining Rape Internationally: A Comment on Akayesu." *Columbia Journal of Transnational Law*, Vol 44, 2006.

MacKinnon, Catherine. "Rape, Genocide, and Women's Human Rights." *Harvard Women's Law Journal*, Vol 17, 1994

MacKinnon, Catherine. "On Torture." In: K. Mahony and P. Mahoney (eds.). *Human Rights in the Twenty-First Century: A Global Challenge*. Martinus Nijhoff, Boston, 1993.

MacKinnon, Catherine. *Towards a Feminist Theory of the State*. Harvard University Press, Cambridge, 1989.

MacKinnon, Catherine. "On Torture." in K. Mahony and P. Mahoney (eds.). *Human Rights in the Twenty-First Century: A Global Challenge*. Martinus Nijhoff, Boston, 1993.

Marks, Stephen. "From the 'Single Confused Page…" Human Rights Quarterly, Vol. 20 (3): 459, 1998.

Marshall, Jill. "A Right to Personal Autonomy at the European Court of Human Rights." European Human Rights Law Review, 2008, 3, 337-356.

Martin, Elizabeth (ed.). *Oxford Dictionary of Law*. Oxford University Press, Oxford.

McDonald, Gabriel Kirk *in* Sienho Yee and Wang Tieya (eds.). *International Law in the Post-Cold War World*. Routledge, London, 2001.

McGlynn, Clare. "Rape as 'Torture'? Catharine MacKinnon and Questions of Feminist Strategy." Feminist Legal Studies (2008) 16, 71-85.

Meron, Theodor. "Rape as a Crime under International Humanitarian Law." American Journal of International Law. Vol. 87: 424, 1983.

Mill, John Stuart. *On Liberty*. Penguin Classics, Suffolk, 1974.

Miller, Fred. *Nature, Justice and Rights in Aristotle's Politics*. Clarendon, Oxford, 1995.

Morris, Virginia and Scharf, Michael P. *An Insider's Guide to the International Criminal Tribunal for the Former Yugoslavia*. Transnational Publications, N.Y., 1995.

Morsink, Johannes. "The Philosophy of the Universal Declaration." *Human Rights Quarterly*, Vol. 6(3), 1984.

Mukamana, Donatilla and Collins, Anthony. "Rape Survivors of the Rwandan Genocide." *Critical Psychology*, 17: Critical Psychology in Africa, 2006.

O'Byrne, Darren J. *Human Rights: an Introduction*. Harlow: Longman, London, 2003.

O'Sullivan, Noel. *Political Theory in Transition,* Routledge, London, 2000.

Olujic, Maria B. "Embodiment of Terror: Gendered Violence in Peacetime and Wartime in Croatia and Bosnia-Herzegovina." Medical Anthropology Quarterly, 12(1), 1998.

OMCT, Violence Against Women, OMCT, Geneva, 1999.

OSCE, Office for Security and Co-operation in Europe. *Preventing Torture*. OSCE, 1999.

OSCE (ODIHR). *Preventing Torture: A Handbook for OSCE Field Staff*. OSCE, Warsaw, 1999.

Pateman, Carole. *The Sexual Contract*. Polity, Cambridge, 1988.

PBS, "Rwanda Today: The International Criminal Tribunal and the Prospects for Peace and Reconciliation. An Interview with Helena Cobban.", 2004, http://www.pbs.org/wgbh/pages/frontline/shows/ghosts/ (last accessed 21/01/2010).

Pearce, Hannah. "An Examination of the International Understanding of Political Rape and the Significance of Labeling it Torture." International Journal of Refugee Law, 2002, 14(4) 534-560.

Peel, Michael. *Rape as a Method of Torture*. Medical Foundation for Survivors of Torture, London, 2005.

Philips, Anne. *Democracy and Difference*. Pennsylvania State university Press, Pennsylvania, 1993.

Provost, Rene. *International Human Rights and Humanitarian Law*. Cambridge University Press, Cambridge, 2002.

Radacic, Ivana. "Rape Cases in the Jurisprudence of the European Court of Human Rights: Defining Rape and Determining the Scope of the State's Obligations." European Human Rights Law Review, 2008, 3, 357-375.

Ratner, Steven and Abrams, Jason. *Accountability for Human Rights Atrocities in International Law: Beyond the Nuremberg Legacy (2nd Edition)*. Oxford University Press, 2001.

Rawls, John. *Collected Papers*. Harvard University Press, London, 1999.

Reitan, Eric. "Rape as an Essentially Contested Concept." Hypatia, vol. 16, no. 2 (Spring 2001), 43-66.

Roberts, Adam and Guelff, Richard. *Documents on the Laws of War (3rd Edition)*. Clarendon, Oxford, 2000.

Rodley, Nigel S. *The Treatment of Prisoners under International Law*. Clarendon Press, Oxford, 1999.

Rodley, Nigel S. "Conceptual Problems in the Protection of Minorities: International Legal Developments." *Human Rights Quarterly*, Vol. 17: 61, 1995.

Rose, Nikolas. *Powers of Freedom: Reframing Political Thought*. Cambridge University Press, Cambridge, 1999.

Rosenbaum, Allan S. *Is the Holocaust Unique? Perspectives on Comparative Genocide*. Westview Press, Bolder, 2001.

Rwanda Today: The International Criminal Tribunal and the Prospects for Peace and Reconciliation. An Interview with Helena Cobban.

Schabas, William A. *Genocide in International Law*. Cambridge University Press, Cambridge, 2000.

Schulhofer, Stephen J. Unwanted Sex: *The Culture of Intimidation and the Failure of Law*. Harvard University Press, London, 1998. Harvard University Press, London, 1998.

Sharlach, Lisa. "Rape as Genocide: Bangladesh, the Former Yugoslavia, and Rwanda." *New Political Science*, Volume 22, Number 1, 2000.

Shaw, Martin. *War and Genocide: Organised Killing in Modern Society*. Polity Press, Cambridge, 2006.

Shaw, Martin. *What is Genocide?* Polity Press, Cambridge, 2007.

Sherif, Yasmine. "International Humanitarian Law and Human Rights Law." OCHA, NY, 2000.

Short, Damien. *Genocides*. Zed Books, London, (forthcoming 2011).

Sivakumaran, Sandesh. "Male/Male Rape and the 'Taint' of Homosexuality." Human Rights Quarterly 27 (2005), 1274-1306.

Sorenson, Susan and White, Jacqueline. "Adult Sexual Assault: Overview of Research." *Journal of Social Issues*, 48 (1), 1991.

Sparkes, A.W. *Talking Politics: a wordbook*. Routledge, London, 1994.

Squires, Judith. *Gender in Political Theory*. Polity Press, Cambridge, 1999.

Strumpen-Darrie, Christine. "Rape: A Survey of Current International Jurisprudence." *Human Rights Brief*, Volume 7 Issue 3. http://www.wcl.american.edu/hrbrief/v7i3/rape.htm (Printed 05/07/2006)

Taylor, Charles. *Multiculturalism and 'The Politics of Recognition'*. Princeton University Press, N.J., 1992.

Thomas Katie. "Sexual Violence: Weapon of War." *Forced Migration Review*, Issue 27, January 2007.

Triffterer, Otto (ed.). *Commentary on the Rome Statute of the International Criminal Court: Observer's Notes, Article by Article*. Nomos Verl.-Ges., Baden-Baden, 1999.

Tuck, Richard. *Natural Rights Theories: Their Origin and Development*. Cambridge University Press, Cambridge, 1979.

UNITED NATIONS DOCUMENTS:

- A/55/290. Question of torture and other cruel, inhuman or degrading treatment or punishment, 11 August 2000.
- A/CN.4/453 and Add. 1-3, "Fifth Report on State responsibility by Mr. G. Arangjio-Ruiz, Special Rapporteur," Yearbook of the International Law Commission II (1) (1993).
- A/CONF/183/9. Rome Statute of the International Criminal Court, July 1998.
- A/RES/S-23/3. Further Actions and Initiatives to Implement the Beijing Declaration and Platform for Action, 16 November 2000.
- CAT/C/GC/2. General Comment No. 2, 24 January 2008.
- E/CN.4/1999/68/Add.4. Integration of the Human Rights of Women and the Gender Perspective of Violence against Women. Addendum. Report of the Special Rapporteur on violence against women, its causes and consequences, Ms. Radhika Coomaraswamy, in accordance with Commission on Human Rights resolution 1997/44, 21 January 1999.

- E/CN.4/Sub.2/1985/6. Whitaker report on Genocide, 2 July 1985.
- EGM/GBP/1997/Report. Gender-based persecution Report of the Expert Group Meeting, Toronto, Canada, 9 - 12 November 1997, United Nations Division for the Advancement of Women Department of Economic and Social Affairs.
- G.A. Res. 91-I. The Crime of Genocide, 11 December 1946.
- GA res.217 A (III). International Bill of Human Rights, 10 December 1948.
- G.A. Res. 3318(XXIX). Declaration on Women and Children in Emergency and Armed Conflict, 14 December 1974.
- GA Res. 260A (III). Convention on the Prevention and Punishment of the Crime of Genocide, 9 December 1948.
- International Criminal Court (ICC). Elements of Crimes.
- UN Doc. A/760. On Genocide, 9 December 1948
- Security Council Resolution 995. Establishing the ICTR, 8 November 1994.
- S/25704. Report of the Secretary General Pursuant to Paragraph 2 of the Security Council Resolution 808, 1993.
- S/1994/674. Final Report of the Commission of Experts, 1992.
- S/1994/674. Final Report of the Commission of Experts pursuant to Security Council Resolution 780 (1992), Annex, UN Doc. S/1994/674, 27 May 1994.
- S/RES/1325. Impact of Armed Conflict, 2000.

Waldron, Jeremy. *Nonsense Upon Stilts: Bentham, Burke and Marx on the Rights of Man*. Oxford University Press, Oxford, 1988.

Wall, Steven. "Collective Rights and Individual Autonomy." Ethics 117 (January 2007), 234-264.

Watson, James Shand. *Theory and Reality in the International Protection of Human Rights*. Transnational Publishers, N.Y., 1999.

Weitsman, Patricia A. "The Politics of Identity and Sexual Violence: A Review of Bosnia and Rwanda." Human Rights Quarterly, 30 (2008), 561-578.

Wentraub, Jeff and Kumar, Krishan (eds.). *Public and Private in Thought and Practice: Perspectives on a Grand Dichotomy*. The University of Chicago Press, Chicago, 1997.

Women's Caucus. "ICC—Grave Breaches: The Torture Cluster." 16-26 February 1999,
http://www.iccwomen.org/wigjdraft1/Archives/oldWCGJ/icc/iccpc/021999pc/torture.htm (last accessed January 2010).

Women, Law and Development International and Human Rights watch Women's Rights Project. *Women's Human Rights Step by Step*. 1997.

Wood, Neil. *Reflections on Political Theory: A Voice of Reason from the Past.* Palgrave MacMillan, London, 2002.

Young, Iris Marion. "The Ideal of Community and the Politics of Difference." in Linda J. Nicholson. *Feminism and Post-modernism*. Rutledge, London, 1990.

INDEX